AFRICAN ETHNOGRAPHIC STUDIES
OF THE 20TH CENTURY

I0130921

Volume 74

THE AFRICAN TODAY

THE AFRICAN TODAY

DIEDRICH WESTERMANN

Routledge
Taylor & Francis Group

LONDON AND NEW YORK

First published in 1934 by Oxford University Press for the International African Institute.

This edition first published in 2018
by Routledge
2 Park Square, Milton Park, Abingdon, Oxon OX14 4RN

and by Routledge
711 Third Avenue, New York, NY 10017

Routledge is an imprint of the Taylor & Francis Group, an informa business

British Library Cataloguing in Publication Data
A catalogue record for this book is available from the British Library

ISBN: 978-0-8153-8713-8 (Set)
ISBN: 978-0-429-48813-9 (Set) (ebk)
ISBN: 978-1-138-60029-4 (Volume 74) (hbk)
ISBN: 978-1-138-60030-0 (Volume 74) (pbk)
ISBN: 978-0-429-47102-5 (Volume 74) (ebk)

Publisher's Note
The publisher has gone to great lengths to ensure the quality of this reprint but points out that some imperfections in the original copies may be apparent.

Disclaimer
The publisher has made every effort to trace copyright holders and would welcome correspondence from those they have been unable to trace.

THE AFRICAN
TO-DAY

BY

DIEDRICH WESTERMANN

WITH A FOREWORD BY
The Rt. Hon. LORD LUGARD

Published for the
INTERNATIONAL INSTITUTE OF
AFRICAN LANGUAGES & CULTURES
by the OXFORD UNIVERSITY PRESS
LONDON : HUMPHREY MILFORD
1934

PRINTED IN GREAT BRITAIN

Gratefully dedicated
to the
UNIVERSITY OF THE
WITWATERSRAND

FOREWORD

WHEN seven years ago the International Institute of African Languages and Cultures came into being with the object of co-ordinating and focusing the results of the work and research which different European nations and individuals were carrying on in Africa, it was felt by its promoters that success in their object would to a very great extent depend on whether it could secure as its two Directors men of International reputation, who would be recognized as outstanding authorities on African problems. The choice with no dissentient voice fell upon Professor Westermann and Professor Maurice Delafosse. On the death of the latter he was worthily succeeded by Monsieur Henri Labouret.

The Institute disclaimed the role of a purely academic institution and set itself to the difficult task of serving as a clearing-house for information in regard to linguistic and cultural questions for all who were engaged in work in Africa—whether as officials (Administrative or Technical) or as Missionaries, or in private enterprise. In furtherance of this objective it publishes a quarterly journal—*Africa*—with articles by selected writers in French, English, and German, of which Dr. Westermann is Editor assisted by the Secretary, Miss Brackett.

It also decided to publish a series of monographs

on various African problems. Several have already been issued, and others are in course of preparation. The present volume by Dr. Westermann, which has been unavoidably delayed by the Author's visits to Africa, is intended as an introduction to this series— and also to the programme of sociological research which the Institute is undertaking. It is the product alike of long African experience and of wide reading, and should be of great practical help to Europeans in Africa—whatever their calling—and to students in Europe of African sociology and psychology.

Dr. Westermann first went to West Africa as a missionary, and his remarkable linguistic ability soon enabled him to acquire several African languages and led to his appointment as a Professor at Berlin University. Obviously the first step in furtherance of the Institute's task of opening up common avenues for investigation and research to which Africans might contribute their share was to devise an orthography at once scientific and practical, and not overburdened with strange symbols, for the writing of African languages—a task which had baffled scholars for many years. Dr. Westermann's script has been widely adopted as fulfilling the desired conditions.

The next task was to ascertain the groups to which the various languages in the African babel of tongues belonged, as a preliminary to closer investigation and selection. With these objects in view he was invited to go to the Gold Coast, to Nigeria, and to the Southern Sudan where the dialects of the Nilotic tribes offered a virgin field for linguistic study. The Governments concerned defrayed all expenses and have expressed most cordially their recognition of the services rendered. He has also visited East Africa and the Union of South Africa. The Institute then decided to invite original compositions in their own vernacular from Africans,—for which prizes were offered. Professor Westermann again was, of course, the reader and judge of these essays and stories.

He has always maintained that the language of a people is the expression of its soul, by which alone a key to their thoughts could be found. Possessed of this key he was able to obtain a deep insight into the life of the African, and to probe the meaning of much in his conceptions regarding the supernatural world, and the spirits of the dead—as the chapters on this subject show—of which the Negro is generally unwilling to speak to the white man. His work for the Institute, his recent travels in all parts of the Continent, his wide reading of books for review in *Africa*, have combined to deepen his knowledge and to familiarize him with the opinions of other Anthropologists—while his unassuming modesty has made friends wherever he went and opened the way for fruitful discussion.

The result so far as it can be packed into so small

a volume is contained in the pages of this book, which I feel it would be presumptuous in me to praise. I can only recommend it cordially to all who are interested in Africa, both for the abundant information it contains on the facts of African life as they reveal themselves to a specially qualified observer, and for the sane and moderate views expressed on debatable questions.

LUGARD

25 *January* 1934

CONTENTS

CONTENTS

I

ANTHROPOLOGY AND PRACTICAL
WORK IN AFRICA

I

TO-DAY, and for a long time to come, the fate of Africa is indissolubly linked with that of the white race. Africa will become what Europe and America make of it. Under the complicated conditions of modern life Africans are not in a position to take their future into their own hands, nor is Europe disposed to surrender its control over Africa. The great riches of raw material, both vegetable and mineral, as well as the capacity of Africa for consuming European goods, surpass even the hopes entertained at the time of the beginning of the colonial era, but the enterprise and capital of Europe and America are indispensable both for the exploitation of these riches and for setting up the regular exchange of goods between the two continents. The African is of necessity being drawn into this economic movement and is undergoing fundamental changes. The future of the African races will depend on the question of how far and in what manner

B

they are able to adapt themselves to the new conditions of life created by the white man's activity in
Africa. The destiny of a continent and its inhabitants
has been handed over into the white man's hand. In
whatever position he may find himself in Africa, consciously or unconsciously he is taking part in the
shaping of this destiny. In some way or other he is
influencing the African, and this is the more true
because the African is not only ready to work under
and with the European and to learn from him, but
even sees in him his ideal. This contact of two such
different cultures creates a number of problems and
at the same time a human responsibility.

European penetration is bound to undermine
African civilization, thereby threatening the vitality
and the moral basis of the people's life. The whole of
Africa lives to-day in a state of transition from old to
new. How the Natives will emerge from this conflict, whether they will be in a position either to retain
the vital elements of their culture and racial qualities
and develop them organically, or to adapt themselves
to entirely new forms of life, will depend largely on
the attitude which the white man adopts towards the
African.

In the Africa of to-day the European and the
African are interdependent. Africa cannot be opened
up without the co-operation of the African. Even
where the climate permits the white man to establish
a permanent home for himself, the work of the Native
is indispensable to him, and this is true to a still greater

degree of the tropical regions. It is the African who builds roads and railways; he works in mines and plantations, on farms and in the white man's household, in workshops and offices, as teacher and preacher; he consumes our goods and sells us his produce; he takes a growing part in the administration of his country; he pays taxes for public purposes and is becoming more and more the efficient fellow worker of the white man in every sphere. As progress in Africa advances greater demands will be made upon the African, and his share in the volume of work will become more.

Just as the European cannot live and work in Africa without the help of the African, so in the same way the African needs the European. Africa and the Africans have during the last half-century advanced in many spheres, and this advance is largely due to the initiative of the European. Without his intervention the African might to-day be at the stage where he was centuries ago. In the future also he will not be able to dispense with European guidance and the white man's knowledge, skill, and dynamic force. The work of European educators has already achieved much, but it is only in its beginnings. When it has succeeded in embracing the whole population of the continent, then the African will be able to fulfil the tasks which will fall to his share in the new order of things.

The co-operation of white and black in Africa has been described in the phrase: 'Black brawn and white brain.' There is some truth in this saying, but not the whole truth. From it we might conclude that for all time the African has been destined to serve and the European to rule. Even to-day, however, the African is doing brain-work to a not unimportant extent, and the distance between him and the European in this sphere will diminish in the future. To-day the predominance of the European is incontestable, and wherever he lives amidst Africans or takes them into his service, he will be inclined to maintain this state of affairs. No one can begrudge the European going to Africa for his own advantage. It may, however, be doubted whether it is possible to go on doing this for ever at the cost of the Native races. A fruitful development will be possible only when all the inhabitants can share proportionately in the prosperity created by man.

We must go a step farther, and admit that in the relationship between one race of mankind and another not only utilitarian but also humanitarian and ethical issues are at stake, and that they must not be left out of account if we wish to keep the best of our own culture. If, however, the ethical problem is not to degenerate into mere sentimental contemplation, and therefore to be condemned to complete sterility, it must be based on knowledge of the facts. We must learn to know the African and the conditions of his life. This is true in the first instance of the administrative official, the educator, and the missionary; but it is also important that every European, whether he be planter, settler, merchant, engineer, or officer, should understand the African, and especially that he should learn to appreciate the changing African. We must realize that the penetration of European civilization has come to him as a revolution, as a fundamental disturbance, which has deprived him of his natural balance and created for the time being situations which may appear to the European strange, contradictory, or repellent. If we are not to succumb to these impressions, and if we are to find a clear line for our actions, one thing above all is needful: a real, objective scientific knowledge of the actual conditions, their interrelation and their interpretation. Many errors of the past, involving wars and punitive expeditions, loss of both Native and European life, misunderstandings and bitternesses with all their consequences, might have been avoided if those responsible had been in a position to understand the African and his motives.

If the study of the African is to be fruitful in results, it must fulfil two conditions. It must be unbiased; and it must not leave the human side out of account. Most Europeans are interested in the Africans, not for his sake but for theirs, and they are therefore always prone to import their own point of view into such an investigation. Even in important questions affecting the inner life of people, such as education, we are in danger of considering not the needs and the interests of the African, but of our own aims, whether these be political, economic, religious, or of a generally civilizing nature. These aims may not be openly expressed, but when it comes to practical organization, they are bound to play a part. Thus the real task and scope of education are perverted. It would be better, even for our own practical purposes, to take time to study the African as he is and to start our work on him from his standpoint instead of our own. The problem involved is great enough to justify a purely objective investigation.

It is, however, impossible to start such a study in the same way as one would initiate an investigation into the kinds of soil and the variations of climate of a country. We have to do with human beings who both as a race and as individuals have their human value, their possibilities of development, and their destined part to play, and who cannot therefore be regarded as mere instruments of European enterprise. Something more than sentiment was involved when General Lafayette said: 'The last of the Negroes may always say to the first of the whites : "Am I not a man, a brother?"' Without making some such admission it is inconceivable that we should be able to co-operate with a strange race and treat it justly. This does not mean a minimizing of racial differences or of cultural variations. It does not imply an ignoring of the social gulf which actually exists between the two races and which corresponds to a great extent to the wishes of both. It does not deny that, as things are to-day, the white man must be the leader and the African the led. It does, however, recognize an ultimate basic equality which underlies all inequalities, and this recognition should be ever present in all our dealings with the African.

To the claim that scientific preparation is necessary for effective work in Africa and with Africans, the objection will be made that successful administrative, missionary, and educational work has hitherto been done without scientific or technical knowledge. That is true. Science is not a panacea. Common sense, personal tact, and practical wisdom, as well as sympathy based on an understanding of the human elements concerned, are all necessary. Many practical men have honestly sought out a path and found one; and the greatest achievements in Native policy and education are due to men who had no opportunities for acquiring technical education as we understand it to-day. Among such men it is only necessary to mention a name like Lord Lugard. Not every European, however, who comes to Africa is a genius. Moreover, those people who have had to seek out their own methods have emphasized the necessity both of systematic study of the problems and of giving the prospective worker in Africa an opportunity of becoming familiar with them before he begins his work. It should not be necessary for every one to start from the very beginning, to learn by his own experiences, and to pay for his lessons out of his own pocket. He can profit from the work of his predecessors and from the knowledge of experts. The problems of to-day are too serious, complex, and urgent to be mastered by mere muddling through.

The methods of practical men without technical training have often consisted simply in transferring indis-
criminately to Africa the institutions and customs of
their own country; and these methods were bound
to lead to mistakes and misunderstandings.

2

Social anthropology is the science to which we look
in the first instance for help in our problem; we expect
it to teach us a true knowledge of the African and his
civilization and its processes. Anthropologists have
rightly complained that in the past their advice has
often not been heeded, and that misunderstandings
and disasters might have been avoided if the lines of
conduct laid down as the result of anthropological
investigation had been followed. This is true to some
extent, but on the other hand it must be admitted that
anthropology has not always been able, nor found it
necessary, to present the results of its studies in a way
in which the practical man could make use of them.
Even to-day some anthropologists protest that there
is no such thing as practical or applied anthropology.
They definitely refuse to make their knowledge serve
any practical purpose, because they fear that such an
aim will cause them to deviate from the road of science
and will dull the keen edge of their investigation. Now
it is certainly true that all scientific work must, in the
first instance, be an end in itself, and this is true of
anthropological research in Africa. On the other hand

no one can blame the practical man, confronted with the problems arising out of his daily duties, if he looks around for guidance and expects the science of anthropology to give him what he needs. Anthropology is after all the science of man, and, when investigations are conducted in Africa, it is the science of African man. When a science is dealing with a living problem such as man, and with an unexplored problem such as African man, it seems obvious that the result of such research should throw a new light on matters with which the practical man has to deal. No one will dispute the fact that biology is a science and that it has rendered eminent practical service. It would be strange if the same were not possible in the case of anthropology. It would be strange too if the anthropologist, like every serious worker in whatever sphere, did not have a natural desire to make his work serve his fellow men, though this might be done in such an indirect way that the practical outcome was not apparent to the outsider. A science whose advocates definitely refuse to consider their task as being in any way a service to mankind may have its right to existence questioned.

What we have in mind when we speak of applied or practical anthropology is a purely scientific method of investigation, which, however, does not consider present-day problems as unscientific and therefore overlook them, and which is not above presenting its results in such a way that the practical man can apply them to his problems.

The main reason why anthropology has hitherto not fulfilled the hopes of the practical man is that it was too much interested in the past. Attention was turned backwards; the main concern was not man, but his civilization and its history. Moreover, it was concerned with civilization not so much as it affects the life of the individual and the community, but rather as an object for comparison with other civilizations, in order to explain their interrelation and their origin. These problems are no doubt important; and investigation of earlier forms of human civilization has a peculiar charm and will always claim attention. The study of the past may also be a means of understanding better our own present, since many phenomena of life only reveal their real meaning when we can go back to their origin. The historical method of anthropological research has to fulfil an important task, but its pursuit involves the danger of neglecting matters which are of scientific interest and of much greater human, that is to say anthropological import, because they deal with the actual life of man and its present changes.

The task of social anthropology is not only to study the political organization of a tribe and from that to reconstruct a previous phase of that organization. It must also raise such questions as the following. How does this organization work in the life of to-day? How is it related to the whole culture of the tribe in question? How has it been affected by modern foreign influences? What conditions of change, adaptation, or disintegration can be recognized, and what is the effect of this disintegration and modification on the individual members of the group? It is important to understand not only the structure of the Family, but also the significance of the Family for its individual members and for the maintenance of communal life; whether it educates individuals to assume personal responsibility, or neglects this education, or makes it impossible; what factors to-day threaten the continuance of the Family. Land-tenure, and its significance for the social cohesion of the group; the valuable and dangerous elements in the individual or communal form of land tenure, and the effects of modern changes; primitive economics and jurisprudence; questions of population and hygiene; the new social order which is being evolved under the influence of foreign civilizations; the new mental outlook; the emergence of individualism; the principles of indigenous African education and the effect of European education; the fate of the old pagan religion and the growth of new religions with their forms of community life; the indigenous beliefs underlying social cohesion, tribal allegiance, and obedience to tribal authority; the incentives to increased economic effort; problems such as these, and in fact all phenomena of cultural change and of a changing humanity, come within the sphere of work of the anthropologist.[1] He is the person who by means of his scientific

[1] Cf. B. Malinowski, 'Practical Anthropology', *Africa*, vol. ii, p. 22.

equipment is able to study them, and he has the advantage of being impartial.

Even the representative of historical ethnology will do well not to ignore the problems of modern life. Those phenomena which seem to him to be old and autochthonous, and therefore a worthy object of his study, are in reality the results of innumerable past changes, and it should be of interest to him to be able to watch such changes actually taking place under his eyes and to see their effect on the life of the people concerned. A scientist, whose whole aim is to find out the truth, can hardly pass by opportunities such as these, for in them he can see factors at work which have been responsible for previous changes and can study their effects. It is true that the present-day changes in Africa are different in kind and intensity from any previously known. They have often led to unpleasing distortions of the Native civilization and even to its complete destruction, but that should not lessen their importance for the anthropologist. Even if civilizations are destroyed men and women remain, and it is necessary for us to find out how they, as living beings, adapt themselves to a changed environment and create new ways of life.

3

Anthropological field-work is carried on not only by fully trained anthropologists but to a large extent by persons who, without possessing the necessary technical training, are anxious to obtain knowledge of the people among whom they are working, moved thereto either by scientific inclination or by the necessities of their calling. The majority of these are missionaries and administrative officials. The former have the special advantage of long residence in the country and intimate knowledge of the language; their work leads them to live in close contact with the Natives and to make themselves familiar with their customs and views of life. Many excellent and well-known monographs on African tribes have been written by missionaries, and the work of the professional anthropologists has in the past been largely based on the material so gathered. This co-operation will always be welcome. An investigator seldom remains long enough in the field to get a thorough knowledge of all phases of Native life, and he does not always learn a Native language sufficiently well to handle it with ease. If the missionary is at all interested in anthropological matters, has some experience in scientific work, and knows the language as he ought to, there will always be departments of life to which he will have access in a way quite impossible to any other investigator, however highly trained.

It is, on the other hand, intelligible that the anthropologists, the more their young science develops, will make higher demands on field-workers and point out the deficiencies of the productions of non-professional workers. Amateurs lack technical training and scientific experience; they are not sufficiently familiar with the actual problems at issue and cannot always

distinguish between the important and the less important. This may result in essential details being overlooked or expressed with such lack of accuracy that
the material is almost valueless. Unconsciously the
amateur may succumb to the temptation of looking
at things from the point of view of his own precon-
ceived ideas, and the objectiveness of his statements
will be endangered, or they will be represented in a
wrong light. The amateur should, wherever possible,
try to acquire at least the elements of anthropological
training, and then his work will give greater satisfaction to himself and will be of more use to others.

While the missionary and the official as a rule confines his studies to a small region which he knows
well, the anthropologist may investigate a problem or
a group of connected problems in their wider aspects,
his objects being to study the culture of a people, or
of a group of tribes as a whole, in its structure, its
function, and its interrelations. No culture is autono-
mous and autochthonous. All cultures have been
fertilized from without. The investigator who studies
culture contacts will want to know how groups are
influenced by their relations to each other; the attitude
of one group towards receiving cultural elements
from another; what contributions each has made to
the total culture of an area; what constitutes the unity
of a culture area; and in what way the single groups
have separately assisted in the evolution of the culture
common to all of them; how they have changed the
cultural elements or allowed them to fall into neglect,

and what are the causes of such occurrences.[1] It may be desirable to trace back into the past the growth of a cultural element and its contacts; in other words, to apply historical standards. The historical and the functional methods are not mutually exclusive but can very well supplement each other. The important point is that the present shall not be forgotten in the past and it should in all circumstances claim the greater interest.

One means of collecting anthropological data should not be overlooked, namely the recording of texts in Native languages. They will as a rule not be sufficient to form the basis of a complete anthropological picture of a tribe, but they are most valuable as complementing the work of the technical anthropologist. It is our duty to let the Native speak for himself where this is possible, in order to get his method of expression, and to understand his reasoning and explanation. Documents of great linguistic, anthropological, and human value may in this way come to light. The collecting of such texts becomes urgent as the last opportunities of doing so are quickly passing in the greater part of the Africa of to-day. Any one can see that the younger generation, if it has attended school or come into contact with European life, has only the slightest or perhaps no interest in its heritage from the past. Since we Europeans have been the destroyers, we should feel ourselves

[1] Cf. F. Krause, 'Ethnology and the Study of Culture Change', *Africa*, vol. v, p. 383.

responsible for collecting and preserving these evi-
dences of a phase of humanity which is rapidly passing,
and for making them accessible to students of future
generations.

No one is better suited for collecting such data than
the Natives themselves, provided they are able to
write their own language. The growing interest
which the Natives are showing in the investigation
of their own tribal life is to be welcomed and should
in every way be encouraged. We can understand how
they resent being regarded by the Europeans as
objects of investigation. As in other spheres, so in
this, they may claim to become active partners with
the Europeans, and it is the task of the field-ethnolo-
gist to educate them along these lines.

4

In the changing Africa of to-day problems have
arisen, and are ever arising, which fall into the sphere
of social anthropology. It is the appreciation of this
fact which has led to the foundation of the International Institute of African Languages and Cultures.
The work of the Institute as laid down in its constitution is to provide an international clearing-house for
research in African linguistics, anthropology, and
sociology, and to bring about a closer association
between scientific research and the practical problems with which persons working in Africa have to
deal. The Institute has no intention of founding a
new school of anthropology, but it proposes to draw

the attention of anthropologists to existing problems, in the solution of which we require and ask their co-operation. It desires also to show the practical worker in Africa that he can derive advantage from the help of the anthropologist and will do well to learn from him.

From the beginning the Institute has been careful not to duplicate the work of already existing institutions, but on the contrary to help forward their work in every way possible. Neither does it intend to interfere with those anthropologists who are working along historical lines, as it is convinced of the value of such investigations. The Institute is, however, calling the attention of anthropological field-workers particularly to present-day problems, because it feels sure that there will always be a sufficient number of investigators devoted to the historical method, who will see that this aspect is not forgotten.

In the following chapters an attempt will be made to focus attention on some of the problems that have arisen in Africa and to show their connexion with the science of anthropology. The anthropological facts mentioned are only given as illustrations. No sort of completeness has been aimed at, either from the point of view of anthropology, or of present-day problems. The subjects discussed have mostly reference to West Africa, with which the writer is personally familiar. The examples also have been largely taken from that part of the continent, and only occasionally have examples from other parts of Africa been given.

II

MAN AND RACE IN AFRICA[1]

I

WHEN the Ewe in West Africa wish to characterize a person as friendly and kind, they say of him, *enye ame*, 'he is a man'. Inversely the phrase *menye ame o*, 'he is not a man' means 'he is selfish and cruel'. Both expressions correspond in their wording and sense to the Latin *humanus* and *inhumanus*. The human ideal is the same in the case of the ancient Roman and the Negro. The present-day European and African also both partake of human nature, and are therefore not essentially different.[2] For this very reason they are capable of understanding each other and of working together, even although for the time being the one may be the teacher and the other the pupil. We initiate the African into all our occupations, from factory-worker to university teacher, from simple artisan to senior official and doctor. We are, furthermore, introducing him to our European literature,

[1] Cf. C. G. Seligman, *Races of Africa*, London.

[2] S. H. Driberg, *At Home with the Savage*, London, 1932, pp. 36 ff.

which is the purest expression of our own culture, and in doing so we take it for granted that he can understand and assimilate it. These facts themselves show that we do not recognize a fundamental difference between ourselves and the African. Many a European has learnt to know Africans as friends in the true sense of the word who have allowed him to forget the differences of race. There is truth in what De Kat Angelino[1] says with reference to the Dutch Indies: 'The key to every colonial policy lies in the appreciation of the essential solidarity of humanity as a whole and in the elimination of racial pride.'

By this we do not mean to deny that differences exist, differences not only of race but also of culture, of innate ability, outlook, and mode of life, which can make themselves so strongly felt that they threaten to make a mutual understanding difficult and in some cases almost impossible. If the traveller on the Upper Nile steamer sees a group of Shilluk, almost or entirely naked, their bodies rubbed with cow-dung and ashes, their long hair bleached bright-red, with depilated eye-lashes, lying on the bank in apparently complete apathy, he may well believe that he is dealing with a wholly strange type of being, from whom he is completely separated. He would change his opinion, however, if he could talk with them in their own language and could learn that they have a tradition extending over 400 years, a complex, well-organized

[1] *Staatskundig Beleiden Bestuurszorg in Nederlandsch-Indië*, The Hague, 1929, vol. i, p. 592.

system of government with a king at the head, and a highly developed religion; and that they are as capable of being educated as any man and have a definite feeling for what is dignified and good behaviour.

While we recognize that there is a common basis of humanity in all races, we have no reason to ignore these racial differences or to minimize them. On the contrary we admire in them the richness of creation. We see the goal of human development, not in uniformity but in specific qualities and capabilities, brought by each race to complete development as its contribution to the general civilization of mankind.

Racial and cultural differences exist not only between Europe and Africa but also within Africa itself, and strictly speaking the term African should not be used without qualification. The people of Africa are divided into a number of races, each of an individual type, and even within the races variations are found which have been caused by intermarriage, by environment, and by history. Indigenous races and civilizations have influenced each other, and moreover for thousands of years streams of foreigners and of foreign culture have flowed into Africa from outside. The result to-day is an extraordinarily rich diversity.

2

Leaving aside the Semites in the east and north, the Indians in the east and south, the Malays in Madagascar, we regard as ancient inhabitants of Africa three races: Pygmies, Hamites, and Negroes. Of these the Negroes come first in number and importance, and to them our main attention will be directed, whilst the two other races will be dealt with only in brief outlines.

Pygmies.

As the name indicates, the Pygmies are distinguished by their small stature. They have a light-coloured skin which is usually covered with light, downy hair. They live, in small groups, in various parts of the southern half of Africa. P. Schebesta (*Africa*, vol. iv, p. 402) estimates the number of Pygmies and Pygmoids in Central Africa as 80,000, the majority of whom are to be found in the Belgian Congo. They are not sedentary, but move about as hunters and collectors, each group in a definite district, to which it claims a right of ownership. Any kind of regular work and earning of a livelihood are unknown to them. They do not practise agriculture or possess cattle, but are dependent on what a day's roaming in bush or forest offers them.

Possibly the Bushmen of South-West Africa are racially connected with the Pygmies, although this is not certain. They differ from them in some respects, notably in their rich mythology and religion. The Hottentots appear to be a cross between Bushmen and Hamitic immigrants, in which the Bushman element predominates.[1]

[1] Cf. T. Schapera, *The Khoisan Peoples of South Africa*, London, 1930, pp. 51 ff.

The Pygmies and Bushmen possibly represent an old type of mankind in Africa. It may be safely assumed that they were formerly more widely distributed in the continent than they are to-day; that they retreated before advancing Negroes and Hamites, and either became their servants or entered into a relationship with them in which they exchanged their game for the agricultural products of the Negroes. The material culture of both Pygmies and Bushmen is poor, and their social organization primitive. How far and in what way the so-called Bushman drawings in South Africa are connected with the forefathers of the present Bushmen, and whether the Bushmen are linked up with such primitive tribes as, e.g., the Ndorobo and similar groups in East Africa, is not sufficiently known. The Bushmen drawings will have to be studied in connexion with similar productions in North Africa and south-western Europe.

Pygmies and Bushmen stand everywhere at a disadvantage compared with Negroes, owing to their small numbers, their cultural inferiority, and their unstable mode of life, which avoids intercourse with strangers as much as possible. Their nomadic habits require wide areas for their subsistence, and these are taken away from them in an ever-increasing degree. The invading Hottentots were the first to oppress and decimate the Bushmen. From the seventeenth century onwards both Hottentots and Bushmen were pressed by Europeans from the south and later by Bantu from the north. The South African Korana

Hottentots are to all intents and purposes eliminated or bastardized. Of the Nama in the south-west, who have fought desperately against threatened extinction, an insignificant remnant of some 20,000 survives and these have lost any unity as a people. The Bushmen see their existence more and more limited. They give to-day the impression of an unhappy people living under precarious conditions in arid regions, into which they had to retreat. Negro and European have contributed with equal cruelty to their downfall. Even to-day when the Bushmen have ceased to be every man's prey, they seem to be unable to adapt themselves to new modes of life. Attempts to settle them and so assign to them a place in the present order of things have had only moderate results. When for a period they do submit to the unaccustomed restraint, sooner or later the irresistible impulse to wander awakens and all good intentions are frustrated.

Hamites.

This name embraces peoples who are akin to the European and Semitic races. They are light-skinned, with a straight nose, thin lips, narrow face, soft, often wavy or even straight hair, without prognathism. As a result of their wide distribution and of miscegenation many variations have evolved. It is even not certain whether all the people whom we call Hamites really had their origin in a common race. They represent an Asiatic immigration, and consequently live pre-eminently in the north and eastern borders of

Africa. The Berber (Amazigh) in North Africa and the restless Tuareg of the Sahara form the Libyan branch. The Hausa are composed of Negro groups with a distinct Hamitic influence, probably from North Africa. The more important representatives of the eastern or Kushitic Hamites are the Beja, Danakil, Galla, Somali, and (mixed with Semites and Negroes) the majority of the inhabitants of Abyssinia. The Fulani are perhaps an offshoot of the Kushites, they live in scattered groups from Senegal to Lake Chad. To the eastern Hamites also belong the groups of peoples classified under the name of Hima; they occupy the Lake Regions (Tussi, Hinda, Huma, Kitwara, Nkole) and may be connected with the Kushitic branch. The Masai and tribes related to them (Bari, Nandi, Tatoga, &c.) show strong Hamitic influence but are on the other hand relatives of the Nilotes. The Nilotes are a group of mixed Negro and Hamitic peoples found chiefly in the Anglo-Egyptian Sudan.

The significance of the Hamites in the composition of the African population consists in the fact that as nomads and as conquering warriors they have not confined themselves to their original homes, but have pushed their way into the countries of the Negroes. Owing to their racial superiority they have gained leading positions and have become the founders of many of the larger states in Africa. Their influence is strongest in East and South Africa and in the Sudan, i.e. the territory between the Sahara and the forest lands. Most of the peoples living in these regions are a result of crossing between Hamites and Negroes.

The majority of Hamites are cattle-owners, and this has no doubt intensified their racial qualities. The calling of herdsman leads man more into the loneliness of the wide steppes than the sociable life of the farmer. Owing to the constant necessity of protecting himself and his cattle against human and animal enemies, he is thrown upon his own resources. He must look for fresh pasturage, and often enough win it by conquest. He has little to lose, with the exception of his herds, which can easily be moved, and is therefore more inclined to settle disputes by war than is the sedentary Negro. The Hamite is proud, reserved, self-conscious, and warlike. He has accustomed himself to live as an aristocrat among the Negroes, and to look on them as his subjects. Their chief occupation, agriculture, seems to him unworthy. Cattle-breeding is the only activity worthy of an aristocrat; agriculture is left to the inferior classes. His relationship to the European is different also from that of the Negro. He does not see in the white man a superior being but a kinsman, and the Fulani addressed the first Europeans who came to them as cousins. This racial self-consciousness, which is quite natural to the Hamites, is still more marked in places where they have accepted Islam. As a rule they are indifferent or inimical to European civilization and education. It costs them a great effort of self-denial to admit the superiority of the white man, and to adapt themselves to the new conditions of life created by him. As economic values are more highly esteemed to-day than aristocratic privileges, they are in danger of being relegated to the background in comparison with the Negroes. The Fulani came to northern Nigeria as conquerors and a ruling caste. The Hausa, a happy mixture of Negro and Hamite blood, are far superior to their former lords in industry, and the latter lose in importance if they do not lose their character as an individual people by mixing with the Hausa, as is so often the case.

That it is possible for the Hamite to accustom himself to a settled abode and to agriculture is proved by the example of the Berber and Galla, who have long since taken this step. Many Fulani in the Western Sudan have also become agriculturalists. Similarly a large part of the Masai (Kuafi) in Tanganyika Territory, after they had lost their cattle through wars and rinderpest, became sedentary agriculturalists. It may be assumed that this intelligent and highly gifted race will, before it is too late, enter on the progressive paths of to-day, and that the wisdom of the European administrators and educators will succeed in winning them over, so that they may take the place which befits them in the future common life of Africa.

The Negro.

The Negroes are, apart from their mixture with other groups, a homogeneous race. The division into Bantu and Sudan Negro is a linguistic one and not a

racial distinction. It must, however, be pointed out
that within the Negro race through migrations and
other influences there has grown up an extraordinary
richness of type which presents great differences of
outward appearance and also of culture. The Nilotes
in north-east Africa and the Akan on the west coast
both have Negro blood in their veins, but in spite of
that one would hardly venture to think that they were
closely related. In his physique and his political evolution the Negro owes much to the Hamitic immigrants, but he has his own distinct racial qualities. He
is physically well developed; his agriculture and his
rich material culture have accustomed him to constant
activity. He is a willing and skilful worker, shows
himself docile and of great adaptability. In contrast
to the Hamite and Pygmy it was easy for him to adapt
himself to the conditions of to-day, and so he has
become in all spheres of life the pupil and helper of
the white man. He seems to have a special aptitude
for art, but he is also an artist in life. His innate cheer-
fulness, his care-free nature, and his amiability allow
him to conquer the heavy blows of Fate more easily
than the members of many another race.

Questions of race come into the sphere of physical
anthropology and so lie outside the task of the Institute. On the other hand, however, problems of the
adaptability of a race or a mixed race to new circumstances are important for our purpose. It would be
interesting to know if the assertion that the Bushmen

and Pygmies cannot be employed by Europeans is really a fact, or if the lack of success lies in the circumstances that the attempt has not been carried on over a long enough period or made on wrong lines and methods. Another important fact to know is how the races and mixed races differ in intellectual gifts, in will-power, in general capacity, and reliability. Lastly, we should know whether in all these differences there can be seen indications of special methods of education suitable for the people.

III

SOME OBSERVATIONS ON THE NEGRO'S MIND

I

IF the Negroes are one race, it is permissible to inquire into the characteristic traits of this race. In doing so, the differences which come to light in the separate peoples and tribes must not be left out of account, but it may be assumed that a certain amount of fundamental common qualities will be discovered. We are still not in a position to-day to draw final conclusions. Investigations carried on up to the present do not afford a sufficient foundation for such statements, because they have embraced only a few tribes, and are inadequate in scope. They deal with the group and its culture and neglect the individual. The spiritual life of a group will, however, be fully understood only through a knowledge of the largest possible number of individuals, and a picture of the whole must be founded on such knowledge. Individual differences in temperament, endowment, and sphere of interest are as significant in the case of the Negro as in that of the European. We need accurate observations on the development of the characters of individuals, under the influence of the Family, of village life, of play-fellows, of initiation and other groups, among which the individual passes his life. Comparison should also be made between the life-histories of persons who spend their days among the old untouched customs and those who live under modern changing conditions. Intelligence tests and other aids of modern experimental psychology can be useful, though they only deal with one side of the human being and not with his whole personality.

Another reason why we must be cautious in forming judgements is that the Negro is only just beginning, after thousands of years of relative seclusion, to take part in the cultural life of humanity and to enter into competition with others and thereby to develop his powers. It is impossible for us to form any definite conclusion about his future evolution. Experience has already shown the falseness of many previous judgements, and the capabilities of the Negro have developed in a way that would have seemed impossible to many half a century ago.

It has not been proved that the Negro in general intelligence and 'educability' is substantially inferior

to the white child. That, however, differences conditioned by race and environment do exist, appears to
be evident from the intelligence tests undertaken by
R. A. C. Oliver in Kenya. The subjects for his investigations were the pupils of the Prince of Wales
School, Kabete, a secondary school for European boys,
and those of the Alliance High School, Kikuyu, who
are of Bantu stock. The two main facts emerging from
this comparison are (1) that the average African score
in the intelligence test is about 85 per cent. of the
average European score, and (2) that about 14 per
cent. of the Africans reach or exceed the median European score. According to the same author the average
American Negro score is about 80 per cent. of the
average white American score, and about 20 per cent.
of the American Negroes reach or exceed the median
European score; but the difference between these two
averages is much less than the difference between the
most able and the least able of either group. The most
eminent American Negroes of all are probably the intellectual equals of quite eminent whites.[1] Mr. Oliver
cautions us against premature conclusions from this
result. It would be astonishing if children of peoples,
who for centuries have enjoyed systematic mental training and have produced the present world-civilization,
did not exhibit superior mental capabilities to those
who are the first generation to go to school and whose

[1] R. A. C. Oliver, 'The Comparison of the Ability of Races:
with special reference to East Africa', *The East African Medical
Journal*, September 1932, pp. 160–204.

parents lead in many respects a primitive life. To obtain sure results, the investigation will have to be extended to a number of tribes living under various conditions and in different parts of the continent, and especially to such groups as have for several generations been in close contact with the active life of modern civilization, and who therefore have had an opportunity of developing their intellectual ability more fully than those living within their native confines. Even in this case it is doubtful whether the period of contact has been long enough to have brought about noticeable changes. In the meantime it would be premature to decide whether the intellectual difference between the two races is fundamental and permanent, or only temporary.

The intelligence, and at the same time the moral principles, of the African find a significant expression in his folk-lore, that is in proverbs, riddles, and stories. They are not all on an equal level, especially the stories. These depend, in the form in which we hear them, largely on the personality of the narrator, and he may be intelligent, witty, or dull. Of the proverbs it may be said without reservation that they are equal in value to those of European peoples. They give proof of an astonishing power of observation of men and animals, deep and mature experience of life with sane judgement, and frequently also of humour and sarcasm. They are always apt and pointed in expression and extraordinarily picturesque. The inventors of proverbs are mostly men, while many of the fairy-tales owe their origin and diffusion to women and mothers. How the Africans value the two categories is shown in a Twi proverb: 'A clever child is told proverbs and not stories.' Proverbs sharpen the wit, and are a mental exercise, while stories are a mere pastime.

The Negro loves conversation and discussion, and often indulges in them for the admitted purpose of sharpening his intellect. A tale is told which ends with a decisive question, such as 'which one of the three acted rightly?' 'who was the shrewdest?' 'who accomplished most ?' With considerable acumen each member of the symposium tries to support his own view. The Negro is superior to the European, at least to the northern European, in the power of self-expression. In addresses at public meetings we often have an opportunity of admiring the clearness of his exposition, the sharp details in his arguments, his apt illustrations by the use of proverbs. We can only regret that so much cleverness and skill are not devoted to worthier objects than perhaps to a case dealing with the chasing away of a goat or with verbal insults. Not all speeches, however, are masterpieces. There are speakers who are diffuse and childish in their arguments, and it is only seldom that a speaker succeeds, in spite of his merits in matters of detail, in making a speech which follows out one train of thought consistently without losing itself in by-paths. This reveals a certain narrowness of outlook which makes it difficult for him to survey a larger whole. Each of the proverbs is a little masterpiece; they express in concentrated and yet easily intelligible form one single thought. When, however, it is a question of expressing a connected group of thoughts in logical steps, the Negro's power fails him. We can make the same observation with regard to the fairy-tales. They sometimes consist of parts which are only externally put together. The original theme is left, a new one takes its place, and it is often difficult to discover any point in the story.

The attainments and technical abilities of the Negro have in many cases reached a high standard. If that standard has been attained with the aid of external influences, it nevertheless required intelligence and skill to retain, assimilate, and develop what had been acquired in this way. The building of houses; the making of implements; spinning and weaving; the obtaining and working of metals; agriculture; social and political institutions; methods of the education of youth: these are the fruits of much experience and sane knowledge of life. The isolation in which he formerly lived helps to explain why the African has remained stationary at a comparatively primitive stage of civilization. The tribe, or perhaps even a still smaller unit, led its own existence in a relative isolation. The African's culture circle was extremely restricted. His cultural possessions and inheritance were limited to achievements within this small circle, whereas in a larger cultural environment where there are greater opportunities for interchange, the general store of attainments can be enriched. If these limita-

tions are borne in mind, his achievements in civilization are considerable. His sphere of activity is
not by any means confined to what belongs to the
immediate necessities of his existence. His whole
material, social and intellectual culture, his art, his
poetry and the forms of his recreation show that he
has advanced far beyond this narrow circle and has
always striven to gain knowledge of the world about
him and to assimilate it. He has found names for elements in his surroundings which are of no immediate
practical interest for him, and has thus given them a
place in his life. There is scarcely a tree or a plant, an
animal, a hill or a tract of country which does not have
its own name. The individual's store of words is
much larger than one would expect. We have frequently
found Negroes with a vocabulary of 4,000 to 5,000
words at their ready disposal. This is to be explained
by the fact that knowledge is not, as with us, split up
among many social groups so that the smith, the
weaver, the locksmith, and the scholar each has his
own peculiar terminology. Among the Negroes each
normal individual is master of the whole knowledge
and skill of his group, and therefore knows the proper
name for everything.

Close contact with Nature has enabled the Negro
to accumulate a store of accurate observation and
experience, and his knowledge in these spheres is not
insignificant. It is inadequate, however, because his
observation is often superficial; conclusions have
been drawn from it in a most uncritical way; and

instead of further thought on the matter, word-spinning has seemed sufficient. The African there-fore has never progressed so far as the knowledge of true causal connexions or natural laws. He possesses a certain amount of knowledge of Nature, i.e. the beginnings of natural science, but for the greater part it is pseudo-science—knowledge mixed with a child-like play of imagination. There is no lack of attempts to understand the processes of Nature and of human life. How to explain the creation of the world, of man, and of the different races of mankind as far as they appear on his horizon; the remarkable similarity be-tween men and apes; the origin of the constellations, of lightning, thunder, and the winds; the interchange of wet and dry periods, and the waxing and the waning of the moon; the sources whence man obtained the benefits of his civilization and how death came into the world: all these problems have moved the mind of the Negro and he has meditated on them. His meditation, however, always assumed the character of an interesting and amusing entertainment. The interest in problems is there, but it is neither suffi-ciently intensive nor lasting to avoid being intimi-dated when faced with the necessity of real effort. A problem commands interest as long as it is a pleasant diversion, but not beyond that, and not for its own sake. The idea of any event happening from an inner necessity or a natural law is quite strange to him be-cause his imagination and ideas depend so much on impressions of the senses. Behind every occurrence there is for him 'the one-who-causes'. If a tree or a person dies, then some one, a spirit or a man, has been the cause. For inner necessity or natural causes is substituted a personal will. The results achieved moreover soon assumed a traditional form, in which they were then handed on unchanged from generation to generation.

It has been interpreted as a characteristic of the Negro that he lives only in the present and does not trouble himself about the future or the past. That is only correct up to a point. Most of his economic activities demand a certain amount of foresight. The complex systems of education which many African tribes have evolved show a serious concern of the elders for the welfare of the coming generation. The living man makes provision for his existence in the other world; and the idea of personal fame after death is not unknown to the Negro. Nearly every tribe possesses traditions of its past, its ancestors, their deeds and experiences on their migrations; and in many cases one can prove from other sources that such traditions have been handed on with comparative faithfulness through centuries. Many educated Africans show a growing desire to know and to keep alive the past of their tribe, and this has already been developed so far that individual educated Negroes have written the history of their own people.

A great part in historic tradition is played by the explanation of names. There is a constant effort to interpret place-names and the names of persons etymologically, and an event is imagined to correspond to this explanation. The interpretation is as a rule wrong, and the event derived from it a product of the fancy. This is another illustration of the tendency to trifle instead of investigate. The Negro is far from possessing a clear picture of the past. Certain points stand out prominently, but when we go back only a few generations, the past is wrapped in an impenetrable mist. It is impossible for him to fix the date of an event because the calculation of time is unknown. Most languages do not have names for the months of the year; and only in isolated cases does there exist a calendar of festivals extending over several months. Events that have taken place a hundred years ago or less, as for example the coming of the white race, are placed in the very beginning of things.

Concentration on the present makes possible a more whole-hearted enjoyment of the day and the moment, for the past weighs less heavily on the African, and he troubles less about the future than the European. His needs are relatively small, and they can be satisfied without too much effort. It is easier for the Negro than it is for us to live in accordance with the saying of Jesus: 'Sufficient unto the day is the evil thereof.'

2

The question whether 'primitive' man, under which category the African Negro is here included, can think and act logically has given rise to much recent discussion.[1] What has been said in the foregoing pages is a partial answer to this query. In many of his utterances in daily life the Negro reveals a completely normal logical faculty, and the mental processes as well as the actions resulting from them cannot be distinguished from our own. It is, however, evident that there are differences between the mental activity of the Negro and that of the European, and we have already drawn attention to some of the salient points. A significant difference is that the Negro is more dominated by unconscious or half-conscious impulses than we are; for him emotional thinking outweighs logical reasoning, and when emotion is the guide, ideas and actions may result which are not in conformity with logic. This, however, is a difference of degree and not of kind; it is found within Africa as well as in Europe in innumerable gradations. A great number of the conceptions and customs of the African which have been stigmatized as 'illogical' or 'pre-logical' have their roots in religion, and every one knows that religious experience is not fed from intellectual sources alone. It is true not only of 'primitive' African religions but of all religions, that experiences and convictions which spring from them may appear to the irreligious man as irrational. Where religious conviction is admitted as a fact, the beliefs are completely logical and consistent.

[1] Cf. A. Vierkandt, *Naturvölker und Kulturvölker*, Berlin, 1896, where these problems are discussed extensively, and likewise the publications by L. Lévy-Bruhl, e.g., *La Mentalité Primitive*, Paris.

It is an essential sign of emotion that it is of short duration and has the character of an explosion. The difference between emotional and logical thought is therefore one between explosive and continuous mental activity. With the Negro emotional, moment- ary, and explosive thinking predominates. His emo- tions may lead to serious results. Suicide, for example, with the Negro is always a surrender to an overpower- ing emotion. More often, however, his emotion evaporates as quickly as it arose. Two people ex- changing a storm of angry words burst out next moment into Homeric laughter. This dependence on excitement, on external influences and stimuli, is a characteristic sign of primitive mentality. Primitive man's energy is unstable and spasmodic. He is easily fired with enthusiasm for an undertaking and begins his work with great zeal; but his interest dies down quickly and the work is abandoned. Many school and church buildings would have remained unfinished, if constant pressure from the European had not been behind them. Where emotion is lacking, the Negro shows little spontaneity and is passive. He waits for what is coming to him and evades what is incon- venient, or adapts himself to it, instead of bravely confronting the obstacles of life and mastering them. If he is forced into acts which awaken no response in his inner mind, his work is apt to be careless, and he tries to get out of it whenever he can. Such weak- nesses must not be thought to be the personal fault of the individual; they are conditioned by environment, by the social background, and can only be overcome by education. When, however, his interest has been aroused and when the object is not too distant, does not demand too much sacrifice, and is at the same time desirable enough to outweigh momentary unwillingness; in other words, when his enthusiasm or devotion to a cause endures, then he is capable of great and even sustained effort. We need only reflect how long it takes to complete a work of art, a dug-out, a drum, or any implement. The making of personal ornaments, the dressing of hair, and preparations for festivals demand a great deal of trouble and much time; but behind them as stimuli are the satisfaction of vanity, the desire for personal dignity, the sense of beauty of form, or immediate utility. Agriculture, too, demands honest effort; but it occupies only part of the year, and when the season for it arrives, the Negro is drawn into the field-work as if by its own rhythm, and it is a natural thing to do what every one else is then doing. There is also the motive of rivalry with his neighbours urging him to keep pace with them. Moreover, the work is done intermittently, and an occasion is easily found to justify a respite from toil. Once the seed is sown, the ensuing work is made easier by the worker watching the results of his labours and seeing the crops grow and thrive.

It is otherwise when a man works for the European. Then it is a question of an activity in which he personally does not take the slightest interest. A continual tension of the will, a perpetual fight with his quickly roused feeling of distaste are required, and it is this which so easily makes the demands of European civilization appear oppressive to him. This kind of work becomes a dull, laborious routine, and the white man himself a hard taskmaster who makes unreasonable demands. If the Negro does persist in his work in spite of everything it is either because of the force of necessity or the gradual assertion of the power of habit.

The same is true in the case of continued mental work. His interest in a question is seldom lasting, and his power of thought is easily fatigued. It is difficult for him to follow an argument of any length, or to think out a problem for himself with all its implications. He loves to place ideas superficially side by side without a logical connexion, or to connect them with each other according to their external features. This lack of critical thinking and logical coherence makes it easy to understand why he does not always feel contradictions as such. In his religious creed two mutually exclusive conceptions may exist side by side. For a long time to come he will be weak in independent critical and productive thought. His defects in will power are on similar lines. The energy which pursues its aim undeterred by disillusionment and unwearied by new obstacles is strange to him.

The Negro has therefore but few gifts for work which aims at a distant goal and requires tenacity, independence, and foresight. He has never succeeded in larger undertakings, which need plans for a far future and a wider view of acting on a large scale; he works from day to day without clearly picturing the consequences. The Negro is therefore not a good merchant. There are indeed traders enough in Africa, and individual peoples like the Hausa, Mandingo, and Swahili do business on a considerable scale. These, however, are principally tribes which have for a long time culturally, or by reason of a mixture of race, lived under foreign influences, and they too carry on their business, even where a large volume of trade is concerned, in a way which differs widely from the orderly and complicated processes of European enterprise.

We must approach the mental attitude of the Negro remembering always that he is above all a member of a group. The motives for his actions are predominantly social not individual, and are deeply influenced by public opinion. His self-consciousness is rooted in his compliance with the community; it depends on the security of his daily life as guaranteed by the group, not on the independent action of the individual. Personal responsibility is avoided wherever possible. As far as this exists within the limits of the group, it results as it were of its own accord from the routine of daily life and therefore demands no great effort of will. Its omission would immediately break that rhythm and thereby shake the individual's position in the group; for this reason such duties are not easily neglected. This responsibility has reference only to fellow members of the group, with whom he feels closely connected, and not to strangers, among whom is the European. It should therefore not astonish us if the Native is not conscious, in his relations with the Europeans, of the same obligation to truthfulness, honesty, and reliability demanded in his dealings with his fellows. He gives promises to a European without hesitation, even when he has not the least intention of keeping them, because that is the simplest way of getting rid of an inconvenient demand. Moreover that which has not been decided by 'the old people', i.e. the representatives of the group, has no binding force for the individual. It should, however, again be emphasized that the features described here are not found in the Negro race alone. Every one knows that they are human characteristics and are met with in members and groups of our own race as well as among African Negroes.

3

Although the fact that the Negro is largely ruled by his emotions can be looked on as characteristic, this does not mean that a different attitude is impossible for him, and indeed we are observing to-day how he is changing. The African is growing accustomed to regular continuous work, and he is becoming more reliable. If it were not so, he could not carry out the achievements which we see him accomplishing to-day and which require a considerable amount of exactness, continuity, and regularity. Every employer knows that he can educate his workers, that there is a difference between a Native who comes for the first time from the bush and a group of workmen whom he has trained, and who will return to him although they may interrupt their work at times. Among the thousands of employees who, year in and year out, work in offices, workshops, and stores, there are many who in every respect do satisfactory work.

The schoolboy, who without any external compulsion and often without encouragement from his parents, insists on going to school and stands by his resolve for years, shows that there is a new spirit awake and that young Africa is not lacking in perseverance. Though habit and the example of his companions may help him, it is no small matter for a boy to renounce the happy life of African youth and sit instead, day by day, on a hard school bench. It is but natural that some should grow weary on the long road to the goal, but there are others who in spite of all obstacles carry out their plan to the end.[1]

[1] A West African teacher in describing his child life says: 'In my whole school life I never had a real joy because I was so poor. Although I was the leader of my class I was often the last to pay my school fees. Sometimes I had to borrow money and books from the teacher or from good friends, because I was not able to buy them. My clothes and blankets were torn and my hat was so shabby that I had really to be ashamed of it. With respect to food I was very poorly off. Often I had no more than one meal a day. When our school started boy scouting, I was the only pupil among 140 who could not take part in it, because I was not able to afford the money for the uniform.'

The considerable progress which the Negroes have
made recently is no doubt due to their contact with
Europeans. This contact has provided the spark
which kindled the fire, but, to continue the metaphor,
the spark must be fanned to keep the flame alive. The
achievements of Negroes in America show that the
present evolution of the African Negro is only a
beginning. Although the majority of American
Negroes, partly owing to the social disabilities to
which they are constantly exposed, live on a lower
level than the average of other races, a considerable
number of them have attained high standards in business life as well as in arts and sciences, and have produced original achievements which stand comparison
with those of any other race. The American Negroes
have for generations had the advantage of living
continuously in close contact with the permanent
stimulus of European civilization.

4

The mental attitude of the Negro can teach us
lessons as to his education. If it is generally true to
say that the Negro can work successfully only when
his interest has been aroused, and when he is able to
enjoy his work, this is doubly true of the African
child. For him the school is at the outset something
strange, which may for a time stir his curiosity, but
is quite outside his previous sphere. He generally has
no more than a vague notion that the school will
bring him into closer contact with the life of the white

man, which may be useful to him. It is important, owing to this attitude of mind, that it should be made clear to the child at the very beginning that the school and all that he learns there is closely connected with his own life and that of his own people. It must teach him to understand that life better, to shape it better, and to take pleasure in it. The child's natural environment must be the starting-point of the school; it must be the centre round which it revolves and to which it always returns. Where, however, this bond between the school and daily life does not exist, there is a chance of education leading to a purely mechanical acquisition of knowledge, quite unrelated to the inner life. Perhaps more than any other race the Negro has a tendency to imitate. When we remember that the pedagogical training of a Native teacher may be only of an elementary character, we cannot be surprised that in many schools the course of study does not touch the interests of the child, and teacher and pupil content themselves with learning by heart. Zest for knowledge is not awakened and the pupil does not learn because of his delight or interest in the subject but because he hopes that by going to school he will gain an opportunity for a better position in life. It is to be feared that such schooling—and all too often it used to be of that character—has hopelessly mechanized many a healthy receptive brain, destined for better things.

We must work against this danger. The recognized task of the educator in Africa as elsewhere lies in character-building, in training the pupil to become a responsible independent personality with his own ideas and his own initiative, and in giving him a serious vocation. It is not enough for the Negro any more than for ourselves to gain nothing but veneer from what we teach him. It is much more important to allow the vital sources of his life within him to spring up spontaneously, that he should develop his own powers of production not only in the material but also in the spiritual sphere, and thus bring his contribution to the culture of mankind.

5

Our problem has, however, a significance beyond the school and education in the strict sense of the words. The technical culture of the European is more apt than anything else to suppress the life of the emotions and to replace it by cold intellect and pure mechanism. Formerly, work was for the African a source of pleasure; even when it demanded real effort, it was such a stimulus to him that the effort became a sport rather than a task. This is in most cases not true when he works under modern conditions. It is difficult to see how a Negro who used to till his own ground or tend his own cattle, who in his leisure times went fishing and hunting, or practised some art, should enjoy work in the mines or on plantations. New pleasures may be offered him there, but they are not related to his work. Even in the higher professions he often arrives at a point where he looks on his work merely as a daily routine, in which his personal life plays no part. It is not unimportant whether a man is able to enjoy his work because he shares in the proceeds or because the doing of it is a moral duty, or whether it is felt as a tiresome yoke borne unwillingly and solely as a means of subsistence. The latter must end in a blunting of the faculties, when the individual and the group have no values in life and no real aims to protect them from spiritual extinction. In what these values consist; how they can be assimilated and organically incorporated with actual living; are questions with which the investigations carried on by the Institute should be acutely concerned. From anthropologists and psychologists we demand guidance in the solution of complex problems such as the following. How, in the case of the African, is the transition from the emotional to a more intellectual attitude, from explosive to more connected thinking and action, to be effected without forcing the emotional part of him into wrong paths or entirely suppressing it? Is there a definite difference in mental attitude and intellectual capability between the child and the adolescent after puberty, and if so, in what does it consist and what has to be our attitude towards it? On what system must the education of the African be based to transform him from a purely receptive creature to productive man with a cultural character of his own?

E

IV

THE ECONOMIC BASES OF LIFE

The Peasant.

THE Negro is a peasant; he loves the cultivation of the soil and in it finds his real vocation. In a number of African languages the same expression is used for 'to work' and 'to cultivate the field'. Other occupations, such as hunting and fishing, rearing cattle or plying a craft, are only subsidiary to the agriculture which nourishes every household and is the foundation of all material life. The boys go from their tenderest years to the fields with father or uncle, and it is their greatest pride when, after they have reached the age of 10–12 years, the father allows them to start a little field of their own next to his, and helps them to take the first step to economic independence. It is a serious deprivation to the old man when he notices that his strength no longer suffices for helping his family to till their fields, and it is not rare to see the chief and other well-to-do people at work on the farm.

The stages in the evolution of agriculture differ according to soil, climate, and the character of the people. Frequently the cultivation shows a high degree of application and experience, observation of nature, and ability in husbandry. In some parts of Africa one can go for days through well-tilled, carefully weeded, and fertile fields, and considering the primitive resources which are at the disposal of the Negro, we have to give him credit for having reached the highest possible stage of perfection with the means at his command.

As a preparation for tilling fields the Negro considers one measure indispensable, which many a European has regretted: the burning of the bush. This is practised throughout the whole of Equatorial

Africa at the height of the dry season. Although to the Native farmer it seems indispensable, yet in many ways it is a most irrational procedure. Its purpose is to clear the land of grass and bush, lighten the hoeing, fertilize the soil with ash, destroy snakes and other dangerous vermin, and make hunting easier. One useful effect of the burning, besides the fertilizing with ash salt, is that on pasture land coarse, less valuable grasses are in this way destroyed and the growth of fine nourishing species encouraged. At the same time there are harmful results of this method of clearing land, seen in the destruction of the forests, the favouring of steppe-formation and the ensuing gradual desiccation, decrease in protection from wind, lack of shade, and deterioration in the quality of the soil. The re-growth of the forest is systematically prevented by firing, and in this way large parts of Africa have been deforested. It is assumed by experts that south of the Sahara as well as in South Africa desiccation is advancing. It is natural that the Natives should cling tenaciously to their bush-fires, and it may be true that a piece of land can be used continuously for several years only on account of the fertilizing ash. None the less this method is wasteful and primitive, and inconsistent with any intensive agriculture. It will only be possible to eliminate it, however, if we enable the Natives to manure their fields regularly, and it will be a long time before that is possible since the majority of farmers have no cattle and therefore no manure, and artificial manures are too dear.

The working of the ground is done with the hoe, the almost ubiquitous farm tool. The general procedure is for one family to cultivate a strip of land as long as it yields a profitable return. The land is then left to recover for a number of years; it again becomes covered with grass and bush, and after that is made use of once more. Where it is a matter of forest-land, the larger trees are cut down or burned at the root, and the wood is left to rot, or is burned. During the period of cultivation, either the same crop is grown each year, i.e. 3-5 years of sorghum or maize continuously; or there is a regular rotation of crops, during which leguminous plants, ground-nuts, or peas, are planted for the enriching of the soil. Obviously the amount of land required for this shifting cultivation is disproportionately large, as one part is always fallow.

Particularly careful cultivation is found where a dense population or the scanty ground make it necessary to use the soil to its best advantage. The Kabure in the hilly country of North Togo have stone walls round their fields; irrigate them with skilfully constructed ditches; and make use of manure from cattle kraals. The smallest piece of land is used, even when numerous stones have first laboriously to be removed. The whole country, in spite of its mountainous nature, gives the impression of a large, carefully tended garden. Similar examples of a really intensive agriculture are to be seen in other parts of Africa, and they show that the African peasant is very well capable of improving his methods.

The plough in an ancient form has spread from the east and north, perhaps in the train of Islamic expansion, right to the southern extreme of the Sahara and the Eastern Promontory. It has not, however, reached the Negro country, not even in those regions where the presence of cattle, as for example in East Africa, would have made its introduction possible. The Negroes have preferred to hold fast to the old system, and they still do so to-day. Where changes have taken place, they are to be ascribed to the direct action of the Europeans. Basutoland is one of the few countries in which the plough has almost entirely taken the place of the hoe. In other parts of South Africa too, e.g. in Southern Rhodesia and Bechuanaland, ploughs are largely in use, and attempts to introduce them are being made in various parts of the continent. The success of these efforts will partly depend on the success of the warfare against the tsetse fly. We cannot determine whether plough cultivation will spread all over Africa, or whether the greater part of the population will remain faithful to the hoe. The use of the plough involves a far-reaching modification not only of the economic system, but also of social conceptions. In contrast to previous custom it makes the men responsible for the larger share of agricultural activities, and therefore creates a new division of labour between the sexes. Hoe cultivation yields good results, though it is certainly capable of improvement, and it is so closely interwoven with the whole economic system that it

will persist still for many a long year. Every peasant
is naturally conservative, and the African peasant
doubly so. All important food plants are still cultivated to-day in exactly the same way as they were
many centuries ago, and we cannot think ill of the
Negro for refusing to abandon with a light heart
the result of his long agricultural experience. He is
accessible to innovation if it can be adapted to what
is already existing, i.e. if it can be easily assimilated
and means real progress. From the sixteenth century
onwards several food plants have been introduced
into West Africa by the Portuguese, such as maize,
manioc, sweet potatoes, ground-nuts, and tomatoes.
They have spread throughout the tropical part of the
continent, and in many regions have become an indispensable part of the people's food. It was possible
for these plants to spread slowly and imperceptibly
as did all earlier agricultural influences, because they
involved no change in the customs of the farmer and
fitted into their place in the existing system of agriculture.

In contrast to this the attempts made by Europeans
to improve agriculture have had only a moderate
degree of success. We quite often see pupils who have
had excellent training on model farms, following the
old indigenous methods on their own fields. For to
them there are two differing systems: one good for
the European, the other equally good for the African;
and they lack a connecting link between the old and
the new. This may partly be due to the belief that the

European, owing to his greater magical powers, is able to achieve what is denied to the black man. In addition, however, the agriculture of the white man rests on a mass of scientific knowledge that is for the moment not accessible to the black man, who is not able to appreciate the advantages to himself of this knowledge. Moreover, the method taught by the European demands more concentration, precision, and care than the Negro is accustomed to or likes. He has to fight many battles against his own indolence and deeply rooted habits. Instruction will possibly become more efficacious if the experiments are carried out on the farms of the Natives by Native farm demonstrators, with the constant co-operation of the farmer himself, because in this way the farmer will more readily be brought to see that it is a question of his own affairs and not the white man's. As soon as he has convinced himself that the innovation is really useful to him, his innate realism will recommend its acceptance.

2

Conditions are different where the Negro raises plants which he has first known through the European, that is, crops which are destined for export, and are therefore in no relation to Native domestic economy, traditions, and habits. In this case it appears self-evident to him that the directions and teaching of the European should be followed, although even here there is always the danger that he should lapse into his old easy-going methods. On the whole it must

be said that the Africans have succeeded to an astonishing degree in acquiring the skill necessary for
production for export, and their successes in this
sphere have been great. The best-known instance
of this is the cocoa-growing of the Gold Coast, an
industry which is exclusively carried on by Native
planters, and which has in a few decades developed
from insignificant beginnings to one of the important
industries of the world, the Gold Coast alone supplying nearly half the world's consumption of cocoa.
Cotton in Uganda, and to a lesser degree in Tanganyika Territory and other African countries, has
undergone a similar development. Other important
Native exports are ground-nuts, copra, and in recent
times coffee. In the years 1921–31 non-Native
agricultural exports from Tanganyika amounted to
£11,312,000 and Native to £13,881,000 approximately. No less than 68·8 per cent. of the value of
coffee exported is purely Native grown.[1] In all these
cases the inducement of earning money has been
strong enough to encourage the Negro to increased
activity without any external compulsion. Even in
earlier times, before the beginning of the colonial era,
the Natives produced great quantities of goods for
which they found a market with European merchants.
Palm-kernels, palm-oil, ground-nuts, wax, hides and
skins, rubber and ivory have always been important

[1] From Sir Sydney Armitage-Smith's Report on a Financial
Mission to Tanganyika, quoted in *East Africa*, Nov. 24, 1932,
p. 247.

articles of export, for the winning of which the world was indebted to the Negro industry alone.

The entry of the Native producer into the world market was a great change for him. It put an end to the autarchy in which each family and each village led an existence independent of the rest of the world. The Negro farmer is becoming dependent on factors which lie far beyond his control and which he does not understand. He has to take an interest in the international scale of prices; the art of reading, and acquaintance with newspapers are becoming important for him. When the cultivation of an article for export assumes larger proportions, the planter no longer finds time to raise cereals for his own food. He has to purchase them, and thus specialization finds its way into agriculture. He cannot work the plantation with his own people and has to call in the help of workers from outside, thus becoming an employer. This situation can be seen in the cocoa crop on the Gold Coast, and the ground-nut harvest in Senegambia. Some of the workers from other areas settle permanently in the country, and colonies of strangers arise, whose inhabitants intermarry with the indigenous population. The homogeneity of the group is in this way decreased, but at the same time their outlook is widened.

If the cultivation of a product brings in large profits, every one wants to take it up, and, not unjustly, people have spoken of the cocoa-fever on the Gold Coast. The desire to earn money quickly so takes possession of the population, that interest in anything else threatens to die out. It is dangerous from an economic point of view for a country to be dependent on a single product and to neglect other useful commodities as has been done with the oil-palm in the Gold Coast. On the other hand, the reaction of the Native planter to a sharp fall in prices is so radical that he loses all pleasure in planting, lets his plantation go to ruin, and it may become a danger from the spread of pests.

Where in one area the same crops are cultivated both by Europeans and Natives, there is not infrequently a certain opposition from the white planters to the black. This may partly be explained by the fact that the Native planter is considered an unwelcome rival who can produce more cheaply. The complaints that the plantations of the Natives become a danger to their European neighbours, on account of their bad condition and faulty precautions against pests, are, however, not always unjustified. Another factor is that the Native quality is not so good in the more valuable products, their preparation often being careless or faulty. Sometimes the Natives cannot refrain from their old habit of adulterating a product by childish devices for increasing its weight, which may result in damaging the reputation of the produce of a whole colony. Sir Gordon Guggisberg in his account of the Gold Coast[1] gives as the four

[1] *The Gold Coast, A Review of the Events of 1920–26,* Accra, 1927, p. 44.

problems with which the cocoa industry is faced:
(1) Deterioration in the fecundity of the trees owing
to too close planting, careless methods, and lack of
attention to the soil. (2) The abandonment of plantations owing to low prices. (3) The falling off in
humidity owing to too great a clearance of the forests.
(4) Serious diseases. In the same report (p. 41) the
author points out that according to the opinion of
the experts the successful combating of disease could
not be completed in less than thirty to forty years and
at a cost of between £20,000 and £25,000 per annum.

We are confronted with similar difficulties in the
case of other Native export products. They are not
such that Native cultivation should be discouraged
on their account. They will grow less and less with
the improving education of the Native, but they show
that the African will remain for a long time dependent on the help and the teaching of the white man.
Products destined to compete on the world market
require a degree of technical knowledge, exactness,
care, and ceaseless work such as the Negro to-day does
not possess. Where he competes with the European
planter he will only rarely succeed in supplying as
good a quality of the product as the white man.
Certain products, as, for instance, sisal hemp, require
the investment of so much capital, and demand such
specialized labour and machinery, that they are not
suitable for production by the Native.

Although independent Native production is important economically and deserves every encourage-

ment, the systematic development of a colony makes direct white co-operation desirable and in many cases imperative. The productive capacity of a Native working within an organization and under constant direction is, according to the Annual Report of the Department of Agriculture (Tanganyika Territory)[1] many times greater than where the same man works alone. In the Lindi Province, non-native production from a few estates employing about 6,000 labourers accounted for 50 per cent. of the value of exports for 1931; the balance of the population, some 350,000 souls, supplied the other half. 'Practical support to non-native enterprise in a Native territory such as Tanganyika is well worth while, and to achieve steadiness of out-turn and of trade each should be equally supported, as they are in effect complementary and not opposed.' The same Report indicates (p. 16) that while in Bukoba, despite several years of educative effort, the coffee plantations of the Natives are still in poor condition, on Kilimanjaro a far better state of affairs obtains, 'possibly because of the nearness of many non-native plantations'.

Professional schools for instruction in agriculture may be valuable, especially for the training of instructors and demonstrators, and for the education of technical assistants for the larger agricultural enterprises. The teaching given there is sometimes, however, too scientific and too specialized to be of real help to the peasant. He learns things which lie

[1] Dar-es-Salaam, 1932, p. 5.

beyond the horizon of his future sphere of activity, and he accustoms himself to tools and methods which he cannot easily employ in his own village. He should not by his training be isolated from his companions in his Native place. The whole aim of his agricultural training should be to make him a progressive element in his community. This can only come to pass if he remains part of this communal life, and if innovations are such that they can be initiated by every intelligent farmer without too much trouble. It is much better that progress should proceed slowly, should remain within modest limits and therefore be adopted more generally, and thus lead to a lasting improvement, than that marvels should be presented to the Natives from which after all only the European can benefit.

Such a simple, one might almost say natural, form of instruction in agriculture is best given in the elementary school; it is an excellent means for establishing the necessary close connexion between the school and daily life, as well as that between the school and the home. Botany and zoology, nature study and geography, cattle-raising and horticulture have their natural point of departure in the home field, hedge, and forest. If the instruction is given in the right way, it will be so interesting to the children that they will speak about it at home, and repeat on their own fields or on those of their fathers some of the experiments which they have learnt in the school garden under the supervision of their teacher. This will to a considerable extent contribute to making the school of a Negro village a centre of culture, from which fresh life would radiate to the whole community. The flight from agriculture is general and is a serious symptom. In the main it can be explained by the upheavals of to-day which mislead the Negro into hoping that he will be able to acquire a fortune very quickly far from his home. This migration is encouraged to a fatal degree if education, by its academic attitude and its ignoring of village life and its needs, drives the pupils away from the village into the large towns. The conviction of the Natives has too often been that farming and going to school are two different things, unrelated to each other, or even mutually exclusive. The boy who is going to be 'only' a farmer does not need any schooling, and the boy who goes to school does not do so with the intention of becoming a farmer. Let any class of schoolboys be asked who among them wish to be farmers and remain in their Native village, and the answer will be quite unambiguous. This means that the intelligent, energetic, and cultivated section of the youth is turning away from agriculture, and this tendency will gain strength as the school system grows. We should therefore welcome the fact that lately the education authorities have successfully endeavoured to adapt elementary schools to an agricultural community and thus to give them their true place in the life of the Native. In the interests of the African we can hope for nothing better than that his land should remain a land of farmers, and that well-populated farming villages with a cultivated and progressive population will be its chief wealth. We should make it our object to prevent the Negro from losing his joy in agriculture, and also to hinder the growth of a prejudice, which is fortunately being overcome to-day in Europe and America, that anybody who cannot get on at school is good enough to be a farmer. The remedy for this is to show the Natives that a thorough training is not only advantageous but indispensable for the farmer of the future.

3

Agriculture has from time immemorial been closely connected with religious and magical beliefs and customs. For a work of such importance, on which the whole existence of the group depends, the powers of man will, in spite of the utmost industry and care, not suffice. The greater number of West African tribes worship the Earth as a divinity which is the giver of all fruitfulness. The priests offer sacrifices to the Earth at all important agricultural seasons and ask her blessing. When new fields are put under cultivation, they point out the right spot and the best time for the beginning of the work. Even the individual father of a family does not begin his work without sacrifice and prayer, be it to the Earth, to another deity, or to the ancestors. Magic serves to exorcize the hostile powers of rival neighbours or of evil spirits, and to attract beneficent powers, especially that of rain in due season. The planting of seeds is generally left to the women, because they have the gift of fruitfulness and can transfer it to the crops. Among the Ewe, a young girl with her friends has to plant the maize on the field of her future father-in-law. This is her first step into the family of her future husband. Among many tribes of Liberia, the Kpelle for instance, it is the custom for a wife to confess to her husband before the beginning of the field work if she has been unfaithful to him, because otherwise harmful influences will hamper the growth of the crop and lead to disasters in the working of the field. The greatest feast of the year is, for tribes who practise agriculture, the Harvest Home, in which gods and ancestors participate and receive their thank-offerings.

The social aspect of agriculture is almost as important as the religious and magical. The days of field work and the bringing in of the crop have, in spite of the toil they involve, a festive character. The whole community works the field of the chief; the young men together work the garden of each member of their group in due succession; the youth is helped by boys of the same age in his work for his father-in-law; and every day such co-operation is celebrated by a meal with the beer drinking that belongs to it, and finishes with song and dance. In the case of larger groups of workers a drummer is often installed on the margin of the field, and the rhythm of his drum regulates the work.

F

All these emotional elements naturally fade into
the background not only when the Native works on
a European plantation, but also when he begins to
rationalize his agriculture and to cultivate products
for export. It is no longer a question of the maintenance of a group for which he feels himself responsible, but of the earnings of an individual; in place of
mutual help there is now paid labour; for the prosper-
ing of the cocoa and coffee plantations the aid of the
ancestors and gods is no longer invoked, for they have
nothing to do with such matters. The cultivator relies
on the lessons he has learnt from the European. Thus
even for this progress a price must be paid. It elimi-
nates many a superstition and much sluggishness in
work, and compels the soil to greater fruitfulness,
but at the same time it destroys much of the religious
sense and feeling of social responsibility. It creates
obvious differences between the poor and the rich,
which tend to create social friction.

4

The Shepherd.

Cattle were spread over large parts of Africa by the
Hamites. During their wanderings on the southern
margin of the Sahara westwards, and along the east
coast, they took their animals with them; and where-
ever they mixed with the Negroes, the latter took up
cattle-breeding side by side with the tillage of the
fields. This is particularly true with regard to East
Africa, where large coherent groups of cattle-breeders

are found, beginning in the Upper Nile region, east of the Congo basin, southwards to the lower Zambezi and Limpopo, the eastern half of South Africa, and reaching to the west coast (Nama, Herero, Ovambo). Besides oxen and kine, sheep and goats are often bred in large numbers. The cattle are generally of no great value economically. The milk yield is small and the flesh often poor. Milk, and sometimes also butter, are important elements of food, especially for those tribes which have little or no agriculture. Many of the Nile tribes drink the blood of living animals; and the hide serves for clothing and ornament. Nevertheless, it is not the economic value of cattle that occupies the first place in the mind of the Native. This can be deduced from the fact that even the owner of large flocks seldom slaughters healthy animals for the purpose of eating the meat, but only for ritual purposes, such as sacrifices, initiation rites, and funerals. Cattle are rather a possession. The wealth of a man and of a group is measured by the number of cattle owned, and the wars in the past were mostly cattle-raids or conflicts for pasturage. An hereditary feud of long standing between two groups of Nuer arose because the ancestor of one group once stole a calf from the ancestor of another. Cattle are the only medium through which commercial transactions on a large scale can be carried out, in other words, they are a substitute for money. Above all things, cattle are, in all cattle-breeding tribes, the 'bride-wealth' by which a wife can be acquired. If a father has four sons, he and his sons must take care to acquire enough cattle to enable them to marry four wives, and he hopes that the marriages of his daughters will bring him in a corresponding number of cattle. Cattle therefore are perpetually being exchanged between the various groups. They represent capital, the decrease of which must be prevented by all possible means. This capital has been, so to speak, entrusted to the present owner by his ancestors, and he must leave it to his descendants unimpaired. A group without cattle is doomed to ruin.

Old rock-carvings in northern Africa seem to point to the fact that a worship of cattle existed there in the past. Traces of such worship are to be found even to-day, for instance, in the customs and traditions of the Shilluk. The influence of such ideas may perhaps be traced in the extraordinarily close, almost personal relationship, which an owner has with his cattle in East and South Africa. The Nuer boy receives an ox from his father at the end of his initiation. The name of this ox, given on account of its colouring, becomes henceforth the boy's favourite 'praise name'. Any one visiting him greets him with the name of this ox. The two grow up together, as the saying goes; he will stroke and caress it, and dance, leaping round it. If one day it should be slaughtered, he will not touch its flesh.[1] The boys spend their youth in the wide steppes as guardians of the herds and take the happiest memories from them into life. For a man there

[1] Cf. P. Crazzolara, *Africa*, vol. v, p. 36.

is no pleasanter occupation than to be among his
cattle, admiring them, stroking his favourites and
inventing pet names for them. The liveliest conversa-
tions of the old men in the evenings over a mug of
beer always turn on the quantity, kind, and peculiari-
ties of their oxen. It can easily be understood that
with such an attitude the economic value takes a
second place. The breeder's object is not weight of
meat or yield of milk. There is no reason why it
should be, since the object is not to slaughter the
cattle, and since in exchanging them it is the number
and not the quality which is decisive. The breeder's
object is rather the size and form of the horns or
the colouring of his cows. The Shilluk have a
special craftsman, the horn dresser, whose task it is
to give the horns of the young oxen the shape which
the owner desires. Others want special mixtures of
colour, and spend largely in order to obtain a collec-
tion of animals of their favourite colour. In these
circumstances separation from a favourite animal is
a real sorrow, and the idea of slaughtering it for a
merely material purpose strikes the owner as cruelty.

In former times an excessive growth of head of
cattle was prevented by continuous cattle-raids and
by the cattle-plagues which often claimed hundreds
of thousands of victims. The transition of most of
the Masai groups around the Meru to agriculture can
be explained by the loss of their cattle through rinderpest, and their consequent impoverishment. Both
factors have vanished to-day. Wars have ceased and

pestilences are successfully combated. The result is
that the Native ownership of cattle has considerably
increased. Bechuanaland has, with a Native population of 155,000, 426,000 head of cattle, not counting
the numerous young beasts. In Kenya the Native
population of 2,838,000 has a round 5 million head
of cattle, over 4 million goats, and 3 million sheep.
The Native population of the Union of South Africa
owns approximately 49 per cent. of the Union's cattle.
The consequences are that many pastures are over-
stocked; the cattle are badly nourished; and the
pasturage is damaged by excessive grazing resulting
in erosion of the soil, and this becomes a definite
danger to the fertility of the country. It is evident
that in the interests of the Natives themselves this
state of affairs should not be allowed to continue nor
to grow worse. The solution will partly lie in replacing the emotional attitude to the cattle by more
rational ideas. The desire for money and European
commodities must become so keen that the owner
will be ready to surrender part of his cattle for them.
This sounds prosaic and is prosaic, but is there any
other way of saving the Native from the loss of his
prosperity? It is an impossible luxury for a tribe to
keep hundreds of thousands of cattle from which it
receives relatively little in return, and which it cannot
feed properly because there is not enough pasturage.
In West Africa and the Western Sudan, where economic development is more advanced and where cattle-
breeders are not so devoted to their beasts, there is

an active trade in animals for slaughter with the economic centres and especially with the coast towns. This trade results not only in increased prosperity, but also acts as a stimulus for cattle-breeding and the improvement of its quality. The beginnings of a rational attitude are found also in other parts of Africa where the Natives pay their taxes in animals. Only when they have learnt to look on their cattle, not as a precious possession alone, but also as a marketable commodity, will the efforts for improving the quality have an object and lead to success. The large centres of population in South Africa are to-day provided with cattle by white breeders. If the Natives do not learn, more than they have done hitherto, to exploit their cattle in a similar way, their whole wealth of to-day will shrink into insignificance, and they will have to give way to cattle-breeders who make a better use of their land and their cattle. Experience in East Africa, where Natives begin to attach great value to quality and try to improve the herds, though they are mostly still disinclined to destroy useless animals, helps to show that efforts for raising the quality and improving the breeds are not without prospects of success.

5

The Land.

Although in former times there was land in abundance in most parts of Africa, yet each political unit, or each clan, knew exactly the boundaries of its territory and guarded them jealously. Even in the case of stretches of primeval forests the boundary was usually known. This had practical significance in the right of gathering forest products and timber, and the duty of maintaining the roads. In the case of the Natives of Liberia every tribe has from time immemorial had an obligation to keep the roads in good order as far as the limits of its territory. Apart from such factors the claim to the ownership of land which had never been actually used had only a theoretical character, and it is surprising that, in spite of this, wars were not infrequently waged for this claim. It was felt to be an unendurable challenge when a strange group wanted to settle in a country which had hitherto been looked upon as the property of one's own group, handed down as an inalienable heritage from the ancestors.

For a large part of Africa the conclusions apply which were made by the distinguished author, M. Delafosse,[1] concerning French West Africa:

'One of the most outstanding principles is that there is not an inch of land without an owner, not one inch over which a proprietor, and, most of the time, also an occupier, does not claim his rights. On this point, peoples of the north and south, both sedentary and nomadic, all agree, and this is no doubt the reason why even the Moslems are little inclined to adopt the rule of the Maleki law, which permits up to a certain point that vacant land can be "without a master". Moreover, all Natives are unanimous that if the chief of the political body is the

[1] *Haut Sénégal-Niger*, vol. iii, pp. 14 ff.

proprietor of the land, it is only as the administrator of the territory and the legal representative of the group to which in the last resort all the rights to the soil belong. Thus, among Moslem as well as among animists, the chief can alienate no lands on his own authority, except those which he cultivates himself and which constitute in a sense his private property.'

This, however, does not mean that the whole of Africa had been divided among the Natives before the arrival of the Europeans. There were vast tracts of forest, marshland, mountains, and steppes, completely uninhabited, to which no one laid any claim. If such regions were within the political sphere of a greater power, that power could call it its property, but that is not the same thing as the claim of a community which needs the soil for its own existence. The Colonial Governments were justified in declaring such territory as Crown Land and in thus preventing unlawful use of it.

Although the African is always ready, weapon in hand, to defend his land, and although disputes about land between neighbouring tribes or clans were not at all uncommon, he has never handled the land question in an ungenerous way, but has always been ready to grant hospitality to strangers. In all the larger towns quarters for strangers were established, in which members of foreign tribes or peoples live either temporarily for the carrying out of trade and industry, or as permanent settlers. The right to settle is granted by the chief or, in his name, by the owner of the land, to whom the stranger has to give regular compensation either in products of the land or the hunt, or by paying him cash in recognition that the land does not belong to him.

The idea is therefore not alien to the African of renting land to strangers, so long as it is conceived as the privilege of a guest. In the same manner the first Europeans, traders or missionaries, were received as honoured guests and were assigned a place for their habitation. If they did not pay a regular rent, it was expected from them that from time to time they should make a present to the chief or the landowner. This was usual even in cases where the white man wanted a piece of land as permanent property, e.g. for a farm, or a site for a mission station. Consent for such settlements was given the more readily because it was hoped that the granting of such advantages to the foreigner would result in the introduction of commerce into the land and in the learning of unknown arts. The alienation of land became a danger only when it reached such proportions that the standard of living of the Natives was seriously threatened.

The white settler or planter came into the land, often dispatched by his Government or invited by Concessionaire Land Companies, in the hope of gaining a livelihood in Africa or finding a profitable investment for his capital. He found fruitful land in abundance, sparsely populated or uninhabited. What could be more natural than that he should wish to appropriate this land, with the excuse that he would win from it quite different produce, and thus be able to contribute to the increase of prosperity far better than the present tenants could do? It was not only the right of the stronger, but that of the more capable, which he thus could plead on his own behalf. A just compromise had to be found between these claims and the interests of the Natives. There are, without a doubt, parts of Africa where there is room for both black and white, where the population is so sparse that for an appreciable time it will not be able to exploit the land at its disposal, and therefore a part of such land can be given over to European settlers and planters without a qualm. It appears contrary to reason to allow valuable land to lie fallow when there is somebody who has the will and the means to develop it. Sometimes in individual cases it may be necessary to dispossess the Natives of land which they already cultivate and on which they live. Such transactions should, however, be avoided whenever possible. For the African his land is not so much a valuable economic object which can at will be exchanged for another, but it is rather something which has been entrusted to the present generation by the ancestors and must be handed on to the descendants. It is, as the Ewe say: 'The great thing which God has given to mankind to be bequeathed to its children.' It is the resting-place of the ancestors, the home of the gods, and we can thus well understand that a group is sorely averse to parting with its soil. The loss of land will necessarily also have disintegrating results on the cohesion of the group.

In spite of the importance of these points of view, their significance must not be over-estimated by one-sided exaggeration. The Africans, not excepting the agriculturalists, were in the past not so exclusively rooted in the soil as is sometimes assumed. We know of some tribes that it was only a few centuries ago, or less than one century, that they migrated into their present districts, and in so doing often ousted other groups. Until the most recent times there were movements of population even within the boundaries of their present home. Another place was sought for settlement because the soil had been exhausted; because pestilence made further stay unsafe; or because a stronger neighbour was threatening. The worship of the gods of the old land was taken away into the new home. This is shown among the Ewe and their kindred tribes. When they invoke their ancestors with drink offerings they walk a few steps eastwards, pointing towards the earlier home of the tribes where the oldest ancestors are still dwelling to-day, and where the souls of later generations of the dead find their last resting-place.

Whenever it appears necessary to the white man to deprive the Native of part of his land, he will find himself impelled by certain qualms of conscience to justify his proceedings no less to himself than to others. For this purpose a number of excuses have been invented, such as that the land did not belong to the Natives 'from the beginning', but they had in turn taken it away from somebody else; or that they had not made the best use of the land; or that they had forfeited the right of ownership by opposing European domination. These arguments are futile, for they are founded on European ideas which cannot be transferred without qualification to African soil. It is unreasonable to think that the land-rights of the Natives deserve greater respect because they are akin to European views, because land is owned individually, or because land can be bought and sold; and that where such conceptions are lacking, one may take away land with an easier conscience.[1] Arguments like these are superfluous, for it is immediately clear that with the arrival of the European the holding of land was bound to undergo the same fundamental changes as happened with all other conditions of life. It is equally clear that a government, having taken possession of a colony, also takes on the responsibility for the present and future well-being of the Natives. It follows that a readjustment must be undertaken which will regulate the relations between white and black, and provide for the due consideration of the needs of the Natives as the weaker party. The principle should always be that the Natives keep their land, and this should only be departed from in exceptional cases. In any case enough land must be left them to afford the possibility not only of feeding the

[1] Cf. L. Mair, 'Native Land Tenure in East Africa', *Africa*, vol. iv, pp. 314 ff.

present generation, but also of providing for future increases. Further, secure titles must be granted to the Natives, so that the tenure of their lands, whether collective or individual, will be secure, and governments must by legal enactment prevent the Natives' land being sold heedlessly and without fully realizing the results.

The Native systems of land tenure are extraordinarily varied and often exceedingly complicated. It is only possible to understand them if one is completely familiar with the whole social system of the tribe in question. The tenure and exploitation of the soil is intimately connected with the system of kinship, with paternal or maternal right. Besides the utilitarian aspect of ownership, magical and mythological rights to which the Natives attach the greatest significance must not be ignored.[1] Again, there are the interests of the different Native groups: the chief, the clan, the village community. A solution which will satisfy the views of the Natives, leave no bitterness behind, and not lead to the break-up of the unity of a tribe, presupposes a careful and patient study of the tribal structure. Indeed, it may well be said that peace and goodwill among the Natives depends on nothing more than a satisfactory solution of the land question.

The question whether individual or communal land tenure is to be preferred will in each case have to be

[1] Cf. B. Malinowski, 'Practical Anthropology', *Africa*, vol. ii, pp. 31 ff.

decided according to local conditions and prevailing customs. The fact that communal ownership is the older must not lead us to consider it in every case as the better. In intensive agriculture or cattle-breeding the tendency is to private ownership of land, because a real cultivation of the soil is impossible in any other way. Where, as in South Africa, the powers of the chiefs are considerable, they will often obstinately oppose any division. This may be partly because the unity of the group appears better safeguarded with communal land tenure, but may also be due to a fear that the division of the land will prejudice their position as masters of the entire land of the group. Certainly individual tenure affords more scope for personal initiative than communal tenure, and the latter has not infrequently led to complete neglect and thus a dangerous deterioration of the soil.

6

The difficulties are least in the purely tropical regions, in which it is impossible for a European to settle permanently; and in those regions where the population is so dense that alienation of the land seems practically impossible. Here the force of circumstances will automatically make the Natives keep their land. In Nigeria the land question is settled in the following way. In southern Nigeria all land belongs to the Natives; when the Government claims land for public purposes, it pays the owner generally somewhat more than the current market value. Crown

lands exist in small quantities, and they may be sold
only with permission from the Secretary of State.
Forest lands are also regarded as the property of the
Natives. If products are taken from the forest, which
are regarded by the Native community as the property
of an individual or family, the owner must be paid.
As it is desirable to keep a forest reserve for the
preservation of the necessary humidity of the soil,
and as the Natives will frequently take no steps to
create such a reserve, the Government has been
forced to declare certain forest areas as reserves, all
possible care being taken not to infringe on Native
rights. In order to protect the Natives from ill-con-
sidered sale of their land, a Native Land Acquisition
Act lays down 'that no person who is not a Native of
Nigeria shall acquire any interest in land without the
Governor's approval'.

In northern Nigeria, too, the whole of the lands
are, whether occupied or unoccupied, Native lands,
'and all rights over them are placed under the control
and subject to the disposition of the Governor'.[1] This
implies that the Governor may sell land to Europeans,
but this privilege has been exercised to a very limited
degree.

When, in the beginning of the colonial era, the
Colonial Powers could see no means or ways of
developing the enormous tracts of country assigned
to them, they had frequent recourse, especially in
thinly populated tropical districts, to the idea of

[1] *Lands and Native Rights Ordinance,* 1916.

assigning great parts of these lands to Land Companies. Certain rights were allotted to such Companies, with obligations regarding means of transport
and their treatment of the Natives. For the rest they
enjoyed a large measure of freedom. The possibility
of making profits from the undertaking was often
doubtful because they were working under new, unknown conditions, and had to combat great initial
difficulties. Their officials felt themselves bound to
make a profit at all costs, and frequently it was possible
to attain that end only by getting the Natives to work
for them at the lowest rates. Where large plantations
were organized, they had the right of evacuating the
Natives, who then had no other course open to them
than to become labourers of the white man. The
whole system of these large Companies often led to
flagrant abuses. It was later found necessary to re-
strict the amount of land allotted to Companies, and
to restore part of it to the Natives. Even to-day,
however, some of the abuses connected with the
system have not been remedied.

Owing to these and similar experiences the Natives
have taken up a different attitude from their previous
one on the land question. Formerly they were naïve,
care-free, and often casual. They sold their land for
a mere nothing, and allowed the foreigners in a most
generous way to live with them and share their land.
Now they have become distrustful and jealous, and
look with suspicious eyes on every Government
Regulation connected with the land questions. They

G

may even raise objections when a mission begs for a piece of land for a school. A West African chief said not long ago: 'Our land is as dear to us as the apple of one's eyes,' and by this he expressed what many people feel to-day. This way of thinking is most clearly observable in East and South Africa because here, in growing numbers, alien races have settled, which in almost every respect are superior to the Negro. Here it was not a question only of using unused land. The Native was alienated from his property, and the foreigner took his place. The Native had to be content with the land which the foreigner assigned to him, or he was invited to settle on the land of the foreigner as a labourer. Sometimes the only escape left to him was to become an industrial worker, to uproot himself definitely from the soil. The chief differences between South and East Africa consist in the fact that in the latter only parts of the land are suitable for European settlement, and it will always be a question of European and Native land-owners living side by side. Moreover, here the problem was recognized in good time and forces are at work with the object of evolving a just compromise. In South Africa, on the other hand, owing to the greater age and greater diffusion of European settlements, conditions have been stabilized in such a way that changes of a radical nature can scarcely be expected. The situation is made clear by the simple fact that in the Union of South Africa the Natives who comprise more than 80 per cent. of the population possess less than 8 per cent. of the land. The rural population of the Union is estimated as approximately four millions, of which some 2,270,000 live on Native land and the rest as squatters or labourers on farms of the whites. This means that 87 per cent. of the Native population are still rural, and about 600,000 live in towns.

Most reserves allotted to the Natives, of which the Transkei, Basutoland, and Bechuanaland are the best known, suffer from being too small now. Practically all of them are overpopulated. Much bitter feeling has been created by the Land Act of 1913, which made it impossible for Natives to buy land except in areas to be subsequently determined by Parliament; and those areas have never yet been determined. Repeated attempts have later been made to increase the Natives' share in the land; but the opposition to all such plans on the part of the white population was so uncompromising that all of them failed. This is the more remarkable because the aim of this proposed new distribution of land was to bring about territorial segregation between whites and blacks. Most whites regard segregation as desirable. If they are nevertheless not prepared to make a comparatively modest sacrifice for its attainment, it may be estimated how small are the chances of the Natives to see the fulfilment of their hopes of owning more land. In no part of South Africa do the Natives have enough land to be able to live on it and develop themselves 'along their own lines'. Everywhere the

situation is that the inhabitants have to look for a
means of livelihood from outside sources, i.e. in the
service of the white man. It is depressing to hear that
in some reserves thousands of young men are on the
waiting list, and have to wait many years before it is
their turn to have a chance of making their own home.
These humanitarian considerations will be answered
by the objection that the mines need hundreds of
thousands of workers, and that the Native would
never look for work if he could earn on his own land
all that he wants. In the absolute sense this is in-
correct. In West Africa many thousands of Natives
work in European enterprises of their own free will
without being forced to do so by lack of land. Even
if the objection is partly correct, no one will deny that
the situation of the South African Native could in
many respects be improved; that his claim to a larger
share of land is justified; and that if there were goodwill on all sides, it would be possible to give him better
opportunities than heretofore of acquiring land. It
is probable that by the introduction of intensive agriculture the productivity of Native land can be considerably increased, but that will require expenditure
and time. There is also the question to what extent,
and how soon, the Natives will be able to adapt themselves to a rational method of agriculture. If they
spend several months every year away from home
their interests are naturally divided, and they cannot
devote the same attention to their agriculture as a real
farmer would. Also the fate of the squatters is seldom

enviable. Their payment and their standard of life are often meagre in the extreme, and they have hardly any prospect of escaping from the narrow circle of their life.

The consequences of the South African land policy are so disastrous for the Natives, and have led to such unhappy results, that one hopes they will not be repeated in other parts of the continent. There is ample room for the black man and the white in Africa. Even if we admit that the white man produces more than the black, that is no reason for depriving the latter of his opportunities for producing, or for limiting his freedom to any degree. There is no necessity to increase the production of foods and other commodities by every possible means, seeing that the world market suffers from over-production. The unbridled urge for ever greater expansion and for the creation of ever newer and larger enterprises seems sometimes almost madness. The whole of African development could be guided into safer channels if it were progressing at a somewhat more moderate pace, and if the Africans were given time to adapt themselves more gradually to the new circumstances.

7

The Labourer.

Paid labour was, until the arrival of the European, almost unknown to the African. On the other hand the chief had the right to demand certain unpaid labour from his people as service to the community (as for instance the building of roads) or as a contribution to the support of the chief and his court. This was, so to speak, a labour tax, and it scarcely ever became a burden to the population. It lasted only a short time, and part of it fell in the months during which field-work was at a standstill. Further, the community had an interest in seeing these works carried out. The reputation of the tribe would have suffered had they been done negligently or not at all. It was a matter of honour to supply the chief so amply with foodstuffs that he could without let or hindrance receive guests and therefore attract business and traffic to the country. It is, of course, possible for a chief to exploit his claims on the working power of his subjects for selfish ends, but such abuse can be remedied by the administration.

Europeans are inclined to call this kind of communal work forced labour—and on the strength of this expression European employers have argued that forced labour is a familiar idea to the Negro from of old. It is a custom of the tribe, they say, and therefore the European Governments can claim this right to forced labour not only for public but also for private purposes. It is, however, evident that the two cases are fundamentally different, and it is not necessary to dwell on this point. It is universally admitted to-day that forced labour is bad labour both from the point of view of the employer and the employed, and it has therefore been abandoned almost everywhere. Up to a certain point it may be permitted for public ends when it is a question of important enterprises which cannot be executed in any other way. We must not, however, expect the Native to do such work for nothing. From our point of view it might be in the public interest to construct a railway or a motor-road; for the Native it is an undertaking in the interests of the European whom he must serve with his labour. In any case such forced labour must not be paid at a lower rate than free labour. It is remarkable that the local Native Councils in Kenya have started the gradual abolition of forced labour, and have voted money for the payment of road labourers.[1]

Although work for foreigners was something new for the African, he willingly entered their service. Wherever a European settles down, he immediately becomes an employer of a number of Africans, and he could in fact not exist without their manual work. The desire to acquire some of the white man's goods, to see new sights and learn unknown things, the example of his fellow tribesmen, were strong enough to lead hundreds of thousands to the working centres created by the white man. Considered as a whole it is admirable how the Negro has responded to this call and what an enormous volume of work he is doing to-day. As long as work for the white man is no more than a subsidiary pursuit for the Native, and the centre of gravity of his existence remains in his home community, this mass movement towards a more intensive activity of the race is to be welcomed.

[1] *East Africa*, 15 Dec. 1932, p. 336.

The situation becomes more difficult when the worker loses his connexion with his native soil, leaves behind him the natural bonds which bind him to his group, and becomes an individual labourer. It means so radical a change in the conditions of his life, that even with the greatest care and most honest efforts it may be many years before a real adjustment can be made. In South Africa the question has become more complicated because the Negro appears as the competitor of the white worker. The Native when he has become 'detribalized' and a city dweller strives to reach the stage of the white man by increasing his output, and then expects that he will receive the same reward, as his needs increase when he lives in a town. In this way conflicts arise, for white public opinion in South Africa will not tolerate such progress on the part of the Natives. The white man fears that it will endanger his position and the integrity of European culture in South Africa. Hence there is a general tendency to exclude the Native from the ranks of skilled labour.

The Report of the Economic and Wage Commission of 1925 sees as the characteristic feature of South African economics that it is organized 'on the basis of minimum employment of high-rated skilled labour and maximum employment of low-rated general labour'. The latter is composed of Natives and to a small extent of the coloured races, whereas the skilled labour is almost exclusively in the hands of the whites. The average wages of the white

labourer are £1 a day, those of the Native the tenth
part of that. The low wages of the Native are justified,
apart from his lower standard of life, by the fact that
he makes an income from his farming, to which the
majority return after the end of their period of work.
The Natives are told, therefore, that they need but
little land because they are labourers, and as labourers
they need only a small wage because they are also
farmers. Yet the number is increasing of those Native
labourers who live continuously in the towns, who
have adapted their mode of life more or less to that
of the European, and who have to depend on what
they earn as labourers. The Wage Board in Bloemfontein has shown that 75 per cent. of the 26,000
Natives living in this town are detribalized, 'they are
no longer connected with any tribe and regard themselves, and expect to be regarded, as individuals'.
These naturally try to rise into the higher class of
labourers and so increase their income. They are
obliged on account of the higher cost of living in
urban centres to insist on higher wages, and these are
refused on the ostensible ground that the high rates
of pay claimed by the Trade Unions for the white
workers would then be impossible. Their situation
is made worse by the competition of workers from
the Reserves, who offer their labour at so cheap a rate
that the urbanized Native cannot possibly live on it.
During the Great War many mines were forced, with
a view to reducing the cost of production, to expand
the field of work of the black labourers and to engage

them also for machine work. As was to be expected, the Natives showed themselves equal to this new work, and the Report of the Mining Regulations of 1925 bears witness to 'the Native's almost phenomenal advance in efficiency during recent years'. The Report states that if this development were allowed to continue unhampered the result would be 'the elimination of the European worker from the entire range of mining operations'. This apprehension led to the promulgation of a law according to which only whites, coloured people, or Malayans, but no Natives, were to be allowed employment in a number of stated occupations. This example does not stand alone. Indirect as well as direct methods of exclusion can be applied by setting the wages for half-skilled labour so high that it does not pay employers to engage Natives at the price. It is easy to see that this is nothing but artificial prohibition from the evidence given by the Wage Board of Bloemfontein for the year 1929:

'It is common knowledge that in many undertakings Natives and non-Natives are doing the same class and kind of work; in some instances they work side by side. If the Board were to make a recommendation for Native employees as a class of employees, it would, in effect, be singling out certain employees only from a group of employees in the same way as it would if it dealt only with red-haired and blue-eyed employees. The Board holds that employees cannot be classified as Natives and non-Natives, although they may rightly be classified as skilled or unskilled.'

One may admit that the Native is not always an efficient worker, nor is his work always worth more than is paid for it, and also that employers are not in the position to pay good wages for a large number of unskilled labourers. Yet it cannot be denied that the difference in the payment of white and Native work is often unnaturally large and is not justified by the actual work done; and frequently the income of the Natives is below the minimum for their bare existence. Housing conditions are bad, and living conditions in many large towns are so hard that the Natives do not appear to be able to adjust themselves at the present stage of their civilization. Many degenerate into proletarians, and there is a danger that their vitality will suffer under these conditions. They are dependent on every fluctuation in the industrial situation, and to-day are suffering severely from unemployment.

It is quite possible that these may be transient phenomena. The abiding and most oppressive result of these conditions is the attempt, which has been conceived on a large scale and is supported by legal means, to exclude the Native from better-paid work and therefore to make his rise impossible. It must be confessed that there are difficulties on both sides, but the means employed up to the present do not seem calculated to overcome them.

The Five-year Plan of Research published by the Institute says that the anthropological research work

undertaken by the Institute shall 'devote special attention to the changes that are being brought about by
world economic conditions in the traditional social
order of selected African communities, and in particular to the changes in the economic organization
of native society. The material conditions of life
influence in deep and fundamental ways the outlook
and disposition of a people, and radical changes in
these conditions have far-reaching moral and social
consequences.' It is with good reasons that the economic revolution is placed in the foreground, for it is
indeed to-day the dominating factor in the influences
on Native life. Its study is connected with particular
difficulties, because on the one hand it touches directly
European interests and on the other it has most manifold and intimate relations to the whole of Native
life. The subject is, however, of such far-reaching
import not only for the future of the indigenous population, but also for a well-balanced living and working
together of white and black, that an objective statement of the processes, the facts, and their consequences is of great importance. These researches will
require tact, mature judgement, African experience,
and a knowledge of economic interdependence.
Where these conditions are fulfilled, the results of
such studies can render real service.

V

ARTS AND CRAFTS

IT is mentioned in Chapter III that the Negro, like most other human beings, prefers to work intermittently. This does not mean that he spends long periods doing nothing. Men may occasionally be seen in a village sitting about in a leisurely manner—a picture which can also be observed in a European village on a Sunday afternoon or a winter's day. It would be unjust on that account to accuse the Negro of being lazy, for at other times all the people, men, women, and even children are to be found restlessly busy. At the season for tilling the fields, the villages are completely deserted, except for the decrepit old men. Every one is out in the farms and they often remain there for weeks on end, living in temporary huts so as not to lose time returning home every day. One might speak of laziness if the Native neglected the activities falling to his lot, which is really not the case. Apart from those hours of a *dolce far niente*, so natural in the Tropics, his time, even when resting from work in the fields, is occupied, and is never lacking in variety. Nearly every man is in his spare time hunter or fisherman; he has bags, baskets, and hats to plait, nets to knit, cloth to weave and sew; there are drums, dug-outs, and mortars to carve; the house has to be thatched, a new fence round the homestead to be made, and a thousand other things have to be done, so that work is never lacking. The men have in addition to give their time and thought to the administration of public affairs. They are summoned to councils or other meetings, which often last for days; they may have to carry out some office at the chief's court, in the town, in the initiation bush, or in building and repairing roads. Special events such as funeral ceremonies, sacrificial feasts, or public games may require days of preparation.

It is especially the practice of industries and crafts which pleasantly and usefully occupy the leisure times of the year. The simplest form of these is the so-called house-craft, in which the members of the family prepare raw material collected by themselves for their own use, as, for example, plaiting, netting, manufacture of calabashes or pots, and other simple utensils. In most of the crafts there is a tendency to distribute the work and to specialize. Individual craftsmen spring up, or social groups engage in some special craft, with the result that a tribal, caste, or local industry develops. These are conditioned by the occurrence of suitable materials, such as certain plants, clay, iron, salt, which are exploited by a group and the finished articles traded to neighbours. Such tribal or group crafts are, for example, in West Africa those of smiths, gold-smiths, weavers, potters, wood-workers, leather-dressers, rope-makers, boat-builders. In the central and western Sudan there exist also the professions of musician, singer, and juggler who wander from place to place, performing their arts. Smiths at times ply their trade as wandering artisans. In a similar way Arabs are found in parts of the central and western Sudan and even on the coast as shoe-makers and workers in leather, and Hausa travel about as tailors.

The boundaries between industries, crafts, and art are not rigid. The African loves to make even the simplest domestic utensil with care and to give it a decoration however modest. He may devote a good deal of time to the preparation of a tool, and he values it accordingly. It is produced entirely by his own hand, is wholly his own possession, and will last him for his lifetime. It thus, as it were, becomes part of his personality; where desire for money has not been awakened he parts unwillingly with such an object; and this is still more the case if he has inherited it and it is consequently considered as something sacred.

2

The artistic sense of the African is highly developed, and exhibitions of African art have found admirers in Europe. His great powers of receptivity and assimilation are brilliantly in evidence in the sphere of art, and his command of form in sculpture and in music is re-markable.[1] The African learnt metal-working at an early epoch and was by the use of this material enabled to impart to his artistic work a variety such as is seldom found in primitive peoples. The quality of his work is not always equal to that of other backward peoples, a fact which perhaps may be explained by a certain predominance of the practical sense peculiar to the Negro, in comparison with which his imagina-tion is less highly developed.

We still know too little about the development of African art and its dependence on other factors in life. Nevertheless, its relation to certain spheres of life can be established, first among which we will mention economic conditions. It was believed that these relationships could be described by saying that the art of people at the collecting stage of economic life who are dependent on accurate observation of Nature, is naturalistic, and that of the herdsmen and agriculturalists imaginative. This is so far true that the drawings and paintings of the Bushmen are pre-ponderantly naturalistic. Apart, however, from the fact that there is no agreement as to the origin of the Bushman art, such a division is too general and in no way universally true. Even the Bushman art has imaginative products, as, for instance, human beings with the heads of animals. Nor is the art of the agriculturalist by any means without naturalistic

[1] Cf. E. M. von Hornbostel, 'African Negro Music', *Africa*, vol. i, pp. 30 ff.

traits. It is sufficient to remember the numerous portrait-heads and many pictures of animals. A clear connexion with the economic life can, however, be traced in the fact that the agricultural tribes with their fixed abode, their more highly advanced material civilization, and their developed world of religious ideas are the real African artists of to-day, whereas the cattle-breeders have been barren and have even exercised a paralysing influence on the development of art through their nomadic life and their warlike tendencies.[1] Apart from bodily ornamentation and a certain care in the production of their few domestic utensils, they have produced nothing; and they have, during their many migrations from north to south along the east coast, often mutilated and destroyed the surviving works of African art. Livingstone realized this relationship, and he traced a direct connexion between the presence of artistic work and the spread of the tsetse fly, which makes cattle-breeding impossible.

Better conditions for the development of artistic life are found where social and political cohesion is more complete. The caste system mentioned above, which allots certain crafts to certain social groups, leads to a far-reaching division of labour which makes it possible for the individual to devote greater attention to the crafts or to art, and to lift them on to a higher plane than is possible under simpler conditions

[1] Cf. H. Baumann, *Afrikanisches Kunstgewerbe* (Hassert, *Geschichte des Kunstgewerbe*, vol. ii), from which book I have taken several of the following details.

H

of life. Still more fruitful has been the influence on
artistic creation of the formation of large States such
as Loango, Congo, Bakuba, Balunda, Baluba, the
Cameroons grasslands, and in Upper Guinea, Benin,
Yoruba, Dahomey, and Ashanti. Here it was the
ambition of the rulers to foster art and to adorn their
palaces and capital with works of art. Artists and
craftsmen were summoned in order to work at the
king's dwellings and to represent the prowess of the
ruler on panels of bronze, as in Benin, or in drawings
in relief, as in Dahomey. The artists enjoyed high
favour and were often rewarded with offices at court,
or promoted to the nobility, with the effect, however,
that this art became a mere courtier's art and was
estranged from that of the people. No one but a ruler
had the means for producing the precious works in
bronze, ivory, and gold,[1] such as are found in West
Africa, and as the best artists gravitated more and
more to the court, so artistic production in the rest
of the land waned. Certain crafts were monopolized
by the rulers and made not unimportant sources of
revenue. The Bamum chief Njoya had his own dye
works and as many as 300 looms working on his
account, and the production of certain coloured pat-
terns was forbidden except in his own workshops.

Like all other forms of activity, art is closely allied
to tradition, as can be proved from the fact that it
takes its most important motives from religious life.

[1] It may be said that the art of Benin was to a large extent
dependent on the wealth acquired through slave-trade.

It will seldom occur to an artist to deviate from the
accepted norms. The inventions of new shapes or the
creation of works into the production of which he
has not been initiated, seldom suggests itself to him.
Skill in art is often regarded as a magical power, and
only those works are produced for which one has the
necessary 'medicine'. This does not exclude all individual invention, as, for instance, in the case of many
pictures of beasts and the portraits or symbolical
representations of men, but such invention is limited
to certain well-defined spheres, and is almost entirely
excluded in representations of religious and magic
life, where suitability for purposes of ritual depends
on strict adhesion to traditional form. The richly
developed West African art of figure sculpture represents the fathers and mothers of the group, and therefore is the handmaid of ancestor worship, to which
this art is indebted for its ·finest fruits. These sculp-
tures are at the same time examples of the influence of
social institutions on art. In regions where mother
right prevails female ancestors, and in patriarchal
countries male ancestors, are the more common
subjects.

African art has had many stimuli from abroad. In
East Africa it has felt the influence of Arabian, Indian,
and Persian art. In the Congo and the coast of Upper
Guinea the effects of a culture stream which seems
to have emanated from the South Seas, make themselves strongly felt. The so-called Sudanese cultures,
which cut straight across the continent from the Nile

to the Upper Niger, show a certain homogeneity in
that they have been culturally fertilized for thousands
of years from Europe and the Near East by way of
North Africa, Egypt, and Abyssinia. To them belong
the famous bronze castings in Benin, and the beautiful
terracotta figures from Ife, for which we may assume
oriental or Indian origins. In West Africa, however,
they have been reproduced in such perfection both
with regard to artistic form and technical workman-
ship, that they may rightly be regarded as authentic
African works of art.

Although Africa in its artistic creation has not been
inaccessible to foreign influences, its connexion with
Europe in modern times has hardly had any fruitful
results. In the ivory works of Loango there are
European and Christian *motifs*; and similarly the
artists in Benin have copied European models. European melodies have often been introduced, and in
South Africa have almost ousted Native music, but
all this cannot be called an enrichment or fertilization.
The efforts to introduce European forms of utensils
by technical schools affect only small circles and have
no relation to popular art.

The chief reason why the contact of Africans with
European civilization has been so lacking in results
for African art, nay more, threatens to ruin this art,
is that European penetration destroys the foundations
on which African art has hitherto been built. Art
flourishes best in stable and secure conditions, in a
certain prosperity which gives the artist, even if he

be only a simple farmer, sufficient leisure and freedom from care to be able to devote weeks, even months, to the production of one vessel. This peace can no longer be enjoyed to-day. New tasks and aims monopolize the mind. One can hear old people complain that their children no longer have time to learn the traditions and customs of their tribe because they go to school and have to learn so many other things. The complaint is justified and applies to art also. Young people who wanted to devote themselves to art or to a craft had to go through a long apprenticeship formerly before they could be accepted into the guild. To-day such apprentices are found only rarely because money and reputation are more easily obtained in other ways, and who is anxious to choose a craft as his life-work which is obviously dying out and is daily losing in esteem? The chiefs have no longer either the inclination or the means, as they had before, to attract to their courts artists and craftsmen who would work for years on end at a single work of art. Even in Africa the pace of life has become too rapid, and the chief has new tasks to fulfil. He is a busy official, collecting taxes, hearing cases, supervising his subordinates, and dealing with a variety of affairs. At the same time he can add more lustre to his name by filling his house with European things. He can hand on his image to posterity more beautifully by means of an enlarged photograph than by a wooden statue. Moreover, the religious roots of art are withering. Where ancestor-worship ceases and the worship of the gods decays, man automatically ceases to depict them.

To this we must add the great superiority of European utensils of all kinds. They are not always beautiful and may at the beginning offend the cultivated taste of the African, but they are practical and durable, and therefore nothing can interrupt the triumphal progress of European ware all over Africa. Up to the end of the last century raw material was frequently introduced from Europe and worked up by the Native. Copper for the Benin bronzes for the greater part came from Portugal. African smiths worked up European iron in addition to the Native product. The weavers to-day mostly use European yarn. Thus the blast-furnaces of the country were put out, and women gave up spinning, but the craft of the smith and the weaver continued to flourish until they too were gradually submerged by the invading stream of ready-made European goods. Some crafts may continue to live on. The goods produced by African weavers show such distinguished taste and are so durable that they still have no difficulty in finding purchasers; and this is particularly true of the beautiful gowns and embroidered shirts which are worn by the Mohammedan inhabitants of the Sudan. It will be a long time yet before the last African pot and calabash, mat and basket have disappeared from household and market. Certain branches of artistic crafts prolong their existence by working to satisfy European lovers of curiosities, but in such cases the art work, which up till now has been surrounded by a halo of myth, becomes a purely secular trade carried on for the purpose of profit and loses its religious meaning, easily involving the degeneration of its form.[1]

It will be regretted that African crafts are, if not wholly, at any rate very largely doomed to destruction. The development is, however, inevitable. The Africans are travelling the same road from primitive to civilized technique as we and other peoples have done, only in Africa the transition is lacking in intermediate stages.

We should, however, not look exclusively on the negative side and should not speak of the destruction of African craftsmanship without pointing out that under European guidance new crafts have arisen out of the old, and are to-day giving to many thousands of Natives opportunities of developing and applying their good taste and technical abilities. For what they have done they deserve every acknowledgement, and also every encouragement. The time is not in sight when Negro Africa will be a manufacturing country. It will primarily remain a market for European goods. At the same time there is room enough for such productions as can be made by the indigenous craftsman. The rule should be that anything which can be made as well and as cheaply in the country itself, must not be imported from abroad.

[1] Cf. F. Grébert, 'Arts en voie de disparition au Gabon', *Africa*, vol. vii, p. 82.

Under these conditions the Negro artisan will always find a sufficient local market, apart from the many opportunities which he will have of practising a craft in larger European enterprises.

The situation is not so simple with regard to art in the strict sense of the word. No one can say whether it will survive or have a new birth; all that is certain is that at the moment it is threatened with rapid decay. It cannot be otherwise in a phase of transition, and no one can be made responsible for it. African art drew its best powers from religion.[1] We might therefore assume that the new religion, i.e. Christianity, would also stimulate creation, as it has done in the Middle Ages in Europe. It created a Christian art and up to the present day art uses religious motives. Will it be the same in Africa? The grounds for judgement are few. The African is too ready and too docile a pupil of the European, and too firmly convinced of the superiority of the white man, to assert his own genius. Only few Europeans have an eye for the possibility of enriching the Christian life of the Natives and making it more part and parcel of their being by means of African art. It should be a noble task for the missionary to summon a recognized artist, as, for instance, a sculptor in wood, to his aid in the construction of a church or any similar building, and to entrust him with its adornment. It certainly would be possible for the African artist to give artistic ex-

[1] Cf. E. von Sydow, 'African Sculpture', *Africa*, vol. i, pp. 210 ff.

pression to his Christian faith in this way. Hitherto Christianity has for the majority of the Africans been a European institution, and so they are inclined to think that the more faithfully its representations follow European models the better. In this view the African is consciously or unconsciously confirmed by many missionaries. It is only when the new religion has succeeded in really striking roots in the heart of the African people that we may hope for an African Christian art.

The Government, too, can assist in the fostering of art. It would, no doubt, rejoice the African's heart if the co-operation of Native arts and crafts were demanded in the erection of representative public buildings; if exhibitions of African works of art were organized in the large centres; or if the educational authorities were to offer prizes for works of art. Attempts have been made in the schools to have recourse to African *motifs* in painting, drawing, modelling, and carving, and to consider African taste. Experiences in this field have been encouraging and show that the artistic sense has not died out in the youth of Africa. Similarly, individual missionaries have striven to open the doors of schools and churches to African music, but their efforts have not found many imitators. Translations of European hymns, European church music, and musical instruments have long ago made so secure a place for themselves in the African churches and are so much beloved that their banishment is unthinkable. Hymns in particular are an integral part of African Christian self-expression, especially as there are many texts of hymns which have been written by Africans.

It is specially regrettable that the Africans themselves have lost their belief in their own art, and that the educated classes are showing them a bad example in this respect. As long as they have no appreciation of the wealth of beautiful things that their own race has produced and content themselves with adorning their houses with newspaper illustrations, we cannot have much hope.

The decay of African art represents a real loss in the values of life. The question arises how can it be avoided? Is there any means of preserving the art? Can it be revived and newly fertilized by influences from Europe? Can European art take the place of African art, and in what way, and by what means? Is there, on the other hand, enough vitality in the artistic endowment of the African? Is it deep enough to bear new blossoms after the unrest of the transition stage of to-day? Has his artistic productivity been definitely doomed to death, and will it be his fate in this sphere as in others to be confined to imitation? These questions deserve to be pondered. The necessary condition for answering them is a real knowledge of African art, from which we are still far removed. The African Institute should not omit this important section of African life from the series of its researches, and it should in particular study ways and means for keeping alive or reviving the interest of educated Africans in the art of their own people; for many of them have less understanding for this fine flower of African genius than the peasant in his bush village.

VI

LIFE IN THE FAMILY

I

WHEN some fifty years ago the question arose in an Ewe chief's family whether one of its sons named Foli should go to school, an old grandmother was asked for her advice, and her counsel ran as follows: 'Our forefathers who settled in these lands knew nothing about books, but they knew how to rule the towns; even although you, Foli, do not learn from books, you yet remain the son of a king. If it is the will of God that you one day become king, sit upon the royal stool and rule the country, it is in the hands of God, not in the hands of men. My ancestor Lako knew no books when he came from the Gold Coast to Glidyi Kpodyi and founded the town there, and he ruled the town until God called him to himself. Therefore I myself do not approve of Foli learning from books; for the son of a king does not wear shoes nor carry an umbrella before he is a king. If now he goes to school and learns to read, he will adopt the white man's custom, he will wear shoes and carry an umbrella, and in doing these things he will break the sacred laws of our family. Therefore it is better that he should not go to school.'

This is the voice of the African mother. She is the conserver of the old customs and is honoured as such. The woman as mistress of the home comes into contact with public life and foreign influence less than the man; she mistrusts it and clings as long as she can to the old-time ideas and usages. The heritage from the past is more secure with her than with the man, and she it is who, as a mother and a grandmother, first instructs the children about that which was formerly held right and proper.

Older women are mostly held in great esteem, and the influential position of the king's mother among the Ashanti, for example, is well known. Among the eastern Ewe the maternal aunt of the king is considered one of the leading personages in questions related to the royal family. The hut in which the sacred symbols of the tribe (stools, drums, trumpets) are kept is entrusted to her care. Where clan organization is still active in West Africa the oldest woman in the group usually enjoys as much respect as the leading male member. In times of crisis, or when an important decision has to be made, her advice is sought. When in 1866, in the hinterland of Liberia, the slaves of a chief were to be sold in order to pay off the debts of a deceased member of the chief's family, they revolted and fortified themselves in the town allotted to them. Their resistance, however, weakened and they would have surrendered if one of the women had not roused them to resist to the very end. Women may have within the tribe their own organization headed by a woman who is responsible for the conduct of the female members of the group and settles all affairs relating to them (Avatime, Fipa, and many others). Among the Yoruba the *iyalode*, 'mistress of the court', occupies among the women of a community a position analogous to that of the male village chief. Disputes between women are brought before her and are settled by her and her female counsellors. Within a household the *iyale*, 'mistress of the house', is responsible for the settlement of any affairs of the female members of the household. Certain tribes (e.g. Sukuma, Nyamwezi, Shambala, Mende) admit women to the position of chief in default of a male heir, and it would in such cases occur to no one to pay less respect to his ruler because she is a woman. That the woman as ruler is regarded as an exception, however, is seen from the fact that she may not bear children. She is virtually a man and holds her office as the representative of a man.

The woman has her well-established place in the family and community, and she knows well enough how to assert her position and her rights. She is primarily the mistress of the household, responsible for its maintenance, for the provision of the food, and for the upbringing of the children. Between man and wife there is a strict division of labour. The man has the tasks which demand greater physical strength, such as clearing the bush, constructing the woodwork in the building of a house, the making of fences, the cutting of roads, and the work connected with cattle. Field-work is usually distributed among both sexes, but there are tribes in which the wife does no field-work at all except a little help in planting, and others in which the whole of the agricultural labour falls to her share. The division of work is sanctioned by tradition, and neither the man nor the woman would wish to deviate from it. It is not a question of socially lower or higher work, but of man's work and woman's work, and both are held in equal

respect.[1] Where the old order still exists the woman
will refuse to allow the man to undertake part of her
work or vice versa, because public opinion would
not approve of it. Men may in exceptional cases help
their wives with work which strictly speaking should
be their share alone. This is, however, in the nature
of a personal favour, and the man does not like doing
it openly because he might easily be laughed at and
suspected of being under his wife's thumb.

In most tribes, and particularly in agricultural communities, the heavier share of the work falls to the lot
of the woman. Her work is continuous, while the
man works for shorter periods and can always separate them by intervals of rest. The wife has to provide
the daily food for the family and so is occupied from
early morning till late at night. Assisted by her
daughters she must every day fetch water and fire-
wood, often from a long distance. As the supply of
food is in West Africa mostly kept in the field, she has
to carry the daily ration into the village. It is a common sight to see the woman returning home in the
evening with a heavy load on her head, and a child
on her back, while her husband and protector walks
in front, or follows her, carrying nothing but his gun.
The preparation of the food, the toilsome grinding
and pounding, the manufacture of utensils such as

[1] Cf. I. H. Driberg, 'The Status of Women among the
Nilotics and Nilo-Hamitics', *Africa*, vol. v, pp. 404–21; H.
Baumann, 'The Division of Work according to Sex in African
Hoe Culture', *Africa*, vol. i, pp. 289 ff.

pots, gourds, baskets, and personal adornments, the spinning of cotton, the care of the children, occasional fishing and gathering of fruits : all these make ample demands on her time. During part of the year she has to work in the fields, and one cannot help admiring the woman who hoes her farm from morning until late in the afternoon, bent almost double over her work in the blazing sun with a child on her back or one left crawling about in the shade of a tree. Shortly before sunset she returns to her home, and has to prepare the chief meal of the day, heat water for her husband's bath, tend the children, and perhaps grind corn for the next day. With all that she still finds time to spend hours over her own or her neighbour's coiffure, to take part in the village dance, to tell stories to her children, and to trade.

This seemingly excessive amount of work has, however, not made her the slave of her husband; every African woman would reject such an insinuation with scorn. On the contrary, it is because she bears a heavy responsibility that her position in the family and with her husband is an assured one. She supports her husband and his children, and her husband shows his recognition of this service by complying, as far as possible, with the woman's wishes and plans in household affairs. If he is taking part in a meeting of the village council, and it continues beyond the hour of his meal-time, he feels ill at ease, because he knows that his wife is waiting for him with food, and may give him an unfriendly reception if he comes late. If he makes certain disrespectful remarks about the quality of the food, without good cause, this gives the woman a legal right (among the Ewe) to leave her husband. In fact it may be said the man depends on his wife not only for his meals, but also for his comfort and his peace of mind. The women know how to prevent decisions of the community council which appear to them unjust from being carried into effect. They depart in a body and betake themselves to the place of some neighbouring chief, until such time as their husbands have changed their minds and begged them to return (Ewe).

The fact that the family is not a completely independent economic unit, but only a common household, has also favourably influenced the position of the wife.[1] Every adult member only contributes a part of his work to the expenses of this household, whereas the proceeds of the remaining amount are his own exclusively. In this respect an extraordinary individualism has developed within the family. The husband as well as the wife, and also the children as they grow up, all have their own property. The crops in the common field belong to the husband. He sets aside a part of them for the maintenance of the family, the other part the wife sells for him, gives him the money and herself receives a commission. The wife has besides the common field, a little personal plot of land, the fruits of which she sells on her own

[1] In what follows the conditions among the Ewe are described.

account. It is not unusual to find a wife carrying on
a regular farmer's business independently, engaging
men and women to cultivate a field for her, whom
she pays with a part of the profits. Further there is
hardly any woman who does not trade, and many
make considerable profits. Thus a woman, besides
her duties as a housewife, can acquire a fortune to
which the husband can lay no claim whatever, and it
is not unusual to see a wife who is the creditor of her
husband. Similarly, the children, especially the boys,
try to acquire a little capital, which the mother or her
brother keeps for them, by working a small plot
of land, by selling fuel, rowing the women to market,
and doing sundry small services for relatives or
friends. The remaining expenses for the household,
for the clothing of the children and for paying a
magician or a doctor, and in short for all the inciden-
tals of daily life, are also rigidly divided between the
husband and the wife.

The far-reaching economic independence of both
husband and wife makes it difficult for any close
union to arise between them. This is especially the
case in polygamy, where each wife in turn cooks for
four days for her husband and shares his home, but
for the rest is comparatively independent. Husband
and wife live in a common homestead, they share the
children and at least partially the work in the field.
For the rest the main interest of the husband is with
his equals in age, his economic undertakings and
matters of public life; whereas for the woman her

centre is, apart from the younger children, her inter-course with the other wives and neighbours and her own relatives. The fact that she remains a member of the clan in which she was born is of practical impor-tance for her social position. Her people take care that no injustice is done to her. She feels herself more closely linked to them than to her husband, knowing that she will always find a refuge with them. In religious matters too husband and wife are usually independent, since each one serves different gods, worships other ancestors, or belongs to another cult group. In the case of the illness of a child, husband and wife together will make a pilgrimage to the shrine of the husband's god, where the priest will offer sacri-fices and prayer for them. These are, however, almost the only occasions which husband and wife share in common. At public celebrations or meetings men and women each have their own place and find their way separately to the place of meeting. That is also the case with the modernized Natives. It is thought unseemly for husband and wife to be together in public.

The wife is expected to obey the husband. In case of disobedience, disorderliness, and the suspicion of unfaithfulness he may beat her; he may also bind her hand and foot so as to give her time to reconsider herself. But he is careful in taking these measures, for she will complain to her family, who may threaten him with taking her away. The wife's method of address to her husband is *fofo*, which means 'elder brother'; she kneels as she gives him his pipe. This submissiveness has, however, vanished to-day except on certain ceremonial occasions. Husband and wife treat each other as a rule as equals and often as friends.

The obligations entered into on the conclusion of a marriage do not end with death. The woman and her offspring remain the property of the group into which she has married, and a brother or other relative of the deceased husband takes her as his wife.

A marriage can be dissolved by a wife running away from her husband, or by his dismissing her. If efforts at conciliation fail, a separation is pronounced, and the rule applies that the party desiring the dissolution is the one that suffers economically. If the wife runs away, her clan does not get the bride-price back, but if the husband dismisses his wife, he has to give back the bride-price. Moral guilt is a minor consideration, and is left almost wholly out of account. The woman who has left her husband is received by her clan and easily finds an opportunity for a second marriage. Dissolutions of marriages are, however, not frequent. Immediately after the outbreak of a quarrel the group leaders begin to use their endeavours to restore peace. Everybody is anxious to avoid scandal, to avoid disturbing the amicable relations between the two groups, and to prevent above all things the extremely long-drawn-out discussions concerning the return of the bride-price, because these may easily lead to lasting enmity. Thus many a wife is forced to remain with her husband even if she has good reasons for complaining of bad treatment.

Polygamy under the form of polygyny is a universal custom. Whoever has sufficient means marries more than one woman. Those who do not are rare exceptions. The woman first married is pleased to see her husband take a second wife. For her it means an improvement in her position, as in this way she becomes the chief wife and mistress of the house, who exercises supervision over all the other wives. With her husband she has a privileged position, and generally enjoys his confidence in a particular way. At the same time it means for every individual woman a relief from work, for this is now divided among several and every one therefore has more time for her own affairs. The man marries his wives, except perhaps the first one, generally with a view to acquiring more property. In pre-European times wives and slaves represented the only possibility of investing capital. The man who had them in considerable numbers was rich and respected. That this result was not always achieved is shown by the proverb of the Ewe: 'When he had married twice, he bought meal, but with the third he had himself to work the grindstone.' Even his personal welfare is not secured by polygamy: 'When a husband of many wives gets sick, he will die of hunger' (Twi). Marriage with several wives is, however, recommended on other than economic grounds. The wife wishes in patrilocal marriage to see her relatives from time to time, and these visits extend over weeks and months, especially if her home is in a distant place. If her father or mother dies, she must keep the death-vigil of four to six months in the house in which the dead is buried. In some places the wife goes some months before the birth of her child to her parents and there waits for her confinement. Soon after the beginning of her pregnancy up to the weaning of her child, the man must have no connexion with his wife, that is to say, during a period of from two to three years. All these obstacles, rooted in the ancient customs of the people and therefore insuperable for the individual, to which in the case of some women are added a certain unruliness and obstinacy, make it seem advisable to the husband not to be dependent on one wife only.

The forms of marriage are various. By far the most common in West Africa was the betrothal of children, by which a man assured a wife for himself or his son. There were few girls who had not been promised to a man in childhood. An Ewe man would throw a little stone at a pregnant woman with the words: 'If you bear a daughter, she shall be the wife of myself or my son.' If after the birth of the child the mother accepted from the man the present usual in such cases, the child was looked upon as promised, and as soon as she grew up her people would tell her: 'That is your husband.' Before the marriage the girl was asked for her consent, but more as a matter of form. The girl had already known for a long time who was her bridegroom, she had consistently accepted presents from him, and her refusal would have been condemned as perversity and disobedience to her parents.

Though the division of labour between husband and wife does not by itself express a different evaluation of one sex over the other, the man in many respects dominates the woman and feels himself her superior. This results from his greater physical strength, the consequence of which is that the man alone bears arms and is looked on as the protector of the woman. The defence of the common weal and also the administration is in the hands of the men. The husband represents his wife in the law courts. In public worship the woman recedes into the background. No woman can dispose of herself. In questions of marriage the woman's advice is asked, but it is the man who decides. The husband has the right to chastise his wife.[1] He is in law the owner of his wife and thus in the legal sense adultery is possible only on the part of the wife, for it is a damage to the husband's property, for which he can claim compensation. Thus there arises a class morality in favour of the husband.

The value placed on the woman's character is illustrated by proverbs which in similar forms are found among many tribes. It would be a mistake to con-

---

[1] When a Kpelle man tried to beat his wife because she had disobeyed his orders, she said to him: 'You are not a man to beat me,' and in the ensuing struggle he was definitely defeated.

sider them as the only criterion. Much that is said may be meant half playfully, but they give indications of the judgements a man passes on women.[1] 'Woman is a mat which must be beaten.' 'Woman is a thorn that pricks.' 'Woman is a misfortune.' 'If a woman looks nice, it is through her husband' (he had to pay for her finery). 'When a woman makes a drum, it leans against a man's house' (woman depends on man). 'All women are alike.' 'Women like to be where there is money.' 'When women say to you, "you are handsome", that means debt' (when women like you, you are sure to get into 'women palaver' and will soon have to pay adultery-fine). 'All the man's earnings are spent by the wife.' 'If a woman is left alone, a scamp marries her.' 'Whoever follows the counsel of his wife will drown.' 'Woman is cold water that kills, deep water that drowns.' 'No one trusts anything valuable to a woman.' 'Whoever has a sister does not know what will be his nephew's clan-name.'

It is quite possible that similar criticisms on men and their ways may be a topic of conversation in female circles, though they have not been recorded.

2

The most important task of a woman in the life of a tribe is child-bearing. For this task she is prepared as a girl usually between the ages of ten and fifteen. The preparation consists of the young girls receiving

[1] Of the following proverbs the first three belong to the Ewe, the following five to the Twi, the remainder to the Fulani.

instruction from older women, possibly from their own mother, about sexual and marital life, about their conduct towards their future husband and their duties as housewife. In some tribes they undergo certain ceremonies, the chief purpose of which seems to be to secure fertility and to facilitate delivery. In these an excision or similar surgical operations take place. It is unanimously agreed that these operations are value-less, or at any rate do not have the effects ascribed to them by the Natives. They are on the other hand often injurious to health and may endanger the sur-vival of the mother or the child. In many parts of Africa the preparation for marriage is confined to the seclusion of the girl for a certain period in a special hut, where she is well nourished and instructed by her mother or her father's sister about the duties of married life.

Marriage is an institution of public life, which for the security of both parties is surrounded by definite customs and laws. In it one group delivers one of its members to the other for the purpose of the propagation of the group. The separation, however, is not complete, for the departing individual remains a member of her or his former group, which continues to have an active interest, as before, in his or her well-being. This means that both the contracting groups normally stand in a friendly relationship to each other, and this is frequently expressed by the fact that children of the one group regularly marry into the other.

The married couple may reside in the man's village (patrilocal) or in that of the woman (matrilocal), or there may be compromise, such as is found among the Kpelle, when the couple first live with the parents of the woman, with frequent visits to those of the man, but usually in the end, after some years, settles in the man's group. In the purely matrilocal marriage (the terms matrilocal and patrilocal are applicable really only to the children, as these grow up in the mother's or the father's place) which obtains in part of Central Africa, the dominant idea is that the group does not wish to part with a daughter, but that rather she is to bear children for her own group. The husband has therefore to live in his wife's group as a guest, or only a frequent visitor of his wife and her people. His position is thus somewhat shadowy, and he remains an outsider in his wife's family. His chief merit is to cause as little annoyance as possible by behaving himself suitably. His interests are, as before, in his own group, while his own children remain remote from him, for they belong to their mother's group and her brother is responsible for their education. The husband may also have other wives in other groups, and it is easy for him to separate from one of them. The position of the woman in such a marriage and within her group is naturally a commanding one, for she it is who assures the continuity of her own group.[1] The matrilocal family is found in

[1] Cf. W. C. Willoughby, *Race Problems in the New Africa*, Oxford, 1923, pp. 102 ff.

matrilineal groups, i.e. in groups where relationship
is determined by female descent. Likewise in those
matrilineal groups which are patrilocal, that is, those
in which the woman follows the man to his place,
the man has only a limited power over his children,
for they also belong to the mother's group, and are
brought up by it. These forms of family life seem to
be on the decrease in Africa, and it appears unnatural
for a father not to have control over his own children.

When a group hands over one of its daughters to
another group it is obvious for it to expect compensation for the loss of one of its members. The most
natural course appears to be that the group A receives
for the daughter given away to group B a daughter
of group B, who is then married to a son from
group A, so that a regular exchange of women takes
place; this arrangement is practised, for example, by
some Ewe and Guang groups. In this as in every
other form of marriage, however, the man or his
group has to perform certain services or to give certain gifts to the group of the bride. A form widely
distributed in West Africa is that the young man,
together with the members of his own age-group,
helps his father-in-law for several years in working
his fields, and has in addition continuously to make
presents to the girl and her people. Among pastoral
tribes the bride-wealth consists of cattle. The idea of
compensation is, however, not the only point of view
in the handing over of bride-wealth. It is at the same
time a form of insurance for the good treatment of

the daughter, a pledge for the friendly relationship between the two groups, and it contributes to the respect felt for the bride and her group among the man's group. In each case it is the act legalizing marriage and is consequently of great social significance.[1]

The Africans rightly defend themselves against the assertion of superficial European observers that women are bought and sold by them. If it were so, the woman would be the slave of the man, which is true neither in law nor in fact. The husband has no unlimited rights over his wife. Once he has legally married her, the Ewe cannot sell even a slave-woman, much less a free woman. It is open to him to 'pawn' his wife, but only with the expressed consent of her family, and generally only when this family is in the husband's debt, so that his wife is at the same time his 'pawn', a condition from which certain rights in the economic work of the wife accrue to him during the time that she is pledged.

The wife herself estimates her value and the consideration which she will enjoy from her husband and his family according to the amount of the bride-wealth paid for her. The position of the husband to his wife and her relatives is from the very first ambiguous if his payments were small, or if any part of them is still owing. He must be prepared on the occasion of their first quarrel for his wife to reproach

[1] Cf. Gordon Brown, 'Bride-Wealth among the Hehe,' *Africa*, vol. iv, pp. 145 ff.

him sarcastically with his unpunctuality and to threaten to cease to do her duties. For the African who has not been influenced by European ideas, a marriage concluded without bride-wealth means a humiliation and even dishonour to the wife, and even the educated, and most of the Christian Natives adhere to this view. The modern entry in a Register of Marriages and the service in a church are gladly accepted as a valuable addition, but they do not make the contract between the parties superfluous, for it seems to them to give a better guarantee for an orderly married life than the sanctions derived from Europe.

3

Although institutions of family life are in their nature of a conservative character, they have in the course of their history undergone changes. All tribes have marriage ordinances which prohibit the marriage of persons within certain degrees of relationship. But these rules, according to the confession of the Natives, are no longer regarded with the same strictness. Many Ewe tribes prohibit marriage between persons who have the same taboo because they are looked upon as members of the same family, and therefore as near relations. Other tribes of the same people do not only allow such marriages, but favour them on the ground that the taboos mostly consist of food restrictions, therefore if man and wife come from different taboo groups, inconvenience arises in the preparation of meals. The children inherit the taboo of the father, but the wife is pledged always to follow her own taboo. She may not eat food which is allowed to her husband and her children. On the other hand, if man and wife have the same taboo, all these difficulties are avoided. It is also given as a reason for marriage among relations that the fortune remains in the same family. Though these considerations may be only of a secondary nature, they are to-day undoubtedly a frequent reason for the breaking of traditional rules.

It is asserted by Natives in various parts of Africa that monogamy was the universal rule in earlier times. It will hardly be possible to prove that this is true, although there is evidence that points to it. It is, however, certain that the possession of many wives by one man became possible only where economic conditions were so far developed that individual property played a great part in social life, and an aristocracy of property was evolved. If this property was invested in women, it was inevitable that the woman herself should become an article of property. That happened frequently, and from it customs were developed which to a large degree deprived marriage generally, and not polygamy alone, of its value. If the man has not sufficient means to acquire a wife, he borrows part of the cattle or money required from a relative. For the lender that is a safe investment of his capital. When the woman, who has been married with the aid of his money, has daughters, and they in their turn marry, then, if not earlier, he or his heirs receives back the loan with ample interest. The result of such loans may be very complicated debts and claims which may drag on through generations, so that a man can be responsible for liabilities arising from transactions in connexion with a marriage which took place long before he was born.

The position of the wife too is influenced by the fact that in marriage economic considerations are placed in the foreground.[1] She becomes the property of the group into which she is married. If she does not fulfil the expectations placed on her, for instance if she is childless and shows herself incapable of work through frequent illnesses, she can be sent back as worthless, and her group tries to give another woman in exchange for her. A man's wife, like any other property, passes to his heirs, and it is not rare to find a man marrying the wives of his father, with the exception of course of his own mother. Often the brothers of a man have a priority claim to his widow after his death. This is expressed in some West African languages (e.g. Twi, Ewe) by the brother addressing the wife of his elder brother as 'my big wife' and that of the younger brother as 'my little wife'. It is obvious that in such cases there can be no question of the woman having a voice in the matter of her marriage. There are tribes among which custom ordains that after the death of a man, his widow may herself declare which one among his relatives she will marry, but just as often she is simply allotted to a new husband. If a girl has been betrothed as a child, her husband

[1] Cf. S. Knak, *Zwischen Nil und Tafelbai*, pp. 244 ff.

may easily be forty or more years older than she. As
a rule he will have other wives, and the young girl
will have to live in subjection to them. It has happened over and over again that a girl has refused to
submit to such unnatural compulsion and has begun
a liaison with a young man and remained true to him
in spite of all threats from her parents. In such cases
the group will come into the painful position of being
compelled to return the presents and other payments
made years before for the girl. If the daughter, however, like an obedient child, gives way, then perhaps
after the marriage the relationship with the earlier
friend may be continued, with the result that the
guilty party has, when discovered, to compensate the
husband. It is not exceptional for a husband to make
a profitable business out of the unfaithfulness of his
wives.

4

Marriage and family life have in many ways been
deeply influenced by modern developments. In many
cases the economic conception of marriage has been
strengthened, and at the same time the moral values
inherent in the old institutions have been weakened.
Through the introduction of European ideas of
money, 'bride-wealth' has at times reached a sum
which has made it almost impossible for a man of
limited means to acquire a wife, or has involved him
in such debts that he cannot free himself from them
to the end of his days. Absurdly high expenses are

often incurred in the wedding celebrations, which
have also to be borne by the bridegroom and may
exceed his financial resources. This has resulted in
such intolerable conditions that colonial governments have seen fit to limit the bride-wealth by legal
enactment. The result has been that the amount,
which was meant to be the maximum, has in the eyes
of the population become the average or rather the
minimum under which no wife can be had, and to
which the bridegroom must add 'voluntary gifts'.
There are educated Natives who, as their fathers did
before them, invest their capital in wives and thus
increase their wealth: every wife having her own
dwelling and household; she receives from her husband a small capital with which she begins a business;
and she supports herself and her children out of her
profits.

It is no longer the two clans which make the
marriage but two small groups out of each clan, perhaps two families, and often it is the bridegroom as
an individual who negotiates with the bride's parents.
Marriage from being an affair of the community has
become individualized.

Under former conditions, close relationships, which
both parties were concerned in maintaining, were
created between the groups in question by a marriage.
The bridegroom was obliged to visit his bride and her
relations at regular intervals; he was bound to work
in the field of his father-in-law; and from the yield of
his hunting and fishing and of his work he had to give

a part to the parents of his bride. He was obliged to try to make himself pleasant to them and to retain their favour, and thus opportunities arose of getting to know each other intimately. The educated Native no longer has time for all this. He pays the bride-price in cash, or perhaps sends it to his father-in-law in a postal order or a cheque. The arrangement is thus in danger of becoming a mere commercial transaction. Where polygamous marriages are frequent and there-fore girls are in great demand, there is a tendency to lower the marriageable age in order to secure as soon as possible the high bride-price offered for the girl. Such a practice may seem justified by the fact that sexual maturity may set in before the body is fully developed, but it is of course harmful and should be discouraged.[1]

The relationship between man and wife is also changing. If the husband is absent from the home for a part of the year as a worker in a European business, the burden on the wife can become even greater than it was formerly, because she alone becomes responsible for the work in the house and in the field. While formerly the maintenance of the family was dependent on the joint farm work of both husband and wife, it now devolves in an increasing degree on the cash earnings of the man. He becomes the bread-winner of the family and has to support his wife and children. This is true to a wide extent, not

[1] Cf. James W. Welsh, 'Can Christian Marriage in Africa be African?' *International Review of Missions*, vol. xxii, pp. 17 ff.

only of employees and labourers, but also of artisans
and of most town-dwellers who work regularly in the
service of Europeans and have fixed salaries or wages.
The woman may contribute by trade or handicraft to
the expenses of the house-keeping, but the chief part
of the burden now, quite differently from olden times,
falls on the shoulders of the man. Similar developments may take place in rural districts, for instance,
where the plough replaces the hoe. Only the man can
handle the plough, and the agricultural activity of the
woman is thereby reduced to a minimum. The same
thing happens where products for the world market,
such as cotton, coffee, cocoa, and ground-nuts, are
produced on a large scale. For such work, which extends over a large part of the year and demands a
certain technical skill, the strength of the woman
alone is not sufficient. The man must help regularly,
and perhaps even engage labour, and often it is not
long before the principal share of the work falls to
him. Even among the purely rural population the
custom is rapidly growing that the man takes a larger
share than before in the field-work, so that the woman
can more often remain at home. One might welcome
this as progress by assuming that the wife would now
devote herself better to her household and the up-
bringing of her children, but this as a rule does not
happen. It could only be expected if the wife had been
trained for it, which is seldom the case. Her demands
grow greater the more she gives up the character of
the peasant and becomes a townswoman, who no

longer 'soils her hands on her husband's field' and has much free time. She expects her husband to provide her with the means for acquiring clothing fitting her rank. When he is not able to do so, she tries to acquire the necessary means herself, and in West Africa, begins by trading a little. Many wives of educated Natives sit for hours every day in the market, where there is plenty of entertainment, and perhaps do less for their household and their families than they used to do when they came home from the field late in the afternoon, and the whole weight of the housework was on their shoulders.

5

The family is the centre of the social organism. If the Africans succeed in preserving it intact during the transition period, in purifying it from unhealthy elements, and in saving it from degeneracy, there need be no anxiety about their future. Here in the first place we must think of the small family, consisting of husband, wife, and children. The larger units also, such as the extended family and clan, may preserve their significance for a long time to come; but it is a necessary consequence of modern developments that the small family should stand out more clearly than in the past from other social groupings and gain in value in the estimation of the Natives. From a purely theoretical point of view it matters little whether the family is patrilocal or matrilocal, i.e.

whether the children are brought up by the father or the mother's brother. Practically there is no doubt that the future belongs to the patrilocal family, and it is easy to understand that progressive Natives, and also missions, prefer it because according to modern ideas of the family, father, mother, and children belong together, and it seems the natural duty of the father to take the responsibility for his children.

It is sometimes asserted that the intervention of the European in existing conditions of African culture and customs shows lack of understanding and is only a disturbance. This is often true. Many efforts at reform have been directed by people ignorant of Native customs and have done more harm than good. Often enough beautiful customs have been destroyed by unthinking enthusiasts, and the intervention of missionaries has misled the Native into disguising his real attitude and becoming dishonest. It is also true that the African family in particular has borne the chief burden of community life, and it has developed so many good qualities that we can only speak of it with respect. It was adapted to the manner of life carried on before the advent of the Europeans, but it was not for that reason in every respect ideal. Together with much that was admirable, it included much that was barbarous and backward. It is, moreover, decaying, and it is evident that something new must arise to take the place of what is declining. To smooth the path for such new development is the task of the educator, and he may thus be compelled

consciously to guide the new development into channels other than the old.

The starting-point of the family is marriage. There
are two aspects of this institution which have become
the objects of lively discussion: bride-wealth and
polygamy. Few Natives wish to discontinue the payment of bride-wealth. It seems indispensable to them
to ensure respect and durability in marriage. The
family represents a great public interest, and it can
only fulfil its task if it is established on a life basis.
Even under existing sanctions it happens that marriages dissolve. These cases, however, will be far
more frequent, it is argued, if there is no guarantee
by means of bride-wealth, which has to be repaid if
the wife of her own free will returns to her clan. The
result of this view has been that marriage has become
almost exclusively a matter of public law, and that
the personal element is made to recede into the background.[1] A man does not marry a girl whom he is
fond of, or whose friend he has been, but one whom
the clan has chosen for him. It cannot be denied that,
although many such unions have resulted in lasting
and happy marriages, they still imply a suppression
of personality in favour of the community and a loss
of dignity for the wife. This is clearly shown when
a young girl is forced to marry an old polygamist; or
when the wife passes by inheritance like other goods
and chattels, which almost always means for her an
entry into a polygamous household; or when her

[1] Cf. S. Knak, loc. cit., pp. 214 ff. and *passim*.

clan will not release her from a marriage which has become impossible for her; or when the father applies the bride-money obtained for his daughter to purchasing another wife for himself in addition to those he already has. With the Guang the corpse of the dead husband announces when questioned who shall bury him and as a reward marry his widow. Endless time and ingenuity are wasted in cases of succession in following out the complicated threads of the claims and obligations arising from the bride-wealth. The most wearisome lawsuits and family feuds are due to this cause. The whole system of payment for a bride is degraded by the fact that avarice plays such a vital part in it, and that every feeling of personal dignity may be lost through it. The bride values her bridegroom, as she does herself, not according to his personal merits or achievements, but according to the price he is able to pay for her. A change has, it is true, recently occurred in this case in so far as girls who have enjoyed a school training are preferred, especially by educated young men, but a correspondingly high gift must be given for them, so that from this point of view even the education of a girl can be turned into a source of profit by her father.

Even in Christian communities the attitude to this custom has hardly undergone any essential change. Many missions are fighting against it, but hardly anywhere with complete success. The idea that the bridegift is necessary for the making of a legally valid and lasting marriage is too deeply rooted to be eradicated in a few generations. It is true that resolutions are passed in the Church Councils forbidding or regulating such payments, but as long as they are due to the initiative of the missionary and not to an expressed desire of the Natives themselves, they will have but little effect. The question therefore suggests itself whether the custom cannot be retained in a purified form. In itself there would be no objection to the young man or his family making a present to his wife's parents on the occasion of his marriage. One might compare this with the dowry usual in Europe, but the difference is that in the latter case the dowry is an advantage to the young couple and destined to help them to start their own household, whereas the African bride-gift rather has the character of a payment to the 'owners' of the girl. In West Africa this gift does have other characteristics, because the bridegroom, besides his payments to the relatives of the bride, must make personal presents to her, the greater part of which consist of a chest full of clothing and ornaments.

The custom of the bride-gift exists in a peculiarly rigid form among the cattle-owning tribes, i.e. among the Bantu in East and South Africa, where the price is paid in cattle (*lobola*). This question Knak has discussed in his book, *Zwischen Nil und Tafelbai*, pp. 215–43. Knak is of the opinion that the custom could be maintained in an improved form, and lays down the following principle as the chief condition. The bride-gift must bear the character of a voluntary offering, which the father or the relatives of the bride may not claim by right, and the bridegroom must expressly declare that he or his heirs will in no circumstances base any claims later on the handing over of the gift, i.e. that he cannot demand the repayment of the gift if the marriage is for any reason dissolved. As a matter of fact a transition to such a freer interpretation of the custom is already observable in West Africa. The educated Ewe prefers to call the bride-gift *akpedanu*, which literally means 'thank-offering', an expression of thanks to the parents for the great care they have devoted to the upbringing of their daughter. In many cases also it has long since been the custom to look upon these gifts as a present which is given unconditionally and without any possibility of repayment later. The custom has not yet become universal, but it is obviously making progress. Whether in these cases it is better that the gift should be given by the bridegroom personally, or by him and his parents, or with the co-operation of the clan, must be decided entirely according to local conditions. In West Africa, where the clan has not the same social significance as among the eastern and southern Bantu, it is the father or perhaps the mother's brother who will help the young man in the fulfilment of his obligations, though it seems justifiable and desirable on educational grounds that the obligation should fall chiefly on the bridegroom. The participation of the clan, where it still exists, can be of value, because the clan as such feels its responsibility for the welfare of the young couple. The recipients of the gifts should, however, be wherever possible only the parents of the bride, because in any case the husband will find it easier to discuss the matter amicably with them than with the whole clan. In cases where the husband and wife have separate property, care must be taken that the father alone is not entitled to claim the gift but that the mother has her share.

The problem of polygamy is distinguished from that of the bride-gift in that it is without exception looked upon by all the churches as incompatible with Christianity, and they therefore all aim at its abolition. It is also not quite such a widespread custom as the bride-gift, as a matter of fact the larger part of the population lives in monogamy. Nevertheless, polygamy is a social institution recognized in all tribes. The African wife does not feel that she loses dignity by living in polygamy, and for a well-to-do man it is according to the old custom practically impossible to content himself with one wife; monogamy is for the poor. It is quite true that family life in our sense of the word is impossible in polygamy, that it is a denial both of the real respect due to woman and of Christian ideals, and that there is no lack of jealousies and strife among the wives. On the other hand, there are also not a few cases in which a man may live in real harmony with several wives and the wives may be mutually helpful to each other, live together like sisters, and the children of one wife be treated by the others as their own. In any case, however, the opposition of the Churches is an important factor to be reckoned with, especially as they are supported by certain trends in the social and economic life of the day. Though polygamy is not found in every family, the fight against it means a sharp attack on many ancient institutions of social life. If the Churches demand of the husband, who wants to become a Christian, that he shall dismiss all his wives except one, it compels him to dissolve legally concluded marriages without a reason that is considered by society as adequate. The woman then returns to her clan and in most cases will find another husband, but the question arises what will become of the children of the dismissed wives. Their fate will be decided according to the prevailing law of their tribe. In any case the result is that father and mother will not be able to share in the up-bringing of the children. If they belong to the wife, she will take them into her new marriage, and here they may be neglected and not well treated by the new husband. A man may find himself in a conflict of conscience when as a married Christian, the duty falls on him to marry his deceased brother's widow. If the wife of a polygamist wishes to join the Christian Church, she is as a rule not in a position to dissolve the marriage, since she has not the means to repay the bride-money, and her family will not recognize her grounds for separation as adequate and therefore will refuse to consent to it. Many Churches have therefore consented to the compromise of receiving the wives of polygamists as members, but this regulation can only be looked on as a transient phase. Monogamy is also made more difficult by the long continence which is expected of the man during his wife's pregnancy up to the weaning of the child. It may be objected that this difficulty has always existed in the case of monogamy; but actually the fact is that, at least in many tribes, the continence of the husband and wife is confined to intercourse with each other but not with others. It is rather a moral than a social problem.

For the Churches the obligation to monogamy has at present the result that their male members are in a minority. The number of couples married according to Christian rites is an exceedingly small one, while those men who cannot be full members of the Church on account of their conjugal relations still maintain a loose connexion with it, and, as they frequently belong to the well-to-do classes, even contribute to a considerable extent to the expenses of the congregation. The consequence is that the large majority of the Church members are women, especially in places where the wives of polygamists have been admitted into membership. Similar conditions exist in South Africa, and the reason here is that the majority of the men are absent at work in the mines.

In tribal life one of the chief reasons for polygamy was an economic one. The wife was an investment of capital and at the same time a welcome help with the work. This reason is losing its importance to-day. There are other profitable investments for acquired wealth. For the town-dweller, and generally for any one who has no agricultural business, polygamy, in cases where the wives do not earn their own living, is a luxury which only the wealthy can allow themselves, since naturally enough such women demand a high standard of living.

Where European and Christian ideas begin to prevail, polygamy is losing respect in public opinion. Sometimes educated Natives plead for the right of polygamy even for Christians; but the idea is general that it does not harmonize with an educated man's mode of life to have several wives in his house. Of course it is possible to evade this point by letting each wife live in a separate dwelling, or by having concubines in addition to the lawfully wedded wife, which many of the educated and well-to-do Natives do.

The general introduction of monogamy would create a new social problem in the shape of the woman who remains unmarried, for in Africa too the number of women is in excess of that of men. Thanks to the arrangement of polygamy every woman found a husband, a state of affairs which would be changed if monogamy became general. A small number of unmarried women, but by no means all, could be absorbed in new pursuits. The old African society had no place for the unmarried woman, and the separated wife or the widow was married again as soon as possible. There were isolated cases of a woman refusing to take a man to whom she had been allotted, and these easily fell into prostitution. It is to be feared that this will be more frequent under modern conditions, especially where the clan life has been broken up and therefore gives no support to the independent woman. Hardly anything is left for her but to go to a large city and there earn her livelihood as best she may.

The Colonial Administrations have often tried to intervene and make regulations concerning bride-wealth and polygamy. It is, however, vain to hope for any considerable success from such measures. They may indeed abolish the worst abuses by annulling the validity of child betrothals for example. Real improvement, however, can only come from within, and in my opinion it must in the main proceed from the power of Christianity. Even among Christian communities family life and married life labour under disabilities and difficulties. It will be a long time before the missions succeed in conquering polygamy and creating a family life which corresponds to the Christian ideal. But in any case it has succeeded in making for many Africans the idea of the monogamous family a goal to be aimed at. The conception that Christianity and monogamy belong inseparably together is so universal in Christian communities that they would vigorously oppose any relaxation of the marriage bond.

6

For creating a healthy family life the wife is primarily responsible. She bravely filled her place under the Old Dispensation, and if she is to be able to do the same under the New, she needs preparation to fit her to meet the new demands which will be made on her. The school education of girls has lagged far behind that of boys, especially in the rural districts. In these the idea is still held that daughters belong to the house and are to be kept away from contact with foreigners. It is contrary to African conceptions that girls should be instructed by a man, and along with boys. Schooling may be good for boys, for it will help them to make a living, but it is considered useless or harmful for girls. The task of the girl is to become a wife and a mother, and for that she can best be prepared by her own mother. The mother needs her daughters in her daily work, and one cannot blame her that she is unwilling to part with them after they have grown up under her care to an age when they can be of help to her. There is no real stimulus for girls to attend school. When a girl has been for two or three years to a village school, which is directed by a male teacher and intended for boys, such training can be but moderately successful as a preparation for her future work as housewife and mother. Nevertheless, we should welcome even this amount of teaching. It will contribute to the awakening of the girl's mind and to making her more accessible to later instruction. Conditions are different in the large centres, where the girls more readily find opportunities of making use of what they have learnt at school either in a profession or by marriage with a man from the educated classes. Here and there it will also be possible in rural districts to arrange for a girls' boarding school, from which, if it is properly directed, a good influence can spread over family life in a whole district. It is necessary, however, that the teaching in such schools shall concentrate on what the girls need in their rural surroundings. The school must be in the closest touch with the village and its family life. It must not aim at being more than a complement to the mother's training in the home. The idea should be combated that the school withdraws the child from the training given by the parents, and thus relieves them of their responsibility. The two must work hand in hand, and the school will have to take great care not to interfere with the authority of the parents, and especially that of the mother.

The efforts of those concerned with women's education should be devoted as much to the adults as to the girls. Such efforts will probably be of a personal and sometimes of a casual character, and the idea would be to appoint fully trained women teachers who would devote themselves to the adult women as well as to the girls. Often the task will fall to the woman missionary, the missionary's wife, and her native helpers. Even if their influence extends only over a small circle, it is still not without effect on the outer world.

Although in most parts of Africa Christianity is still in its initial stages, the influence of Christian family life is clearly noticeable. In many Christian

families there is an atmosphere of cleanliness, fresh-
ness, and sometimes of an altogether new life. The
Christian husband has learned in the school or the
catechumens' class about the Christian order of life
and has been taught to regard his wife not only as an
instrument for work and for child-bearing, but as a
companion and a personality. This teaching and the
new spiritual atmosphere in which he moves will not
be without significance in the relations between husband and wife. The woman's attitude too will change
as she develops greater self-confidence. In the Christian community she enjoys the full right of membership and finds in it, perhaps in a deeper sense than
most men, a new home, which will help her to develop
her personality and free her from the inferiority complex under which many African women are suffering.
Within the Church women have their own independent sphere of activity and responsibility, and it is
not at all exceptional to find that they are the driving
power in the Christian community.

Professor H. Labouret, one of the Directors of the
Institute, has published detailed suggestions for the
study of the African family, copies of which may be
obtained from the Institute. They will be helpful in
collecting the material on the subject. Here again the
investigator should not be content with stating the
data, but should try to understand the process of
change that is going on. The transformation within
the family, the dangers by which its integrity is threat-

ened, do not only form an outstanding subject for the scientific observer, but they also preoccupy many serious Africans, women as well as men, and the problems cannot be effectively studied without their co-operation. After the investigator has made himself sufficiently acquainted with the facts and has gained the confidence of the Natives, he should, where possible, together with other competent Europeans in the country, such as administrative officers, educators, and missionaries, invite small groups of experienced Natives, and in such circles the subject might be discussed. It might also be suggested that the Vernacular Paper should open a discussion and Native contributors be asked to give in written articles their opinion on the subject of the Family. In this way not only would further material be obtained, but the Native point of view would find full consideration, and at the same time the matter would become of interest to the leading classes of Natives and would incite them to further thought on it.

VII

THE GROUP AND THE INDIVIDUAL[1]

I

A FRICAN society is distinguished by the characteristic prevalence of the idea of community. The individual recedes before the group. The whole of existence from birth to death is organically embodied in a series of associations, and life appears to have value only in these close ties. Though there is in them a well-ordered gradation between persons who command and who obey, yet the prevailing feeling is that of equality. Class distinctions as we know them are absent or but feebly developed. They may be of greater weight in countries where there is a marked distinction between a ruling group and a subject people, but usually within a group the consciousness of a strong sense of solidarity is predominant. The

[1] Cf. A. Vierkandt, 'Die genossenschaftliche Gesellschaftsform der Naturvölker', in *Handwörterbuch der Soziologie*, Stuttgart.

group imposes duties on the individual, but it also grants privileges; it takes from its members much of their personal responsibility and offers them its protection. Membership in a communal bond which involves fellowship with the co-members and connexion with the ancestors gives the individual peace of mind and a feeling of security. The introduction into a conscious participation in the communal life of the group and a knowledge of the rules of behaviour resulting from it, form an essential part of education. The most important group formations are family, clan, and village, to which for many parts of Africa, must be added the age grades and the men's associations grown out of them.

The family in its simple form consists of husband and wife or wives with their children. They form an economic unit in so far as they co-operate in the maintenance of their common household. This co-operation is not necessarily complete, for very often husband, wife, and even half-grown children have their own individual property, to which they devote part of their work. On the other hand, the family unit is not only economic, for the members, by sharing common work, care, and experiences, grow into a real living community in which love and self-sacrifice are not unknown. The family ties are less close in matrilocal marriages, where usually the husband does not become a member of his wife's household, but divides his time between his own group and that of his wife. The ties may also be lessened by the narrow relations of each individual to other groups. These find expression in the terminology of kinship names. Each relationship term is applied not to the individual but to a group of persons, who in the Natives' view stand in a classificatory relationship to a given person. For a child, his father's brothers and his mother's sisters stand in the same formal relationship to him as his real father and mother, and hence an African will often speak of 'his fathers and mothers'. If *A* is my father, then his brothers are also my fathers, and I must honour them as my father, and behave to them as I do to my father. This does not, however, mean that the personal attachment and affection between a child and his real parents is not closer than that existing between him and those persons who are more in a formal way his 'fathers' and 'mothers'. In a wider sense all members of the same generation within a group of relations, or group regarded as relations, may call each other brothers and sisters. Those of the preceding generation are for them fathers and mothers, while they call sons and daughters, nephews and nieces of the first and second degree, their children. Since, however, relationship in the male or female line is distinguished, and there is also a gradation between elder and younger, the relationship terms are in this respect even more definite and detailed than ours. The father's elder and younger brother and sister, and likewise the mother's elder and younger brother and sister, and their respective children, have each their own respective designation.

The child has to learn and to use correctly all these names and the corresponding behaviour to his relatives. This makes him conscious of the fact that he is a member not only of his family but of a far larger group which influences his existence on all sides. Even in patrilocal families the child's home is not exclusively that of his parents. He may live for months together with his grandparents, with his mother's brother, or some other relative who wish to have 'their child' with them for some time. Frequently a child is given away as a servant to some elderly person within the group who lives alone and is no longer able to look after himself.

Besides the small family there is the enlarged or extended family. A man lives with his wife or wives, their children, and the husbands of their children, so that there are three or perhaps even four generations in one compound or group of compounds. The eldest male member is the head of the group and all must honour and obey him. The group may be an economic unit, though not as a rule; but the members of the younger generation are bound occasionally to help or make presents to the older people, and especially to the head of the extended family, who in turn has a moral responsibility for them. In actual fact each small family has to care for itself.

2

While in the small and the extended family members of originally different groups are by marriage united into a new unit, the principle of descent is strictly observed in another institution, viz. the clan. The clan is a group of people who feel themselves united by common origin, in which descent either from the father or from the mother is decisive, so that father and mother clans are distinguished. From the standpoint of the children it is a question of patrilineal or matrilineal right of inheritance. When the children belong to the father's clan, the father or his clan is responsible for their up-bringing, and his children are his chief heirs. In matrilineal succession the children are the property of the mother's clan, and the responsibility for them is borne mainly by the mother's brother. His sister's children are his inheritors and—so the Ewe argue—he has in consequence the right to dispose of them. In parts of West Africa he may pawn them, and formerly might sell them in a case of financial difficulty, which was impossible in the case of his own children, because the brother of his wife would have objected. An Ewe man once declared that in old days a man would love the children of his slaves more than his own, because he could sell them! It was, however, exceptional that children were sold, although they were in danger of being seized for debts when they went to neighbouring towns unprotected.

Most tribes show traits of both father- and mother-right. Among the Ewe, for instance, the children belong to the father's clan, and they inherit houses and lands from him. Movable property is inherited by his sister's children, and the father cannot dispose of his children without the assent of the mother's brother. Since they are their uncle's heirs, they are also responsible for his debts, and on them lies the duty of taking blood-revenge in his favour.

The clan owns a piece of land which is divided by the elders according to the requirements of the single families. The land cannot be alienated, for it was handed down by the ancestors, and they are the real owners. The present holders are no more than trustees who have to transmit it undamaged to the coming generation. A member of a clan may have lived abroad for years, but when he returns to the land of his ancestors, a place to live and to make a farm will always be assigned to him.

The natural course of development has tended towards the evolution of private ownership of land. If a man cultivates a piece of land outside the clan land, it becomes automatically his own property. Likewise clan land may become the private possession of a family which has had its usufruct for a number of years. The situation to-day in many agricultural districts is that a man's land only reverts at his death to the clan should he himself have no heirs. In other cases his lawful inheritors receive it and divide it up among themselves. In parts of West Africa development has gone farther: a piece of land may be bequeathed by will to a person, generally to a child, outside the regular hereditary succession. From this there is only one more step to the sale of land. This is allowed when the owner has fallen into heavy debts, as among the Ewe and others. Such a sale can only be carried out, however, with the assent of the leading men of the clan, and after they have confessed themselves unable to pay the debts of their brother in any other way.

3

The village community may originally have been identical with that of the clan or a section of the clan, but in West Africa to-day the majority of villages or towns are inhabited by people of different extraction. Many clans are scattered over a large territory, and very often the village community is, at least in its social significance, more important than the clan. It forms the natural grouping in the daily life of its inhabitants in their work and their recreative activities. It is also the base and centre of the many other associations which claim the individual as their member, such as play-groups of children, work-groups of the young people, age classes, drum and dancing clubs, religious cults, guilds of trades.

4

As the education of the individual concentrates on preparation for the life within the community, in the same way this communal life has itself been the most important factor in the education of the race. In the communal life the most valuable characteristics of the race were developed and thus became the inheritance of successive generations. The individual learns willingly to conform to the group and to serve it; he submits to its authority because only in this way can the community live. On the other hand, the consciousness of being an organic and well-protected member of a group gives the individual a definite self-consciousness and dignity. The African is highly sensitive to blame, contempt, and mockery. He knows no crawling humility, no slavish flattery, and he is not easily embarrassed. As a rule he possesses greater self-assurance than the European. Within his own circle he is never in a position where he does not know how to behave or what to do. In a primitive community work is not specialized in the same way as with us and therefore the non-expert 'layman' who is helpless in everything that goes beyond his special field of activity does not exist. The African is able to enlarge with ease on any subject; in public meetings he deports himself with dignity, and has no difficulty in expressing his opinions in well-turned phrases. He does not suffer from social disabilities, for there is hardly any economic dependence, nor is there a distinction between servant and master, rich and poor. Hence there is no inferiority complex. Every individual is aware of being a valued member of his group, subject to no one, and it is natural for him to maintain this same self-assurance when dealing with the white man, to whom in many ways he feels himself superior. It is natural for him to express his real personality, for everybody knows everybody else, and no one can therefore permanently conceal his real nature. That again compels him to be careful in his daily life, for he may be sure that his mistakes will soon be discovered and that he will fall in the public estimation accordingly. He becomes a social outcast if his actions always run counter to the community's idea of right conduct.

Just as he may expect consideration from everybody if his conduct is normal, so he must respect all the members of his group in accordance with their position in the group. In mutual intercourse there is an expressed courtesy; every one is considerate of every one else, and no one does violence to traditional ceremonial. No West African receives a gift without expressing his thanks, and if possible repeating them on the following day in the company of a 'thank-helper' who assists him. A familiar feature in African life is the visit, paid by a sick man after recovery, or by a woman after her confinements, to those who have shown them kindness during the past weeks. Children from an early age are trained to good manners, and at the age of ten to twelve years they know how to behave with as much decency and dignity as an adult. The highest praise which can be given to a child, or even to an adult, among the Ewe is *ebu ame*, 'he respects people'. It is considered offensive to give way to passion and to shout at any one. Whatever is said in a state of excitement or in noisy tones is not taken seriously, and the speaker harms no one but himself. Self-control is a virtue which is expected from every one, and on the acquisition of which great stress is laid in education during the period of initiation.

Every one is under the obligation to help his fellow members. This readiness to help may be called typical of life in African communities. It would be indecent to refuse a hearing to a petitioner or to any one in trouble. Even children do not accept a present without giving part of it to their friends. Among adults it goes without saying that one must lend one's utensils to one's neighbour; help him in his work, and be useful to him in emergencies, as for instance in the case of a death or any other occurrence in which the individual must rely upon the help of his fellow man. This consciousness that one is always surrounded by friends and can always rely on their support, helps to give to every one both in his attitude to life and in his manner that self-reliant assurance which strikes every one as so pleasing in the 'uncivilized' African.

It is hardly necessary to emphasize the fact that the conditions and qualities described here are not the only ones. They come into conflict with, and yield to, less amiable traits. The disturbing factors are, however, looked upon as unseemly, and efforts are always made to remove their causes. This can only succeed, however, as long as the life of the community is but slightly influenced from without. When social distinctions become more marked; when there is a difference between rich and poor; when individual inequalities begin to show themselves clearly in inclinations and aptitudes; and when a regular system of rulership arises in place of the purely democratic association headed by the chief with relatively slight material powers: then all those unpleasant phenomena of communal life appear which seem to be indissolubly connected with every higher development and to complicate life so infinitely.

VIII

OLD AND NEW GOVERNMENTS

I

THE tribe is a political unit frequently met with in Africa. As an agglomeration of groups and individuals, not necessarily related, which through living in a common territory, having a common leader, one language, and similar customs and usages, it forms a cultural and political unit. In West Africa a tribe will often consist of three elements: the group which migrated to the district; the original inhabitants of that district; and later migrants composed of off-shoots from other groups. Though each of the component parts may be conscious of its origin, they have all been welded together into a close union. The tribe is ruled by a chief, and each individual settlement by a sub-chief who is dependent on the chief in a greater or lesser degree.

Development has not progressed everywhere in Africa as far as the tribal State. There are families or family groups who live independently by themselves and recognize either the father of the family, the priest or the magician as their chief, or regulate their communal affairs by means of a council of elders. On the other hand, several tribes may be united under a paramount chief or king. These larger units mostly originated through conquest, and their continuance was largely dependent on the personality of the ruler. If he was weak there was always the danger that the artificial structure would break down and the state dissolve into its earlier units, because its binding forces were not equal to the centrifugal tendencies of the component groups. When under favourable conditions the composite state endured, the associated tribes tended to assimilate each other's culture and to give up their distinctive life.

These were, however, rare cases, only possible where common language, tradition, and culture made such living together easier. Even where such conditions were fulfilled, it by no means always resulted in political unity. True national states, uniting because men felt themselves one and wished to be one, were exceptions. The rule was that the conquerors settled as a dominating caste in a country and lived on the labour of the subject populace, or the ruler ruled his country despotically with his officials and soldiers. In time the Native population grew accustomed to their position as tax-payers to the ruler and adapted themselves to the new régime. Where the rule lasted long enough and was not too harsh, a certain feeling of union between the ruling house and the subject people may have arisen, but in most of the larger states, the conception of a ruling family sprung from the people cannot be accepted without limitations. The rulers were often strangers and despots, and the feeling of the subjects towards them was shyness or fear rather than respect or devotion.[1] In large areas in West Africa there exist besides the conqueror-kings the old tribal or clan heads, whose functions are to-day almost exclusively religious. They 'make rain' and ensure the fruitfulness of the earth by their sacrifices. The people feel themselves more closely akin to them than to the ruling kings or paramount chiefs.

In the families of tribal chiefs the dignity of the chief can pass by inheritance within certain definite family groups, from which a suitable successor is chosen. The holding of an election may take years, as parties are formed, intrigues begin, and old jealousies are stirred up afresh. The power of the chief is limited. In important decisions he is dependent on the will of his people, above all, on that of the leading heads of families, whose councils dictate the policy of the country. They have the right of censuring the chief or imposing money fines on him, even of deposing him, although use is seldom made of this power. The chief is often hampered in his freedom of movement, because he must observe taboos. Sometimes

[1] 'Le roi! "Dada!" Nous entendons encore l'accent de vénération mêlée de terreur avec lequel les vieux Dahoméens prononcent ce mot!' (A. Le Hérissé, L'Ancien Royaume du Dahomey, p. 5.) Here we had a king sprung from another people ruling despotically.

M

his own person is taboo and consequently no stranger may see him. In such cases another person is chosen to represent him and strangers are given to believe that he is the chief. This latter person may in fact gain so much in influence that he practically assumes the power and the real chief becomes a figure-head.[1] Secret societies may obtain such political weight that they succeed in getting executive power into their own hands.[2] The chief possesses practically no material means to power. It depends on his personality whether he has authority, and is a real leader or merely a plaything in the hands of his elders; whether order and decency reign in his country; or whether, as is often the case, the young people do what they like. He is further bound by custom and tradition. Deviation from such a path might arouse the disapproval not only of his elders, but also of his ancestors. Chiefs have indeed departed from tribal custom. There are instances of men such as Chaka, who forbade circumcision for military reasons, and Moshesh, who tried to put down the persecution of witches and limited the use of alcohol. They were not tribal chiefs, however, but rulers of a larger calibre, who could dare to disregard tradition and public opinion. In the smaller communities certain changes have gradually crept in with the assent of the people, as, for example, when

[1] Cf. R. S. Rattray, *The Tribes of the Ashanti Hinterland*, Oxford, 1932, vol. i, pp. xi ff.

[2] Cf. H. S. Farrow, *Faith, Fancies and Fetish* (Yoruba), London, pp. 116 ff.

human sacrifice was replaced by animals, or cruel customs connected with ordeals were modified or abandoned. The predominant feature of political life, however, was conservatism, and innovations were not looked upon with favour. Barbaric institutions, such as the killing of persons at the burial of the chief, cruel executions, ordeals, the smelling out of witches, have been until modern times recognized features of the administration.

The authority of the chief of the tribe rests mainly on the fact that he is the descendant of the first leader of the group. He is the representative of the ancestors, the custodian of their law and their magic powers, and thus symbolizes the unity of the tribe. In honouring the chief, the tribe honours itself and its own past. Religious duties may be united with his office. He makes the sacrifices to the ancestors or the tribal gods, or at least has to preside over the sacrificial rites.

The religious position of the king or chief can result in less weight being attached to his personal character. He is the guardian of the magic powers inherited from the ancestors, and therefore his person has a certain sanctity. What matters is that these magic powers are maintained unimpaired in him, for they are more important than his personal qualities. This conception may explain a certain custom which once prevailed in parts of Africa: when the king's physical powers decayed, or when his reign had lasted a certain number of years, he was put to death. He was no longer a fitting vessel for magic power, and this must be handed on in another vessel, that is to say, in his successor.

One of the important functions of the chief is to administer the law in conjunction with his councillors and officials. This rests on tradition and has therefore the character of customary law, i.e. of rules which evolved in the course of time and which refer to the behaviour of individuals and groups to each other and to the community. The purpose of this law is to maintain the equilibrium of society so that irregularities which have crept in may be compensated.[1] It is not as important to punish the evil-doer as to make good an injury done. Thus a thief need not necessarily be punished. The affair may be settled if he gives back the stolen property and perhaps pays a fine as consolation money. Similarly, if in the case of manslaughter the injured family is given a person in place of its dead member as well as the fine, the damage has been made good. Negatively, the injured family has the right to kill the murderer or a member of the murderer's family, thus re-establishing the balance between the groups. This may be done through personal vengeance; or by the surrender of the malefactor in public assembly to the injured group for the execution of the death-sentence; or by submitting the matter to the chief and his council. Witches and dealers in black magic are dangerous, not guilty, persons and must be removed in the interest of the

[1] J. H. Driberg, 'Primitive Law in Eastern Africa,' *Africa*, vol. i, pp. 63 ff.

community. The often cruel form of the sentence is perhaps explained by the fact that by seeing it the injured person may receive satisfaction for the discomfort which he himself suffered.

2

The chieftainship is one of those institutions which have preserved their vitality to the present day. It has its weaknesses and defects. It has sometimes led to abuses of power. Many a chief has brought the community entrusted to him to ruin by arbitrary injustice, incapacity, or indifference. Nevertheless, the institution as such enjoys respect and confidence in most parts of Africa. It has had in recent time to suffer upheavals and far-reaching changes, but nowhere has it vanished save where the power of the European has ousted it. Chiefs have had to learn how to adapt themselves. Although the chief's office is combined with pagan religious functions there are to-day not a few Christian chiefs. In this case a way out is found by entrusting the religious duties to a still unconverted kinsman of the chief.

A European Government which has any appreciation of the value of indigenous social bonds of union, cannot afford to ignore a means of integration so important as the institution of chieftainship. No matter whether its colonial policy aims at weakening or strengthening the existing indigenous administration, it cannot, at least in its beginning stage, do without it. This is especially true of the village chiefs.

It is natural that they should retain their former functions, though their position may have changed as
regards details. The problem becomes more complex when it is the question of a bigger chief and a
larger administrative area.

There are three possible attitudes to these institutions. They may be (a) destroyed, (b) metamorphosed
into a European shape, or (c) maintained in their integrity and developed organically. The first two
methods of procedure may be chosen from purely
practical motives, or with the conscious purpose of
causing the decay of existing social and political
organisms and putting European substitutes in their
place, thus bringing about as close a union as possible
between the Native inhabitants of the colony and the
governing colonial power. If practical considerations predominate, the argument will be somewhat
as follows. The indigenous government is a machine
which generally works clumsily, sometimes not at
all, and only seldom well. So many defects and so
much corruption are associated with the system of
chiefs that no serious administration can be built up
on it. If the people were asked whether they prefer
to be ruled by their own chief or by a white administrator, the majority would vote for the white man,
for they are disgusted with the chief's selfishness and
injustice. Protagonists of such a view will point to
Basutoland as a territory with self-government under
its own chiefs, who, however, in important issues
have not realized the weight of responsibility laid

upon them, and do not show themselves equal to their task. As a result of increased cattle-breeding the land is no longer able to maintain its population, and the overstocking of the pastures causes erosion of the soil which threatens to become a danger to the country. It would be better to diminish the number of cattle and improve their quality, and to use a larger part of the land for agriculture. The chiefs are opposed to this idea and, indeed, to any innovation which might endanger their position. The chiefs are as a rule and by nature conservative, since they fear their authority may be prejudiced by modern changes. This has often been the case in the past. If a man produced more than his fellow tribesmen, or in any way distinguished himself, he was immediately suspected of rivalry with the chief and had to face the risk of being put out of the way. Similarly, suspicions arise to-day if any one works on modern methods and therefore acquires dignity and a competence. In this way the chiefs and their administrations can become an obstacle in the path of progress wherever their traditional power is great. They may adopt an attitude of opposition to the educated classes, so that the latter find no proper field for their activities in the purely tribal areas, and easily become an element of discontent. Consequently we find in some South African Native territories, as, for instance, Basutoland and Bechuanaland, a state of stagnation involving a decrease of production and a lowering of the standard of life.

For these reasons—so it is argued—it is a sound policy not to govern through the chiefs, but to hand over the administration to the European official. During a transitional stage the chief may remain as an innocuous symbol of the unity of the tribe, but no power ought to be entrusted to him.

It is clear, however, that the European alone cannot carry on the whole administration. He needs the co-operation of the Natives, no matter whether he governs with or without the chief. All the lower posts in the services of the Administration are filled by Natives, and they are gradually being entrusted with more responsible tasks. If the chiefs are abolished, Native officials will to a considerable extent take their place. They have the advantage of a better general and technical training than the chief himself, and the European can more easily control them. Whether they will have a higher sense of responsibility and justify the confidence of the European more than the hereditary chief may well be doubted. Their position is weaker than that of chiefs because they do not enjoy the same consideration from the population and are not bound to it by bonds of reverence or tradition. It may be confidently asserted that in the majority of cases the Natives will give the preference to the chief with all his disadvantages rather than to the Native official.

In the Transkei Reserve a system of government exists which may be regarded as a cross between direct rule and self-government. The country is divided into twenty-seven districts, each of which is administered by a European magistrate. A district consists of locations each with about 1,000 inhabitants and a Native headman, who is chosen by the people but confirmed and paid by the Government. The administration of the law, therefore, even in matters of minor import, lies in the hands of white officials, and they have taken over the functions of the former chiefs. At the same time there is a certain amount of self-government. Each district has a Council consisting of the magistrate and six Native members, two appointed by the Government and four elected by the people. Its juridical power, however, is small, and is confined mainly to economic matters.

The people as a whole is represented in the Bunga or General Council, which meets annually in Umtata and is composed of three representatives from each district, all of them Natives. The Chief Magistrate is the president, and the eighteen District Magistrates are members without the right to vote. Although the Bunga is only an advisory body, its scope is not inconsiderable. Intended proclamations are laid before it. Its decisions are made known to the Native Affairs Department; their reply is published in the report of the transactions of the Bunga, and they draft the wording of the Proclamation, which is finally published in the name of the Governor-General. The administration hardly ever passes a law with which the Bunga has not declared itself to be in agreement. The duty of the Bunga is especially to protect the

Native customary law and to state its opinion about any proposed alteration.

The administrative districts do not take into consideration the tribal boundaries. The chieftainships exist no longer and chiefs do not as such take part in the functions of government.

The Transkei is thus an example of how a progressive population with private ownership of land has been intentionally detached from its traditional political structure and guided into a modern form of government. It is true that the burden of the executive falls entirely on the white officials, but at the same time a considerable and increasing measure of responsibility is granted to the Natives. The chief is replaced by officials appointed by Government or chosen by the people; in the District Councils and the Bunga the people have representation on a parliamentary basis.

It is remarkable that this system does not appear entirely satisfactory to the Natives. Their main objection is that it excludes the hereditary chiefs from holding that position in the administration which by human and divine right belongs to them. Again and again the Bunga has begged the Government to give back the hereditary chiefs to the people, because they alone possess the necessary authority to guarantee a satisfactory administration. 'A chief is like the sun, a sacred thing to illumine the world; God created a king amongst the people, and He gave him power to govern his people by the laws He made.' The chiefs and headmen they say can nowadays only use their mouths in governing the people, and hence the people do not listen.

The second of the possibilities mentioned above on p. 166 is that political institutions may be preserved in their essence and metamorphosed into European form. Practically this will mean that the Government will, wherever opportunity offers, depose the hereditary chief and replace him by a man who is agreeable to itself. In this way it will break the backbone of the indigenous political order and decree its complete disintegration. The new chief is a creature of the Government, dependent on it and therefore forced to work with it whatever happens. He has no natural authority over the people, but is a representative of the European ruler whose orders he has to obey.

The third method, namely, the introduction of indirect rule,[1] is less simple than the two already mentioned. Its basis is the assumption that the political institutions of the Natives contain values which are capable of development and whose loss would be detrimental to the people. Its object therefore is to preserve these values and enlist them in the service of the new administration. As the forms of political life in Africa are, however, extraordinarily varied, a careful study is the first necessity in every single case, not only for each colony but for each political entity in the colony. Such a study should include the whole

---

[1] Cf. Lord Lugard, *The Dual Mandate*, 4th ed., London, 1929; Sir Donald Cameron, address, published as Supplement to *Extraordinary Gazette*, 6 March 1933.

of the politico-social institutions and values of the group, the position of the person of the ruler, the rules of succession, the organs of administration, the distribution of offices, the legislative and executive powers, land tenure, and the motives which underlie obedience to the existing authorities and foster the sense of social obligation. The authority which is to be the bearer of Indirect Rule must be 'a real authority in the eyes and minds of the people affected, which they are willing to obey' (Sir Donald Cameron). It is also indispensable to examine any changes in the political sanctions and other forms of social life due to foreign influences, including also the attitude of the population to its chief as well as to innovations introduced by European governments or as a result of economic upheavals and social revolution.

The institution of indirect rule does not mean that the position of the chief and his administrative machinery remain the same as before. He becomes a part of the European administration and must adapt himself to it. The principle laid down is that indigenous methods and conceptions shall remain effective in so far as they do not conflict with the universal sense of justice. Even this limitation, however, means many important changes. It will not be possible to avoid the abolition of customs offensive to European ideas of justice. The leading white official must see that business is properly carried out and money conscientiously administered; that public works, schools, and public health works are not neglected; and that the

administration of justice is free from reproach. Many
institutions which formerly were recognized as necessary parts of the law as, for instance, the Ordeal must
disappear. The white official will have to go still
deeper into the actual system of administration. He
will generally strive to form larger units out of small
tribal or village chieftainships, as, for instance, making
one of a group of chiefs of equal standing a paramount
chief, and subordinating the rest to him, which involves depriving them of their existing sovereignty.
Nor will the position of the people to its chief remain
unchanged. On the material side the chief's position
grows stronger. He now has the white man to back
him up, and even has a little police power with the aid
of which he can enforce obedience. On the moral
side, however, this may mean a weakening of the
traditional link and a prejudice to the veneration in
which he was held. He no longer represents the
ancestors but the District Commissioner, to whose
instructions he has to enforce obedience from his
subjects. He must often make far-reaching claims on
them. He has to levy taxes, and in doing so may
arouse the suspicion that he is demanding more than
the Government has fixed—a suspicion which may
not always be unfounded. As in former days, so now
chiefs are surrounded by relatives and other hangers-
on who hope to make capital out of their position,
and the chief is expected to show himself liberal
towards them. The great chiefs especially, who have
been accustomed to rule more or less autocratically,

cannot be expected to adapt themselves without effort to the position of a constitutional ruler with all the limitations that the idea implies. Continuous careful consultation, combined with guidance and control of the organs of government is necessary in these cases lest, strengthened by the authority given them by the Europeans, the chiefs may be tempted to feel themselves too independent and abuse their position to the detriment of their subjects. Authority should as far as possible be decentralized so that the smaller chiefs and village headmen have their rigidly circumscribed functions and a certain amount of independence, and part of the money that they raise in their administrative districts should be set aside for the benefit of those districts.

For the European official co-operation with the chief means a thorough knowledge of the life of the people and a great measure of wisdom and educational skill. He will have to deal not only with those who are ready to learn, but with the incapable, the careless, the unreliable, and even the obstinate, and it is with them and their help that he will have to administer his district. In spite of all the obstacles, however, this system of government is an admirable method of attaining the main object of all education, namely, the creation of personalities conscious of their responsibilities. Though the final responsibility will rest with the white official, that must not hinder him from entrusting real powers to the chief and his administration, so that he may feel himself to be in the confidence not only of the European government but also of his own people. The people must have the conviction that he is their man, united with them for weal or for woe, and not the creature of the Government. Responsibility and healthy self-reliance can be strengthened by allowing the financial administration of the country to remain in the hands of the chief and his officials, so that when taxes flow into the treasury of the chief, a certain part is diverted to the central government for the general needs of the colony and the rest remains to be applied at the discretion of the Native administrators for schools, local and public works, the care of public health, and the salaries of the chief and his officials. Even the law must as far as possible be administered by the chief and his council in accordance with tradition and custom. To prevent abuses and irregularities, written records of all transactions should be kept and these should be regularly checked by European officials. Though indirect rule is based on the conservative element in tribal life, it must at the same time be progressive in the best sense of the word. Its aim should be to assimilate such new elements as are required for development into a really modern administration, whose probity and reliability are beyond question. It should also give the educated class full opportunity of using their capabilities in the service of the community. Indirect rule which does not succeed in enlisting the hearty co-operation of the educated Natives will lack efficiency and cannot be deep-rooted.

The advantage of indirect rule over every other system is that it builds up instead of destroying. It is based on something which already exists and aims at developing it organically. That is a sound policy if what exists has vitality, and this undoubtedly is the case with the institution of chieftainship. It is true that the weaknesses of chieftainship are often sharply criticized by the Natives themselves, but these are generally young people who have either through their education or stay abroad dissociated themselves from the social obligations of their own people and are already really outside it. The majority of the older people speak differently, and even among the younger educated men most are unwilling to give up the institution. There are numberless instances, even in those tribes in which Europeanization has made great progress and the Native administration has been strongly modernized, of peoples resolutely clinging to the institution and of chiefs enjoying consideration and respect in the life of the people to-day which they perhaps never enjoyed before. The people see in their chief a symbol of their pride of race, and his removal would be a blow to their national self-consciousness. The community feeling is so strongly developed in the African and so inherent in his whole existence, that he shows no desire to cast it off with a light heart. It must fill him with satisfaction that he has been able to preserve these bonds intact even to the present day, and to administer his own affairs under European guidance. Many Europeans have

had occasion to admire the loyalty of the African.
This loyalty grew out of the intense feeling of community in the life of the clan and the tribe. Much
of this innate loyalty has been transferred to the
European official, and the latter will best be able to
maintain and increase this capital by honouring the
African's past in his political creations and thus keeping alive in him that self-respect without which no
people can prosper.

IX

THE SUPERNATURAL WORLD

1. Native attitude towards natural objects (*p.* 178). Identification of form and character, of material and spiritual, of whole and its parts (*p.* 179). Belief in separate beings in each individual (*p.* 183).
2. Quality of 'power' in things (*p.* 184). Belief and practice in magic (*p.* 185). Deification of magical objects (*p.* 187).
3. Respect due to age and to ancestors (*p.* 187). Worship of Nature gods (*p.* 189). Religious associations: Poro League (*p.* 190). Festivals of tribal and clan gods (*p.* 191).
4. Religion not confined to material concerns (*p.* 192). Dreams and personal communion (*p.* 192). Feelings of awe and confidence (*p.* 193). Lack of connexion between religion and ethics (*p.* 195).
5. Belief in a 'high god' (*p.* 195). Worship of 'high god' in different parts of Africa (*p.* 196).
6. Destructive effects of modern contact on Native religion (*p.* 197). Initiation schools (*p.* 198). Taboo fellowships (*p.* 199). Causes of decay in Native religion (*p.* 201). Place of religion in African life (*p.* 204). Task of Institute in study of religion as a force in Native life and effects of its decay (*p.* 204).

I

THE world of the primitive African is characterized by its unity and completeness. No sharply defined aspect exists by itself; wish and reality, the possible and the impossible, knowledge and belief, thought and poetry, secular and religious life are interwoven and fundamentally one. Things which we distinguish are to him identical in their essence. It is therefore difficult to study one single feature of African life in isolation. Because it is cohesive one inevitably passes from one region into the other without noticing it; and a correct understanding can only be obtained by surveying the life as a whole.

The tendency of the Negro to regard essentially different things as similar is partly explained by his egocentric attitude. He feels himself to be the centre of his world. He names objects in his environment after the parts of his body (branch of a tree = hand, leaf = ear, stem = foot, front = forehead, top = head), and values them according to whether they harm or help him. In the same manner he transfers to them his own human qualities, attributing to them his needs and desires, his love and hate, his capacity for action, with the result that he treats them in the same way as his fellow men, trying to gain their support and use their help in removing imminent dangers. It might therefore be said that he personifies the objects surrounding him, though it is more correct to say that he places things on the same level as himself. Dead men have in many respects the same quality as the living, for one talks with them and sets before them food and drink. The Kpelle man (Liberia) sees his dead friend wearing his rolled-up burial-cloth on his head, as he climbs the mountain on which the dead dwell. Or he will say: 'We do not see the dead, when they come into our house; they walk amongst us, but we do not see them, for they are covered with chalk (and thereby invisible). If they take something belonging to us, we do not know it; if they eat from our food, or eat with us from the same dish, we do not know it.'

Men can change into animals, and animals into

men. A crocodile leaves the water, hangs up his skin
on a tree, and takes part in a game as a man with the
men of the village (Kpelle). A buffalo trades as a
human being in the market as other men do, and
changes on his way home once more into a buffalo
(Ewe). A man roams at night round the village as
a leopard, is shot, and on the next day he is found,
again as person, lying wounded on his mat (Central
Togoland).[1] In these beliefs, which are found among
most West African tribes, there is a complete identification of form and character. The man, in assuming
the form of an animal, whether, as in the above
examples, by direct magical metamorphosis or by
wearing the mask or the skin of an animal, really
becomes the animal in question; the form conditions
the character.

One talks with an animal as with a man and brings
him sacrifice as to a deity. Food is placed before the
skulls of slain animals and they are prayed to tell their
living companions in the bush and forest how well
they are being cared for, and advise them likewise to
allow themselves to be shot by hunters. The eyes of
a shot leopard are bound, so that it cannot see the
hunter who killed it and so take vengeance on him.
The huntsman, before he goes hunting, washes not
only his own eyes but also those of his gun so that
when shooting they may better see the quarry. A
sacrifice is made to the gun and it is accompanied by

[1] Cf. also A. W. Cardinall, *Tales told in Togoland*, London,
1931, where many examples of a similar kind are given.

prayer that it may not miss its mark. By a motion of
the arm a storm or an army approaching in the distance can be turned away, just as an animal can be
frightened away by the same movement (Kpelle).

These identifications are, however, not followed to
their logical conclusions, and they do not mean that
the African is incapable of making distinctions. He
does so where necessary; and the class system of
the Bantu languages shows a subtlety in distinction
such as no European languages have. Things may be
different in one aspect, but in another, namely, in
their capability of doing harm or good, they are not
essentially distinguished. Vestiges of such a complex attitude are extant among ourselves, when in our
fairy-tales animals and trees talk. With us, however,
this fairy-world is real at the most in childhood and
vanishes later. The Negro, even as an adult, can
relate in all sincerity how in the dawn of morning a
hyena turned into a woman before his very eyes, and
it is quite natural for him to beg forgiveness of a tree
by making a sacrifice before felling it, and excuse
himself by saying that the elders, whom one may not
gainsay, have laid this unpleasant task upon him. It
is in the religious sphere more than in any other
that the logical attitude is constantly set against the
emotional, and the former carries less weight.

The unity of his vision prevents the African also
from distinguishing between the material and the
spiritual. The soul itself is matter sublimated—
breath, a shadow, a flame. It is possible for the

magician or priest to capture the soul of a sick man
which has escaped and is sitting on the roof of the
house or on a neighbouring tree, and having captured
it to restore it to the human body (Ewe). Processes
are regarded as things or beings: illness is a stone, a
piece of wood, which must be removed from the
body, or a being that is wandering about in the body.
If I dream of a far country, then in my sleep I have
really been there, even although I was visibly sleeping
on my mat the whole night long, for there are men
who can leave their bodies, as a snake its skin.

As form and character are identified, so are the
whole and its parts.[1] The whole has the characteristics of the part and the part those of the whole. If
I have a part, then I have essentially the whole; and
what I do to a part, I have likewise done to the whole.
If I carry the tooth of a leopard on my body, then I
have command over the power of the leopard. Anything I do to the nails and hair cut from an enemy
I have done to him. If the Ewe huntsman discovers
the spoor of a wild animal, he strikes the air with a
stick in the direction in which the animal ran. He then
strikes the animal's foot-marks, thus making it im-
potent to run farther and enabling him easily to over-
take it; or he takes sand from the animal's spoor and
ties it in a string, thereby binding the feet of the
animal so that it cannot go farther.

Similar things have similar qualities, and inner re-
semblance is inferred from external similarity. Hence

[1] Cf. A. Vierkandt, *Naturvölker und Kulturvölker*.

one can cure, strengthen, or call forth like by like. Rain clouds give rain, and if I produce smoke clouds, which resemble the rain clouds, then by so doing rain will be produced. The Kpelle stun fishes by beating the water with a twig, the leaves of which contain poison, and they maintain that on the day one does that it will rain. When it rains, the water is set in motion just as it is by being struck with the twig, therefore this artificial agitation of the water will produce rain. An Ewe who carries home a slain animal on his back receives as his share the back of the animal; his back has worked and needs refreshing and the best refreshment for it is the back of the animal. The loins of the animal are given to the wife of the hunter because the loins carry the body when it works; just as a man's body rests on the loins, so the management of the household depends on the woman.

Man himself is not necessarily a unit, but may consist of several independent parts. On the Gold Coast sacrifices are made to one's own soul (the Okra). It is, on the one hand, an integral part of man, but at the same time it leads an independent existence and can be gracious or ungracious to the man to whom it belongs.[1] The Yoruba make sacrifices to their head, so that it may think well; to their stomach, so that it nourishes properly the other parts of the body; to their big toe so that it runs well.

The view that a person may consist of several

[1] Cf. R. S. Rattray, *Religion and Art in Ashanti*, Oxford, 1927, p. 153.

independent parts, each of which is able to act on its
own accord, can even find a linguistic expression, as
when in languages of the Gur (Goor) group (in the
northern Gold Coast and Togoland) the sentence
'he worked with his hand' is expressed literally:
'he took hand it (namely the hand) worked.' This
appears to be the foundation for the *pars-pro-toto*
view. Through the fact that a part is no longer felt
to be part of a whole, but an object in itself, the *pars*
becomes a *totum*, by being taken away from the real
totum. The separation from the *totum* is the first act,
and it is followed by the part being treated as a whole,
e.g. by offering it sacrifices as in the case of the
Yoruba. The next step in mental development will
then be to 'readjust' the part to the whole, that is to
recognize the members as part of the body.

2

The interest which the African takes in things is
not an academic one. They interest him in so far as
they are useful to him or can do him harm, and in so
far as they are effective in relation to himself. Their
essential quality is power. This power is possessed
by gods, men, animals, and things, varying in degree
and in kind. It is the most important factor with
which one has to reckon in daily life. One is exposed
to it every moment and on all sides, and it decides
whether one is to be fortunate or unfortunate. In
itself it is impersonal and neutral, neither good nor
evil, but it can hurt or help man, preserve or destroy

his life. It obeys the will of its possessor and can
become a fearful instrument in his hand. It can also
be transmitted, so that man is not limited to the
resources given by nature, but can acquire others,
and a great deal of thought and consideration is
directed to conserving and increasing this power and
thereby warding off possible dangers caused by hostile
agencies.

We are accustomed to call this force magic, but the
conception is really too narrow, for under these words
we understand something 'supernatural', whereas
with primitive man the distinction between natural
and unnatural, rational and irrational is shadowy. In
Kpelle the word *sale* means medicine as well as
poison and magic, i.e. anything that is effective in a
striking manner. I gain power by eating food, but
also by rubbing in an ointment containing power-
giving ingredients, and to the Native both are of
equal value. It is the same whether I treat a sick
man with a steam bath (as is often done in West
Africa) or a charm. Magician and doctor are one and
the same person, and which of his remedies are to be
regarded as magic and which as medicine is a question
which interests the European but does not exist for
the Negro. A difference does appear, however, in
that many objects possess power in large measure, or
an outstanding quality, which enables them to control
effects to an abnormal degree. This force is claimed
when one's own powers are not adequate. One is indeed conscious that the actions which we call rational

are indispensable; that, for example, the cultivation
of a field depends on such factors as the nature of the
soil, the quality of the seed, rain, and, above all, on
one's own work. Often, however, the rain does not
come, and to produce it more than ordinary human
powers are needed. In fact experience has taught,
that where all conditions are fulfilled, yet the expected
result has not followed, so that something essential
must have been absent. In the ordinary course of
events the rational method of action is regarded as
sufficient. Where it is a question of extraordinary
issues of vital importance to life itself; of the threatened
well-being of one's own existence, of one's kin or of
the community; in a word, where the ordinary course
of life is no longer possible and great issues are at
stake, then extraordinary means are required which, on
account of the occasions from which they arise, take on
the character of the superhuman in the imagination
of the participant.

The magical practices by which power is produced
are to a large extent a technique, which in principle
and in everyday cases may be performed by any person,
but of which certain persons possess a better knowledge and skill whereby they become specialists. Their
art consists in knowing for each individual case the
suitable ingredients and the proportion in which they
are to be mixed, in the same way as the pharmaceutist
mixes his drugs and medicines. On the other hand, it
may become more than a mere technique. There
is something sacred about it, for it has been handed

down from the ancestors of earliest times, and may have its origin in a deity who transmitted the knowledge to a former member of the group. The performance of the magical act is not like any other occupation, but is invested with responsibility, for on it depends the well-being of one's family members or of the whole community; and for its effectiveness it is essential that it should be performed exactly in that way in which it has been transmitted from the forebears. Thus more complex religious elements enter into magical practices and beliefs. In the beliefs of the Ewe and Akan, magic may change into a deity. When a person owns a 'medicine', that is to say a magical object, which shows extraordinary power in healing sickness, in giving children, in producing rain, &c., the owner may one day declare that he has found out his magic (*dzo*) to be a deity (*trɔ̃*), and that he henceforth is going to treat it as such; or the priest of another god whose advice he has asked may explain to him that his magic is a god. He then becomes the priest of the new deity, whose help is now sought by other people and who may attain great fame. The Ewe call these gods *dzo-zu-trɔ̃*, 'magic-become-god'.

3

Aged people possess a large amount of power, especially those who hold a leading position. During their long life they have been able to accumulate forces, and have also inherited them from earlier generations. Their very existence is a proof of power, for it is only thanks to it that during their long life all attempts of hostile forces have been ineffectual against them. In consequence one prefers to have charms made by them, for they not only understand the technique better than others but can also impart to the charm something of their own strength. But just as man does not cease to exist with death, so his magical power is not ended when he dies. For that reason an old man is buried in his hut, in the cattle kraal, or within the settlement, in order that the group may always have control over him and thereby over his strength and goodwill. A man's strength fails when he remains without food. The same happens to a dead man: he needs strengthening. A well-nourished man is in a better, more kindly mood than a hungry one, and this is true also of the dead. Therefore one should not approach the ancestors without a sacrifice when asking for their gifts.

Besides the ancestors, the forces of nature, as bearers of extraordinary powers, early aroused attention. They are thought to be embodied in striking natural objects or phenomena such as rivers, lakes, rocks, large trees, thunder and lightning, the rainbow. They too are endowed with human qualities, but the scope of their power exceeds human limits. Man must try to conciliate them, to press their powers into his service and to avert the peril that threatens from them. Thus they have become, especially in West Africa, the objects of a religious cult. Ancestor worship, on the other hand, which in one form or another is universal in Africa, predominates in East and South Africa.

The worship of nature gods often takes place actually on the site of the objects of worship themselves, as far as that is possible. As it would be inconvenient, however, for the purpose of a regular cult to go every time to a distant river or rock, a symbol of the deity is erected in every village where the god is worshipped. The same necessity naturally occurs when it is a question of phenomena such as the sky or the thunder, or of those gods whose cult was brought from a former home or imported from a foreign country. In this way idols, representations of the gods, came into use. The idol is, in the belief of the Natives, not identical with the deity, but is no more than the place where the deity can be approached and addressed. This takes place through the mediation of a priest; he receives the supplicant, lays the offerings before the god, calls him, and says the prayers.

The adoration of a divinity is not always confined to one natural social group such as the tribe, the clan, or the family. Some divinities, as, for example, Bruku in middle Togoland, have obtained such fame that pilgrims come from all the neighbouring countries to pray his aid, and his shrine has become a religious centre of 'international' importance.

Religion has, moreover, directly created new social structures, for the worshippers of a divinity from different clans or tribes may form a religious fraternity or

sect, which can only be entered after a period of proba-
tion. The sect has a common settlement, surrounded
by a wall, where the leaders dwell, and where the
adepts live carefully segregated from their families
during the time of their initiation, which often includes the learning of a secret language. Thanks
to their feeling of solidarity, and of superiority as a
group of the elect, thanks also to their alleged secret
knowledge and the brilliant festivities which they
institute, these sects exercise a great power of attraction, and they not infrequently have succeeded in
getting the political power of a community into their
hands. Their classical home is the coast of Upper
Guinea.

The religious centre of such a sect is not necessarily
a divinity. There are some, especially in Sierra Leone,
Liberia, and the neighbouring districts, which group
themselves round a beast like a leopard, serpent,
baboon, or crocodile, or even a powerful charm. A
combination of religious and social elements is found
in the societies which emerge from the initiations.
The boys who leave the initiation school enter the
secret league of the men, in whose hands both the
administration of the community and the exercise of
the important religious and magical functions are
concentrated. The best known of these associations
is the Poro League in Sierra Leone and Liberia.[1]

[1] Cf. T. J. Alldridge, *A Transformed Colony, Sierra Leone*,
London, 1910; K. J. Beatty, *Human Leopards*, London, 1915;
J. L. Sibley and D. Westermann, *Liberia Old and New*, London.

Corresponding to it there is the Sande or Bundu of girls or women.

The binding strength of religion in society is most evident in the yearly festivals which are in parts of West Africa celebrated in honour of the old tribal or clan gods. They take place about the turn of the year, that is, after the work in the fields is over, and may be called the climax in the life of the people. They are the occasion which brings the whole community together to a common festival of rejoicing and thanksgiving. As far as possible the members of the clan who are living apart from it take part in it, and everywhere are to be seen scenes of a joyful reunion. It is a thanksgiving day for the god, who has made the harvest thrive and given his children food and health. His idol is ornamented and publicly exhibited; sacrifice is made to him; groups of friends and relations come together in houses, on the village green, or in groves for sacrificial meals. It is also a day of remembrance for those who died in the last year and for the ancestors as a whole. They move among the living, food is set aside for them, and for this one day they take part in the general rejoicing of their own clansmen. The symbols of the tribal ancestors (stools, swords, drums, trumpets) are cleaned, smeared with fresh sacrificial blood, and shown to the people. This is also the occasion on which the sacred possessions of the tribe are explained to the young people and they are introduced to its history. Present and past, living and dead, young and old, the religious and

social unions of the group all come together on this
occasion to form a most impressive whole.

4

Religion has been defined as a provision for life by
supernatural means. This definition is too narrow,
but it does contain some of its true essence. If the
African is asked what he considers the greatest good,
his answer will be: 'Life.' Life of his own person, of
the family, of the tribe. 'Life for the town, life for all
people, life for the king, life for women and children'
are the constantly recurring formulas in Akan and
Ewe prayers. A man's own powers are not sufficient
protection against the many enemies of life, and
he stretches out hands to that which is more than
human.

Yet religion is not limited to the care of material
life. Well-being, good fortune, a happy relationship
with one's fellow men, all these things also belong
to life; they embrace not only oneself but the members
of the family. When a man goes with his wife and
children to the priest asking him to pray to the god
for the life of a sick child, there are motives in this
prayer far exceeding the merely material; and the
same is true when a chief or clan headman sacrifices
to the ancestors for the well-being of the people
entrusted to him.

Even the relationship between the god or the
ancestor and his worshipper can have the character
of personal communion. When the priest rises from

his bed in the morning and has washed his face, he offers the morning salutation to his god as to an old, honoured friend. If the head of the household has to go somewhere, he takes leave of the ancestor, whose symbol stands in his hut, and should he be saved from a misfortune or meet with luck, he will not delay in making a thank-offering to his protector.

The gods and ancestors speak to men through impressive experiences or dreams, and the origin of a cult or the discovery of a divinity may be traced back to such an event. A man roaming through the bush in the midst of the dry season suddenly comes upon a bubbling spring of whose presence no one had known previously; or, while resting under a tree, he has a wonderful dream. In both cases it was a deity who thus revealed itself to the person and demanded to be worshipped by him. It is natural that when a man has so directly been summoned by a divinity to its service, he should feel himself personally bound to it, and that such an experience may mean a turning-point in his life.

Even apart from such extraordinary cases, religion exercises a far-reaching influence on the inner attitude and actions of man. The dominating feeling with regard to the higher beings is a sacred awe, in which terror of the god's wrath and punishment predominates. It is early impressed on the children that they must on no account go too near to the idols and holy vessels, 'for the god will kill you'; and when the god announces his appearance, the multitude feels 'as if

o

cold water had been poured over them'.[1] This fear of the gods may seem to be contradicted by the fact that their images are often completely neglected; but this is explained by the idea that the idol or the shrine is not the dwelling-place of the divinity, only the place to which he can be invited, and where converse with him is possible. If a public religious function is to take place, the temple, shrine, or statue, and even the ways that lead to them, are put in order.

The idea of the divinity and of the ancestors, however, arouses in man not only awe but also confidence. When he is helpless and near to despair, prayer and sacrifice fill him with new assurance and give him back his self-reliance. A hard task will be attacked with greater courage, if we are convinced that we are dependent not on our own strength alone, but that we have a mighty ally by our side. The many religious and magical duties and prohibitions within which the Negro moves often appear to us mere burdens and obstacles. He himself, however, does not feel them to be so. Every charm which he acquires; every taboo which he has to observe; every omen to which he has to give heed; the gods whom he serves; the ancestors to whom he gives reverence; the oracle whose consent he must gain: all these things are like a protecting cloak which he wraps round himself. Each one gives him more confidence in himself, and attention devoted to them is not an onerous waste of time but

[1] Cf. D. Westermann, *A Study of the Ewe Language*, London, 1930 (Text on p. 228).

a reassurance and a satisfaction, for in this way he learns to overcome his dread.

On the other hand there is hardly any link between ethical life and religion. The gods and ancestors are a-moral; they take no interest in the ethical behaviour of their worshippers and are indifferent as to the inner attitude in which they are approached. What they demand is offerings and prayers. If in spite of them they refuse their help, it is through anger that one of their many commandments has been, probably unwittingly, disregarded. Ethics are rooted in the social groups. One is moral and acts morally if one keeps to the norm which regulates the relations of the members of the clan or of another group to one another. These norms are binding, however, only in relation to members of the group; they relate to those outside only in so far as the security and well-being of the clan are affected.

5

Moral conceptions of a higher kind are to be found in the idea of a high-god, who often is identified with the heavens or the sun, or stands in relation to an ancestor. Often the ideas about him have a certain sublimity: he is the creator and guardian not only of his own people but of the whole world. His predominant qualities are might, goodness, and justice. He is benevolent not because mankind prays to him, but because his nature is good. This conviction is expressed in numerous current sayings. There is no question that many West African tribes combine with this belief in a high-god the highest conceptions of good and evil in the moral sense. He forbids and avenges evildoing. This conception has evidently been strengthened by the knowledge that much injustice in this world remains unatoned for and that the weak man has to bow to the strong, and by the resulting conviction that somewhere absolute justice prevails.

In isolated cases this high-god has regular worship, which is different in no essential from that paid to the gods of Nature. More often, however, he is beyond the reverence of man, dwelling in the far-off Unknown, and ideas about him are ill defined. His demands are theoretically admitted, but they only exercise a small, or no influence at all, on practical life. The belief in him is a philosophy rather than a living faith. God is the first cause of everything that is, and He is responsible for the ordering of the world. From this more platonic attitude we can also explain how God and His ordinances are criticized. An Ewe may say: 'God is unjust because He lets my neighbour succeed in everything, and I am sitting here in misery'; or one may say to a worthless man: 'May the god who created you mould no more men.' No man would venture on such expressions with regard to the Nature gods, for they are feared.

Conceptions of the high-gods are not uniform in all parts of Africa, and they are still insufficiently known. Further detailed investigations among many

tribes will be necessary before we can form a clear
picture of the significance of this phenomenon for
the religious life and its relation to other religious
phenomena. The high-god often has an extraordinarily elusive character. On the one side he shows
connecting links with the Nature gods, for the sky
and the sun are natural phenomena, and heaven and
earth as father and mother often form one entity. The
same god has also entered the world of fairy-tales and
plays in it a role which is anything but heroic.[1] On
the other hand there are tribes, among whom anything that is great, strong, or impressive, is described
as the expression of a superior power with the name
of the high-god, so that we get the impression that
he is essentially the same as the primary force which
influences everything. This explains the belief, which
is prevalent in West Africa, that every man has his
own god, i.e. an emanation of that universal force,
which is effective in him and for his good, and yet has
a personal character.

6

Magic and religion are fundamental elements of the
African's life; they influence his thought and action
in all relationships and can with difficulty be separated
from hardly any of his activities. Nevertheless, the
often-heard opinion that the African cannot be conceived without religion needs to be qualified. He is
religious in the same sense as he is social; and just as

[1] For examples cf. again Cardinall, *Tales told in Togoland*.

social life can be upset, and is being upset to-day, so can religious life, the more so because both are so closely related. It is certainly a narrowing of the scope of religion, if it is regarded only as a social function, but nevertheless its social aspect is predominant. Religion is in its most significant expressions dependent on social groupings, and the two are so closely connected that the destruction of the one means the death of the other. Religion is thus drawn into the present whirlpool, and its collapse weakens social cohesion.

Even where conditions are still relatively stable religious institutions are forced to make concessions to new ideals, and, receding step by step, are leaving the field to them. The initiation school of the Poro formerly lasted among the Kpelle for six years. To-day it continues for scarcely three, and even then it is hardly possible for the leaders to bring the young men together. It is not in the first instance indifference or disobedience to the elders which keeps them away, but the demands of new conditions of life which attract them. Formerly it was the rule for a boy who attended a mission school to disappear one day into the Poro bush and to reappear when after a number of years the boys were dismissed. To-day boys who attend a school realize the serious results it has on their future calling if they leave school prematurely. They do not want to escape initiation; they love it, and any one who is not initiated is even to-day a social outcast. The difficulty is solved by the boy going for a few weeks into the bush during the holidays, undergoing a rapid initiation, and then returning to school. The young men who are working on plantations and in other places find a solution in a similar way, and possible objections on the part of the Poro leader may be allayed by a present of money. Poro pupils were not allowed during the time of their initiation to see other people, but were supposed to live in complete seclusion. To-day they take leave for months on end in order to earn money. All this means that the institution is decaying and with it the most important elements of religious belief and practice. It could really thrive only under the old untouched conditions, and the present compromises, so painful to the old people, are but steps to its complete disappearance. It is a loss in religion as well as in social cohesion. The Poro society is the formative element in the community life; by initiation a youth becomes a member of his tribe, and this is the greatest event in his life. To-day this privilege has lost much of its charm. When the young men, after a prolonged absence on plantations or in other centres, return to their villages, they have learned to look upon the symbolic rites of the Poro Order with disillusioned eyes. A cleft between the two generations is opening, and the socio-religious bond which united the community begins to crumble away.

The same is true of another West African institution, which is of even greater importance, because it creates social bonds between tribes and makes inter-

tribal relations possible. Every one has inherited a
taboo from his father, generally an animal which he
must not kill and whose flesh he must not eat. It is
believed that people who have the same taboo are
related and must treat each other as brothers. This
relation is regarded as perhaps more sacred than that
between members of one family, and persons of the
same taboo are bound to help each other in any case
of need.

'It is a kind of free-masonry which is not limited by
ethnic boundaries nor by differences of civilisation, and
which constitutes an exceedingly interesting phenomenon.
For instance, a Mossi of the Pima clan, animist and savage,
who had never left his native country before, finds himself suddenly at St. Louis and meets there a Wolof of
the Noliaye clan, who is a Moslem or a Christian and is
relatively civilised, who on his part has never been in the
Mossi country; the Pima does not understand one word
of Wolof, nor the Noliaye one word of Mossi; after some
moments, by signs which only they note, this Mossi and
this Wolof recognise each other as members of one clan,
and immediately the Wolof takes this Mossi, whose home
is 2000 kilometers away from his, under his protection.'[1]

In so far as these taboo-fellowships are of a religious character, it may be said that here religion has
created ethical values of a social character. Although
no doubt the duty to help a taboo-fellow has its origin
in the belief that people who have the same taboo are
members of one group and are therefore bound to

[1] M. Delafosse, *Haut-Sénégal-Niger*, vol. iii, p. 105.

mutual help and thus to protect each other against strangers, the prevalent idea to-day is that identity of taboo creates a mystical relationship, something like a religious brotherhood. Such relations are, even under modern conditions, still partly respected, but they have no longer their former significance. In purely Islamic regions the Moslem brotherhoods have taken their place. Where Christianity gains a foothold, the taboo is no longer recognized, and in the large centres where the population is crowded together, those prohibitions are only seldom observed. Moreover, to-day it is possible to travel in a foreign country even if one has no kin upon whose protection one can depend, and people are no longer able or willing to receive strangers. As intercourse has increased, hospitality has decreased. Every one is more occupied with his own concerns than he used to be, and gladly makes use of any excuse to ignore the old laws of keeping open house for real or imaginary relatives.

Decay threatens religion also because it is closely bound up with local conditions. What happens when a young man leaves his Native place for any length of time? The gods or ancestors in whose reverence he grew up have their seat in his Native village and can only be worshipped there within the social group. In strange lands there are strange gods of a strange people, with whom he has no connexion and to whom he cannot pray. The thought that his own god or forefather is near him and will protect him everywhere

does not occur to him, quite apart from the fact that
this would presuppose a personal relationship to the
god or ancestor such as does not actually exist. Cult
is not the business of the individual but of the group,
hence he who is separated from the group can no
longer take part in its religious activities. In addition,
the young man in the towns and work centres as a rule
comes into an atmosphere devoid of religion, and it
is no wonder that under such circumstances the whole
religious attitude of mind, and with it the essential
part of his standard of values, are deeply changed if
not completely paralysed. If the resulting feeling of
emptiness is once overcome, the thought gradually
gains strength that a man can manage without religion, that doing so really makes life easier and frees
it from the constraints which were imposed by the
religious duties practised at home. This is the fate of
hundreds of thousands to-day. Their religious root
is dying, and what remains is a crude belief in magic,
a fear of spirits, and some undigested European ideas.
The reverence for that which is greater than man has
been extinguished. When the need for a religious
substitute crops up, such people become an easy prey
of pseudo-religious or political agitators; and when
they return home, they carry the seeds of their decline
with them.

It is not necessary, however, to assume such extreme cases in order to understand the ruin of the
pagan religion. The attack on it has been opened from
all sides. The activity of the mission, the teaching in

the schools, the growing understanding of natural processes, the spreading of mechanical science, the lack of religious feeling of many Europeans, the universal unrest, and the materialistic tendencies of modern life which the utilitarian instincts of the Negro meet half-way: all these things create an atmosphere which is fatal to indigenous religion, and its end is only a question of time. There may, indeed, be reactions here and there, such as the revival of an ancient, almost forgotten cult, or the birth of a new cult with borrowed European, perhaps even Christian elements. They may for a time exercise a certain attraction, and it does happen that educated Natives, even some who have been baptized, take part in them secretly or openly. But these reactions cannot stop the decay. There is nobody in Africa who has a serious belief in the future of indigenous religions; they have never had reformers or martyrs and will have none. All this might be looked on as a natural and even desirable development, but there is in it a danger that the religious sense will be lost altogether. The African has to-day so many interests, and such varied distractions claim his time that his life is completely filled, and he scarcely feels the withering of the religious roots of his life as a loss. He takes a critical attitude even to the Christian religion, for the observation is forced on him that many Europeans make only moderate use of it, and that their sermons on brotherhood stop short at the boundaries of race. To this must be added that the introduction of the Christian religion is for the younger generation of educated Natives a by-product of general education and rarely rests on personal experience. In any case there is one essential difference from earlier conditions: the fact that with paganism culture and religion are identical. Pagan religion is indissolubly bound up with the whole of life, whereas Christianity has a realm of its own, which is not necessarily in such close union with the whole of life as once was the case. There is a gulf between the spheres of religious and secular life which formerly did not exist.

For the African religion is not only a social bond of union of the greatest significance but also the giver of warmth and colour to his life. Most of the communal celebrations, such as sacrificial feasts, initiations, funeral rites, and harvest festivals, have a religious character, and life is the poorer for their disappearance. Above all, religion gave inner strength and peace of mind. If the vanishing faith is not re-placed by a new one, a dangerous barrenness looms ahead for the African, and it cannot be for the good of man or of a community that a large sphere of inner life should lie fallow or overgrown with evil weeds.

On African religions a large number of mono-graphs exist. Although they are not exhaustive and do not nearly represent every characteristic type found in Africa, yet the Institute should not see its primary aim in multiplying the existing material. It seems more important to emphasize certain points of view

which hitherto have found little notice. More significant than the statement of religious institutions and
customs are questions such as these. In what lie the
living forces of a religion and how do they manifest
themselves in the life and actions of the individual and
the community? Do the people know of religious
personalities and religious leaders, or is religion solely
a matter of the group? Which are the individual and
social consequences of decay or loss of religion and
what substitutes take its place? In what way and to
what degree is Christianity assimilated; of what nature
is its influence on the life of the individual and of the
group; and which are the essential differences between
pagan and Christian communities? How far has
Christianity created its own forms of life and
ways of self-expression, or is it simply imitating
Western forms? Of equal importance would be the
effect of Islam and a comparative study of Islamic and
Christian communities in Africa, possibly among the
same people.

X

EDUCATION AND MISSIONS

I

EDUCATION is not something which the African has received for the first time from the white man. The 'primitive' African is not uneducated. Many Africans, men and women, who have never been to school nor in contact with Europeans, show such dignified and tactful behaviour, and reveal so much refinement in what they say and do that they well deserve to be called 'educated'. On the other hand, 'uneducated' behaviour is at times met with among people who have for years been under intensive European influence and in schools conducted by Europeans. The African may sometimes appear lacking in consideration or respectfulness, but as often as not this is due to awkwardness or an involuntary impulse to assert his independence, especially when he is dealing with a stranger, towards whom he naturally adopts a defensive attitude. Shyness may well hide an estimable character.[1]

If to-day the white man has set himself the task of giving the African a new education, his attempt is justified by the fact that under present circumstances the Native system of education is breaking down, and even where it continues to exist it is no longer adequate to modern needs.

The education of young children is in Africa characterized by its leniency. The child is mainly left alone with his playmates and he is expected to find his place gradually among the adults without too much interference from others. In the simple circumstances of tribal life in which all children grow up under similar conditions, hedged around by the solicitude of relatives, not hampered by social disabilities and all having practically the same aim in life, this easy method usually leads to the desired goal. Spoilt children are an exception. Punishments are at this age seldom inflicted, on the grounds that the child is not yet a real person and therefore not responsible for what he does. Behaviour towards a child may also be influenced by the belief that in the child an ancestor has returned to life who has to be treated with consideration.

[1] Cf. E. W. Smith, *The Golden Stool*, London, 1926, pp. 283 ff.

Children's games are largely imitations of adult activities, and in this way they grow up accustomed imperceptibly to genuine work and only occasionally guided by their elders. Girls begin serious work earlier than boys, as the mother soon needs their help. The important thing for children to learn is the proper behaviour towards elder people and towards their equals.

A systematic and intense course of education is imparted in the initiation rites, at the period of transition from childhood to adult life, and of admission to full membership in the group.[1] Both boys and girls have to pass through an initiation, but for the boy the act is of greater significance than for girls. It is the most important event in the life of a young man, for in it he is brought into close contact with the past of the group and with the magical powers emanating from the ancestors. He becomes a new person. By a series of ceremonies the boys are separated from their childhood-life and from the companionship of women and children, in order to be initiated into the spiritual inheritance of the forebears. Beliefs and customs which in the past have sustained the life of the group are through these rites handed down to a new generation. Since the existence of the group depends in the future on the unaltered continuance of this inheritance, the individual has to be adapted to the social norm as handed down by tradition. He

[1] Cf. A. W. Hoernlé, 'An Outline of the Native Conception of Education in Africa', *Africa*, vol. iv, pp. 145–63.

must be formed into a willing member of the community which includes the ancestors.

The details of the ritual are manifold. In parts of Africa for reasons which we do not know, only rudiments of the ceremonies exist or they are altogether absent, as, for example, in most Islamic countries, and also among a number of peoples on the west coast.

In its more elaborate form the procedure of initiation is as follows. The boys are housed in a settlement prepared for the purpose outside the village and are thus separated from the rest of their people. Where circumcision or other forms of mutilation are customary, these are performed at the beginning of the ceremonies, if they have not already taken place in early childhood. The head is shaved; clothes are taken away and burned; and frequently grass clothes are worn during this time. The initiates bathe in the early morning in icy cold water; they have to jump over some object, such as a fire, a ditch, or a bull; or have to run the gauntlet between the young men already initiated: these actions symbolize the separation from the past life. The boys have also to observe certain food taboos and have to undergo tests, flogging, pinching, enduring cold.[1] They have at times to sleep on the bare ground; they are wakened at night and sent away with messages, or given impossible or difficult tasks; and in all this may not manifest any sign of pain or unwillingness, but are expected to

[1] Cf. G. Gutmann, *Die Stammeslehren der Dschagga*, 1. Band, München, 1932.

show unquestioning obedience. By the elders of the group they are instructed[1] in the knowledge and scope of the community, in folk-lore, traditions, magical beliefs and practices, in the moral code, and occasionally also in agriculture and craftsmanship. Sexual instructions occupy an important place, and most of the songs and dances taught refer to sexual life.

After the period of seclusion, rites expressing their rebirth and their acceptance into the group of the adults are performed. They receive a new name, take baths to purify themselves, are sprinkled with medicines, and put on new clothes. In the presence of the old people they give proofs of their achievements and their manly courage, and are then admitted as full members of the community.

Certain elements in the initiation rites are decidedly unpleasing and even harmful; some of the physical operations performed on girls are dangerous to health. The sex teaching, the dances, and the songs, as well as a certain sexual licence, are designed by Native opinion to exercise a moderating influence on the sexual instinct, but this result is certainly not achieved in all cases. Nevertheless, such considerations should not lead to a condemnation of the custom as a whole. It is an institution which has throughout a long and eventful past been the backbone of community life. There are so many educational and moral values in it that its disappearance means a severe loss,

[1] D. Westermann, *Die Kpelle*, Göttingen, 1921, pp. 234–53.

and the Natives themselves regard its decline as a mark of the disintegration of tribal existence. Whether, however, European educators will succeed in retaining the valuable components of the institution and in giving them a place in modern education is doubtful. Not only are the customs already in a state of rapid dissolution, but educational and missionary opinion is divided in judgement on them. The institution is closely associated with religious ideas and may even be called the very core of the religion of a tribe. It is therefore not easy to understand how it can continue to exist in a Christianized community unless it be profoundly changed.

Though its forms and its specifically pagan aspects may disappear, however, this should not necessarily mean that the educational values contained in it and the social attitude resulting from this tribal education should also be doomed to extinction. These values were seen in reverence for the old, readiness for mutual help, a feeling of solidarity, and self-discipline. In order to appreciate these better it seems necessary that the inner side of the initiation rites should be more closely studied than has been done hitherto. Thanks to anthropological investigation we are acquainted with the externals, and also with the symbolic significance of most of the rites. We know little yet about the changes in the inner life of the initiates. In all races the period of puberty is of decisive importance for the life of the human being, and in a certain sense it is actually what many African call it, a rebirth.

A study of the physiological and mental processes in individual life, as influenced by the outlook and attitude crystallized in the initiation rites, might help the educator to a better understanding of his problems.[1]

2

The African educates his child for life in the community. In this lies the real meaning and the strength of his educational methods and aims. Here also lies their weakness, since attention is focused on the group and is apt to neglect the individual. The child is not regarded as a developing personality but as a member of the group. The individual must conform to the type recognized as normal, and deviations from it are looked at askance, for they threaten to break through the framework of tradition and so

[1] K. Th. Preuss (*Der religiöse Gehalt der Mythen*, Tübingen, 1933, pp. 23 ff.) believes that he sees in the initiation rites the idea of a connexion between sexual intercourse and death. As many plants wither when they have borne fruit, so a man goes to meet his death after the maturing of his powers of generation. To escape this danger the ritual of a magically conceived death and resurrection was invented, which aims at preventing actual death. As a matter of fact the transition from childhood to manhood is often expressly designated as a death and resurrection, and on the other hand many myths point to the fact that primitive man regarded death as an unnatural disturbance of the original eternal life. A conception widely spread in Africa is that men were in the earlier stages not subject to death and produced no children; only after they began to produce offspring did they become mortal.

become a danger to the community. Such an education does not entirely rule out the development of personality, but the state of African society shows that it is obviously a hindrance to such development. The adherence to tradition, the fear of departing from what has always been, mistrust of innovation: these are some of the reasons for the stagnation of African life.

The system of Native education further explains why a young man does not plan his life, set himself an aim and exercise his strength in attaining it. The individual as such has no aim in life if his task is to become exactly like the rest. There is no choice of profession for 'birth fixes for life the social status of each individual' (Willoughby). The path is already indicated: the son of the farmer becomes a farmer, the son of a fisherman a fisherman. It is true that there are exceptions, that conditions differ as to peoples and tribes, and that the older attitude is changing to-day. Nevertheless, speaking generally, it is true that the group has built for itself a well-protected but small and never enlarged house, and the air in it has become close and is apt to smother any fresh initiative. Passivity is dominant, and the result is lack of energy and of inclination to break the resistance of one's environment and to build a house of one's own. Life is not faced, but allowed to drift. The fate of man is decided more by external chance and incalculable forces than by personal will and guidance, and resignation to the unalterable is the natural attitude.

European education has in abundance the personal and individualistic note lacking in the Native educational ideal. African tribal life and European school education are in their present form incompatible, and this should be clearly borne in mind. The older people in Africa feel this strongly. Nevertheless, when they send their children to school it is because they realize that it is impossible for them to stem the rising tide, and that a new world is coming.

3

To-day the African youth is no longer moulded exclusively by tribal environment. A wider world is opening for him, a world shaped mainly by European activity. Sooner or later, directly or indirectly, he comes under its influence, in towns, mines, plantations, and other work centres; by every innovation in economic life and in technique; through contact with fellow workers; through direct intercourse with Europeans; and through measures passed by the administration. These are the factors that educate him, and shape his life, by giving him a new outlook, new standards of value and undreamed-of possibilities of developing his faculties. One of these educational factors is the school. Its influence on the individual may be negligible. Perhaps he acquires through it no more than a few new accomplishments and habits which are far outweighed by the impact of his other daily environment. This environment, moreover, touches the whole population, whereas only a small minority go to school. Yet the influence exercised by the school may be wide in scope, for it is systematic, it continues for a number of years, and it goes deeper than most of the other contacts with European civilization. Willoughby[1] says of the Bantu: 'Whenever they come much into contact with Europeans, they part with what is most real in their own life and take on what is material and therefore superficial in the life of Europeans.' Now the school attempts to help the African to avoid this mistake by introducing him to the inner side of European civilization, by enabling him to understand the forces behind it and thus to assimilate it. It is even making some feeble attempts to show the Africans 'what is most real in their own life'. The significance of the school as a factor in education is enhanced by the fact that it is looked upon by the younger generation as the surest way into the world of the white man. As every one desires to become a citizen of that world, there is a spontaneous flow of pupils to the school, such as has seldom been experienced before. It would be an exaggeration to ascribe it in every case to a desire for education. It is often no more than a wish to acquire knowledge which will be useful for obtaining a position and earning money. It is none the less extremely encouraging to witness this active acceptance of the possibilities of learning, and it gives the school a brilliant chance of developing into a means of real education.

[1] *Race Problems in the New Africa*, p. 255.

Education is the task of Government. They have only in recent times begun to concern themselves seriously with it, chiefly with the object of training clerical employees. That was natural in the earlier stage, but the problem of to-day is how to succeed in giving a school training to the whole population, and how to shape this training. The time is past when the school could content itself with the development of a small *élite*, and with directing this development on European lines, without reference to the pupil and his environment. The result of this system of education which was adapted to the needs of the European has led to the fostering of the higher and professional schools to the detriment of the elementary schools. That should not continue to-day. The urgent need is for village schools in abundance, adapted to the needs of the villages and destined to serve them. These schools should therefore aim at being self-contained, not merely preliminary stages to a higher school. In other words, they should not be professional schools, but educational schools in the highest and best sense of the term, not alien to the community, but organically one with it.

Christian missions have in most parts of Africa been the pioneers in developing systematic educational work. Recently, however, since Colonial Governments have established their authority, they have turned their attention to the education of Natives and have taken responsibility for it. Thus it has happened that either, as in the case of French Africa,

Government has founded its own school system, or else it has limited itself to organizing certain types of schools, for example, technical and higher schools. On the whole, however, they have encouraged a close financial co-operation between Government and mission schools, and Government has also through regulation and inspection ensured a determining influence in the aims and methods of education. This system is used very extensively in British colonies, in South Africa, and in the Belgian Congo. The exceptions to it are areas with strong Moslem influences where mission schools are only admitted under special regulations. This co-operation between missions and Government has undoubtedly borne good fruit.

The missions have behind them long experience, a staff of Native workers, and establishments for their training. It is to the interest of Government that as large a number of children as possible should find an opportunity of acquiring at least an elementary education and it is desirable that education should be religious. Through the collapse of African religion the Natives are losing an essential part of the values of life. Something new must take the place of the old, and my personal view is that in the circumstances of to-day the new can only be Christianity.

The connexion between mission and Government may, however, not be without its disadvantages. The mission becomes dependent on Government, and would without this financial help be unable to continue its scholastic activities. It may be tempted to devote its main efforts to education for the sake of a maximum grant, and by cultivating those sides to which Government attaches importance neglect its religious functions. Difficulties of the opposite kind also arise. The missionaries have arranged their schools for their own purposes. They have to care for the religious education of Christian children, but at the same time they regard the schools as a means of missionary propaganda, since they are attended also by pagans. For the missionary the interests of his religion or his Church are naturally paramount. This is clearly shown by the character of many of the village mission schools, which often fail to satisfy even the modest claims of a general education. They may even incur the suspicion that they make use of secular knowledge merely as a bait to fill their class-rooms, and then show their scholars the way into their Church.

Like every other activity of the white man, the school, and especially the school in the hands of the mission, has a destructive effect on social cohesion. The missionary aims at replacing the indigenous religion by a foreign one, and in doing so he strikes at the very root of Native life. Religion is so closely associated with all other departments of life that this destructive effect is inevitable, even when the missionary proceeds with the greatest caution, which is not always the case.

There are two main schools of thought among

missionaries about these problems. One school sees Christianity and Western civilization on the same plane. Even if they do not regard them as identical, yet for them they are so closely bound together that the one is not thought of without the other, and the union of the two is expressed in the term 'Christian civilization'. The institutions and outlook of the West are the ideal, and to transplant this Christian ideal to Africa is the aim of their work. Where Native institutions are different from our own, they are unchristian. To succeed in replacing African customs by European or American is a victory of the Christian spirit. According to the personal outlook of the missionary he may in his efforts emphasize the Christian or the civilizing side, but in essence both are one.

Many circumstances commend such a policy. The missionary spreads around him, even without intention, a European atmosphere through his mode of life and his activity. All Africa is tending towards European methods, and the Natives themselves wish it to be so. To most of them Christianity is part of European civilization. It seems therefore natural that the two should go hand in hand.

Missionaries sharing these convictions have nothing to learn from anthropology. Their attitude to African cultures is negative; in their eyes they are barbaric, worthless, and the sooner they disappear and European institutions and customs take their place the better. At best they treat them as negligible, things which one passes over with a smile, as long as there is no danger of their being a hindrance on the road to the complete civilizing of the people.

The other group of missionaries believes that there is a variety of civilizations, each with its own features and its own values. They believe that Christianity comes to a strange civilization not to work its dissolution, but to fulfil it, that is to say, to bring to their full flowering the seeds of humanity which lie unseen in primitive civilizations. They look on it as their first task to make themselves familiar with the civilization of the people among whom they are working. They deem it unreasonable to wish to influence the inner life of strange men and women and guide it into new paths, without knowing that life as it was originally. Pagan religion for them is an object of deep interest, and worthy of that respect which the educated man brings to every form of spiritual life. Where ideas and customs are in a state of dissolution, they are regarded as not less worthy of study, for in them the religious genius of the people is revealed, which the missionary as no other must understand.

These missionaries do not feel called to bring the civilization of a European nation to the African, but to bring the Gospel. This they believe to be supernational, appealing to all men equally, suitable for any type of mankind, and creating in each society its own form adapted to the peculiarity of each people. On the whole it may be said that this second attitude, i.e. the sympathetic one towards African life and institutions, is gaining ground.

Any educator who approaches the civilization of a country with respect will take care that no injustice is done to this civilization in the education of the children, and that they are trained to respect and love it. This will be taken into consideration through life in the school, the subjects taught, the method of teaching, and the books used. It presupposes, at least in the village elementary school, that the vehicle of instruction is an indigenous language.

Since by far the larger number of pupils never get beyond the elementary school, it is essential that this course of training should be of real service to the scholar. It should last not less than five full school years. The pupils must have progressed far enough to be able without trouble to read and understand their own vernacular literature, and possibly also to perfect their knowledge of a foreign language. They must also be able to keep simple accounts. For the rest, however, their education should be as little as possible a matter of book-learning, but a training such as will suit the needs of a future peasant or craftsman. Training of hand and eye, lessons on technical and agricultural subjects must not be looked on as pleasant interruptions of teaching from books. Work in the field and workshop should take the first place and claim the greatest part of the pupil's time. The chief advantage of such a method is that the pupil is not merely receptive, but himself produces something useful. He learns to put his own powers to the test of reality and is thereby saved from over-

estimating the value of intellectual knowledge.[1] If
hand in hand with this there is teaching of physical
and political geography based on the study of the
immediate neighbourhood; and if the instruction
further aims at enlightening the pupil on the indigenous social and economic life of the village, the district
and the whole colony, and at making clear to the
children what new forces are to-day remaking their
country, such studies can well serve to keep the
scholars in touch with their own people and at the
same time make them ready to receive what is new.
The second is as important as the first. The pupils
must not have the impression that something is being
kept from them; on the contrary their eyes must be
opened to all that is good in the new order of life,
with a view to their absorbing it as far as it can be
assimilated.

The teacher will only fulfil his task when he realizes
that his function is not only to instruct the children,
but to live with them and show them how that which
has been learnt at school can be translated into terms
of real life.[1] He must be friend and counsellor. From
this it is obvious that his activities must not be confined to the school, but must embrace the village to
which the school belongs. The village school has one
advantage over the boarding-school, namely, that the
children live with their parents and remain in the
surroundings which are natural to them. There is,

[1] Cf. J. H. Oldham, B. D. Gibson, *The Remaking of Man in
Africa*, London, 1931, pp. 74 ff.

on the other hand, a risk that the influence of the school is nullified by that of village life. If this is to be avoided, the teacher must strive to serve the whole community, to lift it to a higher level and to gain the co-operation of his pupils in this effort. Necessary as is the acquisition of definite knowledge and certain aptitudes, the school should not consider this its only task. It must embrace the whole human being if it would contribute effectively to the creation of a new life for the people. The personal contact of the teacher with his pupils is more important for the formation of character and therefore for the real education of his pupils than the knowledge they acquire.

If, however, this contact comes to an end when the child leaves school, its effects may soon be effaced. When the pupils return to their home surroundings, they will forget much of what they have learnt. To prevent this, the pupils of one or more classes after leaving school should be united in a group or groups and keep in touch with each other and the school, just as is done in the case of initiation groups. The teacher could call them together at periods when their principal work is slack for holiday courses. He could also visit them in their homes and advise them in their work. Valuable help in such an object and in the keeping alive of spiritual interest among the pupils could be rendered by a vernacular periodical.

To what extent elementary schools with the character described can be created will largely depend on the quality of the teacher. If he is to be the cultural centre of his village, from which will radiate new forces to fertilize the old life, he must be at home in both worlds, the Old and the New. His technical and scientific attainments should be as wide as possible. In addition he must have practical common sense, an understanding of the life of a peasant community, a right sense of the value of the powers it has developed, and of the best way of turning them to account in education. He must, moreover, be ready to take part in that life. True education does not come from books, but passes from person to person. The efficacy of a teacher depends on what he is rather than on what he knows.

Although every African teacher does not reach the ideal of his profession, yet their role in the formation of a new life in Africa can hardly be over-estimated. There are among them some with only a modest culture; others who at far too young an age were entrusted with a task for which they could not have been fitted; and some who are complete failures. Yet with all their shortcomings they render a service which has far-reaching effects. In thousands of communities they are the only persons who have had a European education and have thus acquired a wider outlook. They remain in constant touch with the European in later life and are among the very few Africans who read books after they have left school. On the other hand, they live in close contact with the Natives according to Native ways, though perhaps

modified somewhat. They are thus the best inter-
preters of the New to the Old. By the very nature of
their work they are obliged to live in harmony with
the chiefs and representatives of the older generation,
and in this way they acquire an understanding of the
value of the sanctions of tradition, the more so if their
eyes have been opened to them by their European
teacher. Almost all the Natives who have published
books about the culture, language, or the history of
African tribes, and have thus rendered a service to
science as well as to their own people, are teachers or
ministers. Many of them exercise their calling in difficult circumstances, amongst very backward communities, in miserable hovels with quite insufficient
equipment, and often for very scanty remuneration.
When the incomes of Missionary Societies have
fallen, missionary teachers have often suffered deduc-
tions of salary without a murmur. Many of them are
true servants and real idealists and are among the
brightest hopes of the race.

One of the reasons which for a long time prevented
the school from having its real effect on the life of the
people was that, especially in the case of missionary
work, schools were founded on charity and financed
with the help of foreigners, so that the people have
become accustomed to the idea that the mission or
the government will take responsibility for their
upkeep. As a result of systematic education this
attitude is to-day to a large extent overcome, although
it has not entirely vanished. Its early complete

abandonment must of necessity be the goal in view. Communities who want a teacher and school will be able to maintain both just as Mohammedan or Christian sectarian groups are able to maintain theirs. The school is the affair of the community, and the community or the Native Administration, or the indigenous Church, have to provide for its needs. Where this is not done, the school remains a foreign element in the village or town. It is equally necessary that the Native community should have a share in the administration of its school or schools and should feel responsible for its guidance, even though it cannot for the time being dispense with the co-operation of strangers. As long as the school is not under a Native Council, it has not taken root in the community. Indirect rule should be extended to education, for it has up till now been far too direct. What the Annual Report (1930) of Achimota College says with reference to this institution is true of every school in Africa: 'In the education of African children parents should have an effective voice. An education where foreign experts think out problems, foreign experts work out projects, and foreign experts carry them out is doomed, however perfectly benevolent it may be, to be perfectly unimaginative.' In the Council of Achimota according to Statute six of the fifteen members must be Africans, and the Report says: 'that proportion (of Africans) must inevitably increase.'

The position of elementary schools has in the foregoing discussion been given the central place, because they are of primary importance when one is considering the whole population, and consequently their development is of the greatest significance in the education of the race.[1] In the village social cohesion is more vital than in the larger towns. Social relations are more stable, and if interest in them can be successfully aroused through the school much that is valuable can be saved from destruction, and the transition from the Old to the New can proceed slowly like a natural growth without causing too much harm. If the school succeeds in raising the cultural level of the village, this will also make it easier for the educated young people to find their future in the village and to co-operate in its improvement. Missions and educational authorities alike should make a point of enlightening the population about the real significance of the elementary schools. It is a deplorable fact that many educated Africans do not realize the importance of them. Their ideal seems to be the higher school with the purest academic education possible. While these may be admissible in a very limited number and at a later state of general development, the present

[1] In an article 'L'enfant noir', by R. Delavignette, published in *L'Afrique Française*, Nov. 1932, the same emphasis is laid on the creation of rural elementary schools (*écoles rurales populaires*). In South Africa 57·2 per cent. of Native children receiving primary and secondary education were in the sub-standards, 69·2 per cent. in the sub-standards and standard I, 77·5 per cent. in these and standard II. Very few go beyond this, and only 5 per cent. were beyond standard VI.

need is for schools which educate, not for literary studies but for life, schools of which Achimota and Makerere are outstanding examples.

The pedagogic problem is simpler in the high schools than it is in the village schools. Their object is to introduce the Africans to European civilization. Many Africans cannot rid themselves of the suspicion that the European wishes to keep from him the best of his knowledge and skill, and therefore prevent the cultural level of the Natives from rising above a certain stage. The suspicion is mostly unjustified. Every educational authority wishes that the way to the best of European civilization should be opened to the African; and that it should be made possible for him to develop all his capacities without let or hindrance, and use them in life. Such a training presupposes an intimate acquaintance with a European language.

But at the same time also the higher schools should reserve a small part of the time of their pupils for the study of indigenous life, its manners and customs, its history and folk-lore, and also its language. The scanty understanding which the majority of Africans have of their spiritual heritage of the past is deplorable, but can easily be understood in view of the circumstances of to-day. On the other hand, it has been noticed that pupils who have had a really thorough education and have learnt to understand European civilization have had their eyes opened also to the value of their national life. Among the cultured men of the older generation, and especially such as are in responsible positions, there are many who insist on the necessity of building education on the foundation of the heritage of the past. Even when a scholar has assimilated a foreign language, he does not feel himself at home in it, and cannot express himself as completely in it as in his own Native tongue. It would therefore be desirable that those branches of study which are concerned with spiritual life and character-building, such as religion and ethics, as also history and Native life, should be taught in the vernacular.[1]

The language problem in African education is one that has given rise to much discussion; although opinions vary and the actual practices in using or not using the vernacular as a medium of instruction differ widely, there appears to be a growing recognition of its usefulness. More light on the actual facts is needed. In the journal *Oversea Education*, vol. i, No. 2, the question of bilingual school education with special reference to conditions in Wales was discussed. In order to come to a definite understanding, similar investigations should be undertaken in Africa. A comparison, for example, should be made of the general results of an education based on serious vernacular instruction and familiarity with vernacular literature, and one carried on without or with poor vernacular teaching (examples of both cases can easily be found in one country, where general conditions

[1] See Chapter XI.

are equal). The investigation should comprise elementary and higher education; it should not be limited to intellectual achievements, but to the wider scope of character-building, of forming personalities, of the relation of the educated to the Native communities and their influence on them, and it should take into account the results stretching over a number of years. Research of this nature will form a section of a comprehensive study of African child and youth psychology. This is much needed and should form an essential item in the Institute's research plans.

Many missionaries have from the outset recognized the problem of adapting the school to African environment. This is proved by the fact that the missionaries were the first to attack the study of African languages seriously, and that they have used them in their religious and educational work. If a considerable number of African languages now possess the beginnings of a literature, the missionaries have to be thanked for it.

But even under the most favourable circumstances it is inevitable that the religious and educative work of missions will have a disintegrating effect on Native life. It introduces a new order of life, and in many ways means a break with the old. Hardly once in Africa has it happened that a social unit, a tribe or a village, has been converted as a whole to Christianity, thus making it possible to preserve the structure of society in a Christianized form. Wherever Natives adopt Christianity, the Christian unit comes into being within or by the side of the pagan community, and, at any rate in the matter of religion, finds itself in conscious opposition to the latter. The Christians have their own laws, carry out their own rites, and in districts where the European influence is still small, they are distinguished from their surroundings by their standard of life. Participation in pagan ritual, ancestor-worship, and other religious ceremonial is out of the question for them; even harmless pleasures are often forbidden to them by the missionaries. It may also happen that Christians oppose an ordinance of the tribal chief whenever this is in conflict with their convictions or the bidding of the missionary. Conflicts have rarely arisen from this source, thanks to the inherent tolerance of the Negro, for he finds it easy to discover a compromise. The pagans are ready to allow the Christians the rights which are their due, and in cases where a considerable part of the population has become Christian, they submit without objection to the rule of a Christian chief.

It is unfortunate that Christianity comes to Africa split into sects. There are to be found, often in the same place and practically always in the same tribe, communities of several denominations, making another rift in the communal life and providing the African with an object lesson in intolerance, which is quite alien to his nature. It may happen all too easily that the missionary warns his flock against intercourse with those of another creed because they might be weakened in their own belief, and thus he

sows the seed of mistrust and estrangement. The
Native has by nature broad and liberal sympathies,
and we can imagine the irritation he may often feel
when the missionary teaches him in the name of
Christianity to segregate himself from his own Christian compatriots because they belong to another
Church. A West African, who is a faithful Christian,
expressed himself on this point as follows: 'Our
gods live peacefully with one another. No priest
competes with another, but they consider it as a
matter of course that one should serve one divinity,
another man another. Christianity pretends to be a
religion of peace, and yet its teachers bring discord
to us. They separate the inhabitants of a place, even
a whole people, into two or more camps. That we
cannot understand.'

The Africans thus have to share the burdens of the
European Christian Churches; this is the more deplorable since these burdens are in the sphere of doctrine
and ritual, whereas the Christian ideal of life is in
essentials the same for all Churches. When doctrine
and ritual are so strongly emphasized the impression
is easily created that they are essentials, and the fact
that Christianity means a new life recedes into the
background. The missionary should not cease to show
that the important thing for the Christian is something
quite different from following certain usages which
have come from Europe. Where Christianity has been
transmuted into life, it creates its own forms, and
African Christians should be given the possibility of

doing this for themselves. Old African life was rich in forms which brought colour and variety even into the tiniest village. The greater part of this is vanishing to-day, and the new Christian forms often have such a distinctly European character that they appear strange and meaningless to the Natives. The Christians should be encouraged to develop their own customs in daily life, in the great events in family and community, and in the Christian Church. There are numberless beautiful African customs on the occasions of birth, marriage, illness, and death; in connexion with the education of children and their entry into the community of the adults; in seed-time and harvest, and the building of the house. Most of these could be preserved in a Christianized form and would contribute to the deeper penetration of Christianity into the soil of Africa, thus saving the Christian from being cast adrift from the past of his own people. Both school and Church should make it their task to encourage and foster the old folk-songs, folk-dances, drum festivals, dramatic representations and other games, and thus to preserve for the everyday life of the Natives something of its former colour and movement. Recreation is no less necessary than work, and to forbid the former pleasures or let them die out without replacing them by something else is an inadequate method of education.

Christianity is destined to be one of the important factors which will contribute towards social reintegration. Already it has succeeded, as no other institution coming from Europe has done, in producing new vital social groups. The existing Christian communities are proof of this. Many of them show even in their outward appearance signs of a new progressive life. The manner of life of the Christians is frequently on a higher plane than that of the pagans. Their houses are roomier and cleaner; they spend more on the needs of daily life and on the education of their children. They raise considerable funds for the maintenance of their Church. Where the leader succeeds in awakening the enthusiasm of his Christian followers their readiness to make sacrifices is sometimes astonishing, and not infrequently exceeds the limit of what is usual in Europe. The readiness to achieve so much can only arise out of the consciousness that the new community has endowed life with new value for them.

A new Christian communal life is born in the village by the side of the old paganism, the one ruled by tradition, the other by a 'new Law'. The old enjoys the advantage of having definitely fixed forms which have for many generations been considered holy and inviolable. Its followers are in the majority, and it exercises undisputed authority over them. The new communal life is still in the early stages of its development. It is bound by numerous ties to the old, preserves many old ideas and institutions, and draws its nourishment from the roots of the common past. Yet in many ways it is revolutionary and is creating its own forms which are based on new ideals.

In spite of all the weaknesses which can be explained by the qualities of the race and its history, new progressive forces are at work in the Christian groups. Tradition is no longer the all dominant factor; the new faith, when it is part of the inner life, gives a different attitude to all tasks and aims, and creates new values.   There can be no doubt that these new standards have significance for the readjustment of social life. The Christian community is a reality.   It has its offices, in which men and women are trained to personal responsibility; its self-administration; its groups and its societies; equality of rights for women; its regular assemblies and its common task.   It therefore affords the individual ample opportunity for activity as a member of the whole and at the same time gives him the feeling of security, so that the old traits of clan life, brotherliness and readiness to help, find a new home in this environment.

Yet the Church reaches out beyond the individual community. The congregations of a whole area form a unity, a body with common aims, common administration and regular assemblies of the leaders. The members of the congregations get to know each other at the great church and missionary festivals, and exercise or receive the same hospitality as has hitherto only been enjoyed by fellow tribesmen. Teachers and ministers are moved from place to place, thus showing that they serve the whole, and that the interests of the individual congregation must be subordinated to those of the Church. The same forms and rules are in use in all churches and schools; all members use the same books; the dialect in which these books are written generally sets the standard, and thus forms a new bond of union. A special part can be played in this respect by the vernacular periodical which ought to exist in every church. By becoming a forum for the free utterance of opinion, in which every one can take part, and by printing contributions and news which interest all, it can render an important service and be an essential help in maintaining a link between the members of one church.

The Christian Church is almost the only sphere of life in which the African can give free and unfettered expression to his own personality. In all other matters of public life he is the subject of the dominant race, but the Church gives him full or almost full independence and responsibility. All posts in it are open to the Native, and the missions are always working for greater independence for the Native Church. The European is made more and more a collaborator instead of a superior. This is of more importance in places where the African lives under oppressive conditions and where he has lost his tribal life and has thereby become homeless. Here the Church is called upon to give him a new home, in accepting him as a member of its community and in showing him the way to full development and an outlet for his spiritual faculties. The other aspect of this freedom of the churches is the number of sects which have been formed, especially in South Africa, partly as the result of social pressure, opposition to white leadership, or too rigid Church discipline. They often lead a poverty-stricken existence, but they show that the African can stand on his own feet and give the Churches under European leadership proof that an African Church can be financially self-supporting, which is a necessary pre-supposition for self-government.

4

In order to arrive at a just estimate of missionary work and its results, one should not forget that it is undertaken among peoples who live in a state of transition and disintegration, and that the missionary himself cannot avoid taking part in this disintegration. It is inevitable that unpleasing phenomena should grow out of these conditions, and it is un-justifiable to lay the blame for these exclusively on the mission. The missionary cannot always prevent men approaching him and being accepted into the Church who wish to use Christianity and the member-ship of the mission as a cloak for mean and selfish purposes. Many come to him without understanding what Christian life means, and it is no wonder if after a time they turn away disappointed or must be ex-cluded. Also the following factor should not be overlooked. In going over to Christianity a man is breaking away from his own social group and the inherited religion, and thereby leaving behind all sanctions which these institutions embrace and which were regarded as absolutely binding. An individual does not dare disregard a tenet of the pagan religion or fling to the wind a command of the priest, of the witch-doctor or of an elder, for it may mean death to him. With conversion to the new religion the old bonds lose their menace. It is true he enters upon new obligations, but these are to him not nearly of such a fearful and binding character as the old ones. Here it is not a question of community of blood, of revengeful deities or of relentless magical powers, but of a relation based on trust and faith. It needs a deep religious experience or great spiritual maturity to comprehend the reality of such a community and to recognize its obligations. Even if Christianity does impose commands and restrictions on its members, it is nevertheless fundamentally based on freedom and self-responsibility, and this can only be acquired through long and intensive education. Hence it must be realized that many of those who join the Church never quite reach the goal and are only in part of their life Christian, while some only succeed in producing pathetic caricatures.

In the same way all the fruits of missionary schools do not attain maturity, and it is these unripe and spoiled fruits which are injurious to the repute of missionary work. Youths educated in a mission are accused of being presumptuous, deceitful, and un-reliable. One hears Europeans say that they prefer a 'bush-Negro' or a 'raw Kafir' to one trained in the mission. This is an unjustified generalization and it would be easy to quote numerous examples in contra-

diction. The unsatisfactory products of education
are frequently those who have been dismissed from
the schools because of their lack of qualifications and
who now seek a job on the grounds of their supposed
knowledge. The preference for the uncivilized Native
may also be due to the fact that in his inexperience he
is a more convenient tool in the hand of the European
than the more sophisticated Negro who has been in
closer contact with European ways.

Nevertheless, the missionary and the educator
should not turn a deaf ear to the warnings of their
critics. If there were not an element of truth in them,
they would not find such frequent and vehement
expression as they do. They are not so much a reproach to mission as to education in general; but they
are raised against missions owing to the chance cir-
cumstance that education is to a large extent in the
hands of missions. One of the most important causes
of the failure of many pupils to fulfil the hopes reposed
in them is the fact that even in their early youth they
turned away from their own group life. They are
condemned to live between two worlds, the old one
of their parents and their community and the new
one of the school, and they are not fully at home in
either. Too often in the school the pupil is taught to
look down on the old life as on something left behind.
What was sacred and unassailable there is here branded
as absurd superstition, and what is a religious reality
to his parents is regarded in the school as non-existent
or the work of the devil. A violent conflict thus

possesses him, from which he may perhaps never be freed. In the new world of European civilization and religion he does not find a firm footing. The school cannot give him a substitute for what he loses, namely, membership in a group with its own moral standards and obligations. He is in danger of becoming an isolated individual, responsible to no one. He may behave well as long as the missionary has him under his wing, but though he may have adopted Christianity that does not necessarily imply that he has a strong enough grasp of Christian principles to live out in practice what he learned in school when he is thrown upon his own resources. This is especially true of pupils who after leaving school go to the towns where they are exposed to all the lures and temptations of a new world.

XI

LANGUAGE AND EDUCATION

I

IT is natural for us to look upon language as a medium for communicating thoughts, that is, for effecting an understanding between men. However essential this function of language is, it is not its only one. When an Ewe man has a hard piece of work to do, he stimulates himself by repeating the series of his own drinking or praise names in rapid succession, or by asking a friend to call them out to him. Likewise young men while hoeing a field or cutting rice are followed by their girl friends who inspire the workers

R

by encouraging exclamations. A mother talking to her baby, a woman humming as she grinds corn, an excited or a lonely person talking to himself, lengthy greetings exchanged between strangers on the road— none of these have anything, or very little, to do with the communication of thoughts. They are emotional acts, the indication of a need for expression, or are intended to evoke an emotion in the person spoken to. It is easy to understand why the languages of primitive peoples have more of this emotional character than ours, because in our language the intellectual aspect is more marked. Nevertheless, the emotional side is by no means absent in our own use of speech.

Nothing binds people more closely together than a common language. This is realized by every one who, after a long stay abroad, is suddenly greeted in the sounds of his mother tongue. In Africa all the bigger towns have quarters where foreigners speaking the same language forgather so as to feel more at home. It is well known how much Natives living away from home appreciate periodicals in their vernacular, because they form a link with their home, and very often also with their home Church. In Europe we see peoples and national minorities engaged in desperate struggles to preserve and cultivate their language. To communicate their ideas and to make themselves understood in their surroundings it would be as well or even better for them to use the language of the country in which they live. The reason for clinging to their own language can only be that it has a sentimental and a spiritual value for them, and by giving it up they would be sacrificing part of their birthright. Allegiance to a people is closely allied with language: a person who, in a foreign environment, gives up his own language indicates thereby that he separates himself from his people and becomes merged in his new environment.

Europe of the Middle Ages had a universal language, Latin, which for many people was a means of acquiring an education and exchanging knowledge, and which was also used, to a great extent, for purposes of general communication. But as the peoples using it became self-conscious and developed a national feeling, they rejected Latin and began to love and to cultivate their own languages. In spite of the fact that these languages had, up to that time, been despised as clumsy peasant dialects unfit for literary use, they seemed to the people a more adequate means of expressing what they had to say and what they felt,than the foreign language. They felt it to be a violation of their inner life and their national self to be forced to talk and think, to write, pray, and sing in a language which had never become their own. But even among those nations with whom Latin had become the 'vernacular', each came to develop 'their' Latin in their own way, thus again asserting their own individuality. The languages derived from Latin—Italian, French, Spanish, Portuguese, and Rumanian—have become distinct languages, because each is the expression of a distinct nationality. An international language is useful in many ways and for many purposes, but it should never presume to be a substitute for national languages. Standardization and unification in matters of the mind are, when carried too far, the end of all life.

All one's love for home, all that calls up memories of early childhood, of parents and friends, of people who have meant something to one in life, all this is embodied in the sound of the mother tongue. This is true for the people as a whole as well as for the individual, and for the African as well as for us. When we speak or hear our mother tongue, every phrase evokes feelings and visions which are not aroused by similar expressions uttered in another language. It has been said, and rightly, that each person is an individual of its own type that is never repeated, and that it is the aim of education to develop this individuality to the full, and give it fair play. The same is true of nations; each has its own genius which is manifest in its feeling, thought, and will, but is nowhere so clearly brought out as in the language. No language can be fully translated into another, and only an approximation of the meaning is possible, because concepts hardly ever coincide exactly.

Conditions in Europe cannot, however, be compared without qualification to those prevailing in Africa to-day. The European languages were allowed to develop without too much interference. While the influence of Latin gradually receded, a national culture grew up, of which the national language became an integral part, and out of its dialects one written form evolved and a literature grew up. In Africa, on the other hand, languages are numerous and cover small areas. The progress of amalgamation of cognate dialects has not gone far enough, the cultural background of the languages is narrow, and they are to-day drawn into the turmoil of Europeanization. It is therefore much more difficult for them to hold their own than it was for languages in Europe.

The large number of African languages is a natural result of the general conditions of life on the continent. For long periods the tribes or even smaller units lived in complete or nearly complete isolation. Strictly speaking, no individual (in any language) speaks exactly like any other. Within a group of related families, and more so between one village and another, or between two districts, differences in pronunciation, speech-melodies, idiom, and vocabulary, can easily be observed. In normal circumstances these differences are levelled down through intercourse and the influence of the written language, so that on the whole the linguistic unity is preserved. But in most parts of pre-European Africa this intercourse did not exist or only to a very small extent. Each group, when separating from the main body, led its own life, and the stranger, though he might be a neighbour, was looked on with suspicion. The result was that the speech form of each group developed in its own way, until they were no longer mutually intelligible. The original unity was thus split up into a number of independent languages, and this fact in its turn contributed to isolation and distrust which became an ever-increasing barrier.

Other contrary developments, however, also made themselves felt. Where several groups of people lived in a neighbourhood, one among them was often more enterprising than others and thus gained supremacy. They established contacts with their neighbours through trade and commerce or through political conquest. The language of this group became preponderant and showed a tendency to spread. It became useful and therefore desirable to know it. The members of the superior group do not as a rule take the trouble to know the language of a smaller group. If these want to converse with their superiors, it has to be done in the ruling language, and it thus becomes a mark of distinction to know it. The process of linguistic expansion is facilitated if it is a question of related languages. Thus Swahili has spread and is spreading in the Bantu language field, that is to say, among languages closely akin to itself. In the vast Mandingo area, one dialect, Malinke, has gradually become the lingua franca among all rival dialects. In both cases it was a process of natural amalgamation. On the other hand Hausa, although it is, like Swahili and Mandingo, the language of very active trading peoples, has not shown nearly the same power of absorption as, for instance, Swahili, one reason for this being that its structure and vocabulary are different from those of the surrounding Negro languages. Where it is adopted, it is done in a very much simpli-

fied and often in a distorted way. The importance of
Hausa as a means of intercourse lies in the fact that
numerous Hausa settlements exist outside the Hausa
boundary in the Central and Western Sudan and in
the West African coastal lands; but only in rare cases
has Hausa become the second language of a Negro
tribe.

The need for a common language with a wider
range was more keenly felt when the white man came
to Africa and established peaceful relations. Nothing
has contributed more to the spread of Swahili, Hausa,
Mandingo, and Zulu than European penetration.
Where a lingua franca had not evolved, the existing
need created new languages which could easily be
understood and acquired by all the parties concerned.
Best known among these is pidjin-English as spoken
on the West African coast, which is used as a means
for intercourse between Europeans and Natives, and
also between Africans of different languages who
live in European centres. The language consists of
English words which in their pronunciation are
adapted to the African's mode of speech. Grammatical distinctions are reduced to a minimum. This,
however, does not mean that the language lacks
form. New grammatical forms have evolved, and
these are not English but African, corresponding
exactly to the syntactical formations of West African
Negro languages. Pidjin-English is a West African
language which takes its word-material from the
English vocabulary. Similar pidjin forms of African

languages have evolved in the so-called Kitchen-Kafir, a simplified form of Zulu, in Sudan Arabic, Bangala, and in the outskirts of the Swahili expansion.

A pidjin language has as a rule no emotional background; it is solely a means of communication, differing from Esperanto only in having a smaller vocabulary and in being of natural growth. It may, however, associate emotions where it becomes the mother tongue of a group, as is the case with the Creoles in Sierra Leone, and also with people using Bangala in the Belgian Congo and Sudan Arabic in the Upper Nile region. There is no reason why such simplified forms of speech should not occasionally be used for literary purposes.

2

What is the African's attitude towards his own language? The prevailing impression might be that the majority of the younger generation take a very slight interest in it and would be willing to abandon it altogether in favour of a European language. But this is only one side of the question, and it would be wrong to generalize from such a statement. Under normal circumstances Africans cling to their mother tongue just as other people do. Where a lingua franca has spread or where a smaller language is surrounded by a larger one, the local form of speech has in many cases continued to live on for centuries, although for all communications with the outer world the lingua franca may be used. Though in North Africa the

Punic, Greek, Latin, Arabic, and modern European languages have through long periods exercised a commanding influence, yet the old indigenous Berber dialects have not disappeared. When to-day in Africa, in one language area, an attempt is made to use in school and literature a neighbouring language or dialect, immediately there is opposition. This is partly due to tribal jealousy, but also to the feeling that language is a valuable possession the loss of which would impair the individuality and integrity of the group.

Among the older generation of educated Africans there is no doubt a growing appreciation of their national language. While fully realizing the necessity of knowing a European language, they do not want to lose or neglect their own, and many of them are seriously concerned in developing it and making it literary. The annual competition established by the Institute, for vernacular manuscripts written by Africans, is meeting with a very vivid interest among the Natives, and in 1932 seventy-eight manuscripts were offered for competition.

3

The spiritual heritage of the African is to a large extent preserved in and transmitted through the language, and is intimately bound up with it. African religion, the indigenous systems of education, the rules of behaviour regulating life within the group, cannot exist independently of the indigenous language.

In West Africa religious cult groups are found which speak a language of their own, the underlying idea being that the religious teaching and the intercourse with the deity can be done only in the language in which the doctrines and rituals professed by the group were first conceived or revealed.

Knowledge in primitive society is not so much a matter of rational learning as a personal experience, and it is more of an emotional than of a merely intellectual character. This is clearly seen in the teaching given in the initiation schools. During an initiation school the pupils are kept in a continuous state of excitement, and this inner commotion is thought necessary for receiving and assimilating the lore of the tribe as transmitted from the ancestors. What impresses them most is not the matter taught but the circumstances under which they are taught. It may even be done in a language which the present generation no longer understand so that the contents have to be explained by a 'speaker'. It is clear that these emotions and exaltations can be evoked only through the indigenous language, and that the teaching would lose all its meaning when imparted in a foreign language. Not only its charm and attractiveness, but also its sanctity and binding nature would vanish if it were to be derobed of its original form of expression.

Though the African's mental heritage may appear to us poor and defective in some ways, it is not devoid of value. He had evolved an educational system which was well adapted to his life and which produced good results. He has also amassed a store of experience, observations, and achievements, and he has produced an art which commands admiration. No conscientious educator can ignore this, and at least elementary education might very well draw from this material. If this is to be done, it can only be through the vernacular.

How far it is to be done will depend on the attitude of the white educator. It is quite right to say that ultimately the question will have to be decided by the Africans themselves, but it is no less true that the position the Native takes is very much dependent on that of his white teacher and that it must be guided by him. Where a mission has from the beginning of its activity laid stress on vernacular teaching and has provided vernacular books which meet the existing demand, the Natives have learned to respect their own language. They find it natural to read and write it and to have their tribal lore as well as the elements of European knowledge represented in vernacular books. The task of creating an interest in the heritage of the past and of producing a vernacular literature cannot be left to the Natives alone. The white man must take the lead. Wherever a school or a teaching system will seriously take up the cause of vernacular education, the European educators will have to master the language.

Here it is that many missionaries and other educators fail and make a wrong start, perhaps to-day more so than used to be the case half a century ago. In the

Africa of to-day the white man will in many cases come into a milieu which is perfectly conversant with his own European language, and so nothing seems more natural than that he should follow the line of least resistance and limit himself to the use of his own tongue. The pressing demands made upon his time on the one hand, and a shirking of the trouble necessarily involved in the mastering (not in acquiring a working knowledge) of an African language may explain this passive attitude of his. Such an educator will never inaugurate vernacular education, and if it does exist already, he is not likely to pay much attention to it. If, on the other hand, he has learned the language and through it learns to understand the Natives and their forms of life, he will insist on having it used in school and on giving the mental heritage of the people its place in education, for he has come to realize the absolute foolishness of instructing children in a language of which they do not understand a word.

Still greater is the responsibility of the European who undertakes to produce a vernacular literature. He not only needs a thorough knowledge of the language, but in using and even moulding it for quite new purposes he is confronted with a number of problems, the difficulties and importance of which should not be underrated. Questions arise of the right dialect, of standardization, of orthography, of word-division, of word-formation, of finding the right expressions or of coining new ones by composition and without violating the language, and of the introduction of foreign words. The language will be extremely rich and nice in some respects, but it may be poor in others, and often seems to be lacking in just those things which the European wants to express. Only if he is indefatigable in efforts, patience and devotion will he reach his aim. He may realize that the more he studies the language the less he seems to get to the bottom of it, but he will also come to admit that it is a much more flexible and adequate instrument than he at first thought it to be, and that it is capable of development and also of expressing European thought. In fact there is no African language (except perhaps Bushman) in which it is not possible to express everything that is required for primary education. With honest goodwill, it should be possible within a few years to produce the necessary text-books in all the African languages suitable for educational purposes, and in this way to provide a basis for a really popular, comprehensive elementary education. Only if this vernacular educational literature as well as at least a few books for general reading come into being and are actually used in schools will Natives learn to consider their own language as a valuable means of education and instruction; and only when the problems connected with the building up of a literary language have been thoroughly worked out and the language reduced to a simple and consistent way of writing, only then will the Africans be able to enjoy reading and writing their language.

4

An objection frequently levelled against the use of the vernacular is that these languages are spoken by so few people that it is not worth while building up a literature in them. This is true in certain cases, but not in all. A number of African languages are spoken by as many people, if not more, as the numbers speaking some of the European languages with literatures of their own. Swahili may justly be numbered among the important languages of the world. Hausa, Ibo, Yoruba, Mossi-Dagomba, Mandingo, Lulua are spoken by millions of people. There are many other purely tribal languages, such as Zulu, Xosa, Suto, Ganda, Nyamwezi, Ruanda, Luo, Zande, Banda, Efik, the Akan stock, Ewe, Mende, each comprising hundreds of thousands of speakers and some of them with a definite expansive tendency. There is no inherent reason why such languages should not evolve a literature. Great as they are, the diversity and multiplicity of African languages should not be exaggerated. Often what we speak of as a language is really a dialect of another language. The difference between two forms of speech may seem considerable and a mutual understanding impossible. This occurs in Europe as well as in Africa, and yet a closer examination will often reveal significant and essential similarities, not only in the sound system and vocabulary, but even more in structure and idiom. This is to be expected, since all of them have developed in the same surroundings with a common mentality and a similar cultural background behind them. It is this which facilitates the development and spread of linguae francae which are African and therefore not felt to be foreign.

It is obvious that not every language can have a school literature. How far it will be possible in a given case to select and use one written form for a group of dialects or cognate languages will depend on the interest, the tact, and the wisdom of those responsible for education.

5

It is noteworthy that in one branch of African education the principle that a person should be taught in his own language has been followed almost without reserve, namely, in religious education. The missions have realized from the beginning that if they wanted to reach the heart of the Africans and to influence their inner life, they could do so only through the medium of their own language, and they have kept to this principle; even where a considerable section of the people know a European language, Church work is with rare exceptions done in the vernacular, and it is characteristic that most African books and periodicals deal with religious subjects. Only in this way was it possible and will it be possible in the future to build up an indigenous African Church.

6

With modern secular education, however, the situation is different. It is possible and desirable to transfer certain elements of the old indigenous educational principles, of the lore and knowledge of the tribe, into modern education and instruction. But this is not sufficient to give the pupil an adequate outfit for the life of to-day. Even in elementary education he needs an understanding of the new forces that are transforming his country, and he must assimilate at least the elements of these forces in order to be able to use them. Therefore, modern education is bound to take its material mainly from European culture. In principle this might be done through the medium of an African language, and it can be done in the elementary stage. Here again, however, language and culture are connected, and moreover it is natural that under present conditions there should be a very general and very keen desire on the part of the Natives to know the white man's language. This attitude has to be taken into consideration, quite apart from the fact that for every class of higher and also of technical education the knowledge of a European language is indispensable.

Nothing tends to broaden the mental outlook of a man more than learning a foreign language and through it understanding the culture it represents. There is truth in the saying that with every new language one acquires a new soul. How much more so is this the case with the African who, when he acquires a European language, leaves the humble huts of his tribal life and enters the realm of the civilization which rules the world and is more and more becoming the culture of mankind.

In a real sense, this is true only for a very small minority of those who learn a European language, namely, those whose education enables them to read and to enjoy reading European books and thus reach the sources of Western thought. Not to them only, however, is the knowledge of a European language useful. Wherever the African in his daily work comes into close contact with the white man, some knowledge of his master's language is almost indispensable to him. The work he has to do here is practically always carried on in the European language, whether in business firms, in offices, or in most of the workshops. A Native who knows this language will always be preferred to one who does not, the more so because only in exceptional cases will his white employer understand the vernacular sufficiently, and even if he did, as a rule the technical terms required do not exist in the language. The only exception to this rule is perhaps East Africa, where Swahili is largely understood and used by the white population, and the language is, thanks to the influence of Arabic, more highly developed as far as technical terms are concerned. For many Africans living in towns, and particularly in South Africa, proficiency in a European language is a vital requirement, because only on this condition can they hope to be able to compete and to find a place in life.

When within an area a rivalry arises between two Native languages, the one having become literary, the other not, or the one expanding and the other receding, a feeling of inferiority develops in those who do not master the language considered as superior. The same is true in the case of the European language, and this is another powerful motive for so many people, not only children, but adults, wishing to acquire at least some elements of the white man's speech. As conditions are in Africa, the idea of going to school is intimately connected with that of learning a European language and thus becoming in some way or other a member of the socially higher class. Therefore, even in elementary education, it will as a rule not be advisable to exclude the teaching of a European language altogether. Here again it may be possible in the case of Swahili, but not in most other parts of Africa. However slight the knowledge of English acquired in a village school may be, there will always be occasions where the Native can use it and be proud of it.

The really relevant case, however, is that of higher education. The African is a gifted linguist, and even after a few years' instruction may be able to speak English quite fluently. But this does not imply that he reads English books or is even able to understand and assimilate the treatment of a serious subject in a book. In my experience the Africans who do read books are mostly teachers and ministers. It is true they do it because their calling requires it, and their reading is restricted to certain definite spheres, but nevertheless the fact that they exercise their mind and keep in touch with higher culture accounts for the fact that among them are to be found some of the best-educated Africans. They represent, however, only a minority of the educated group, and it seems important for the advancement of the race that a class of Africans should be formed who are not only able to speak English and to read an illustrated newspaper or political propaganda material, but whose education enables them to enjoy studying, digesting, and assimilating a serious book. It is true that the African learns much from personal contact with the white man, and that the personal influence of the teacher on his students is of greater import for the formation of character than book knowledge. But this influence comes to an end when the student leaves the school and is left to himself. Those who are to be the leaders of their people and the channels of the new forces should remain in close touch with the best of what the European mind has produced, and one means of establishing this contact is certainly the reading of European books.

The other side, however, is no less important. The introduction of students into the full realm of European culture loses all its meaning if it implies a neglect of the African's own life and language and thus isolates him from his own people. This is where modern education is easily inclined to make a fatal mistake. Some time ago I came across a Grammar of the Fante language published about a century ago, which had on its title-page the following rhyme: 'Let every foreign tongue alone, till you can read and write your own.' If this sound and natural principle had been followed throughout in Africa, African education would stand on a sounder basis than it does to-day. Just as a knowledge of a European language links the pupil to European culture, so it separates him from his own people. The teaching of a European language is one of the powerful disintegrating factors in African social life. The danger was less great as long as only a small minority of children received a school education, mainly for the purpose of becoming the white man's assistants. Circumstances are altered, however, when education spreads and school attendance becomes general. This is the position to-day, and the time is not far distant when at least in parts of Africa there will be compulsory education. It might be worth while therefore to examine once more the question whether elementary education should be in the vernacular or in a European language, or what should be the relation between the two. Vernacular education does exist, it is true, at least in parts of Africa, but even there it is often no more than rudimentary, one reason for this being that many leading educators do not believe in it. One sometimes has the feeling that teaching in the vernacular is considered as a necessary evil that has to be overcome as quickly as possible in order to hasten to the much more important teaching of the European language. It is natural that under such circumstances the pupils do not attach any importance to the vernacular and are glad to get rid of it as soon as possible.

If boys and girls in an African village are taught in English, or at any rate are given to understand that their main task is to learn English, what will be the result? Are they not systematically drawn away from their own home and their own people? How can we be surprised when such children, after leaving school, find life in their village no longer attractive and try every means to get away from it? Yet after all for the great majority of them the village is the world in which they will have to live and work, and make a success of their life. If our education dissociates the pupil from his own social bonds, what are we giving him as a substitute? He is then naturally drawn towards the white man, but only to realize that this door remains closed for him. If we teach the African that introduction into the white man's world is only one side of his education, that it is equally important for a man to understand and respect his own people and its life forms, and that for every self-respecting person it is a matter of course to stand on the side of his own people and to dedicate the best of his life to it, then we shall do him a better service than if we try to persuade him that his aim should be to become as European as possible.

The same is true where higher education is con-

cerned. A person whose training in knowledge, outlook, and character has enabled him to grasp fully the
living forces of European civilization, should regard
it as his personal responsibility to hand on to his people
what he has acquired and thus become a fountain head
for new life; but he can do this only when he has not
dissolved the ties that unite him with Native society.

The teaching of the vernacular is by many considered as a waste of time; this may be true for the
pure rationalist and for those who regard knowledge
of a European language and education as two almost
identical things. But if education in Africa means the
full development of personality and the organic growth
of a new society, it cannot lose sight of the soil out of
which the existing society has grown and the human
values it has produced. The medium for studying and
appreciating these things and for assigning them their
due place in the new order of things is the Native
language, and from this point of view it is one of the
important means of education.[1]

[1] The educational system of the Belgian Government in
Belgian Congo provides for two classes of schools: primary
schools (comprising five years) and special schools (professional
and normal schools). The medium of instruction in all schools
is one of the main languages spoken in the colony, viz. Lingala,
Swahili, Luba, Kongo. In the lower primary schools (2 years)
no European language is taught, while in the higher classes
and in the special schools French may be taught under certain
circumstances (Cp. J. Mazé, *La Collaboration scolaire des
gouvernements coloniaux et des Missions*, Maison Carrée (Alger)
1933, p. 106 f.).

XII

DISINTEGRATION AND REINTEGRATION

I

IN considering the relations of Africa with other parts of the globe the fact cannot be overlooked that though from prehistoric times onwards foreign peoples have again and again migrated into Africa, yet the Africans have never of their own accord advanced beyond the boundaries of their continent. The desire for adventure never lured them to strange lands. They remained passive and receptive, and waited until others came to them. African life before the arrival of the European was conservative, and tradition was the dominating power. Africa 'has no chapter in the history of the planet'.

This does not mean that complete stagnation ruled either within the continent or in its external relations. From time immemorial there have been influxes of peoples as well as of cultural elements from Asia and to a smaller degree from Europe. From the Near East there came 'Hamitic' groups, whose immigrations probably were spread over thousands of years. Three distinct streams are easily distinguishable: along the north African coast; through the region between the Sahara and the West African forests; and through the East African steppes to South Africa. They stirred up the Negro world, driving out, annihilating, or subjugating many tribes, and made themselves their rulers. In the course of the nineteenth century the Ngoni, a group of the Zulu who have definite Hamitic traits, left their home in South Africa and settled in the region round Lakes Nyasa and Tanganyika. The ethnical and political conditions in southern Tanganyika were completely changed by their violent inroads. From 1860 onwards they devastated and depopulated in the most cruel manner large areas west of Lake

Nyasa and in later years the whole district between the Rovuma and the Rufiji, until in 1897 they were subjugated by the German Government. Part of the conquered tribes the Ngoni annihilated and forced others to join them, with the result that to-day the population represents a heterogeneous mixture of South and East African groups, in which only a few aristocratic families have managed to a certain extent to keep themselves pure.

Of a different character were the migrations of the Fulani. Starting from somewhere near the shore of the Red Sea, they wandered along the southern edge of the Sahara as far as the Senegal. From here they turned back eastwards again and at the same time farther into the lands of the Negroes. They travelled in small groups seeking pasture for their herds, which was freely given them by the Negro rulers. They did not even disdain to become cattle-herds in the service of the Native chief, thus gaining unnoticed a footing in the land as unobtrusive guests. If conditions were favourable, they brought other groups of their people in their train, until they became a factor with whom the Negro government had to reckon. The Fulani soon adopted Islam and became its rigid adherents. This added to their feeling of superiority and their aversion to being the subjects of pagan Negro rulers. In a number of cases they finally succeeded in seizing hold of the political power, as, for example, when they conquered the land of the Hausa in the beginning of the nineteenth century.

Naturally such immigrations often also set indigenous tribes in motion, and migrations took place at all periods within Africa itself. New settlements were formed in suitable, preferably unoccupied, places until some other disturbance occurred or for other reasons the place was no longer pleasing. Occasionally the migrations were due to definite motives, as, for instance, when a people tried to gain access to the sea and to direct trade with the whites. More frequently they did not have a definite object. Hunters followed their game; herds changed their pastures; villages were moved because the soil became exhausted; sections of armies settled in the conquered country or went farther into the unknown, driven by a vague lust of adventure.

Peaceful connexions with the external world were not, however, lacking. Already in very early times merchants from the north and east came to Africa, and trade routes existed to the interior. Gold, ivory, slaves, and spices have for thousands of years been bartered for the wares of the foreigner. Strangers settled on the coasts; in the north, Phoenicians, Greeks, and Romans; in the east, Arabs, Persians, and Indians. It is probable that for many centuries prehistoric cultural influences came from the Pacific, from India and the Near East.

It is therefore inaccurate to say that Africa had lived in complete isolation before its modern contact with Europe. Certainly it was cut off from the outer world on the Atlantic coast, but on the north and the east it had in a restricted degree opportunities of participating in the life of civilized mankind and of profiting thereby. Traces of it are evident in many parts of the continent. The strangers not only brought their wares, but settled in Africa, taught the Africans their arts, introduced new cultivated plants and domestic animals, and familiarized them with new social and political institutions. With the exception of the ass, Africa received all its domestic animals from Asia, and many of its cultivated plants from Asia and America. Such accomplishments as the founding and working of iron and other metals, the art of weaving, the introduction of new food plants such as dura, rice, and the banana, and the raising of cattle must have led to a complete upheaval in life and in social and political institutions. The high cultural development in the empires of Monomotapa on the Zambesi, of Loango, Congo, Lunda, Luba, Benin, and the civilizations of the Mandingo, Hausa, Kanuri, and Swahili, are clear proof to what an extent external influences have been accepted and have taken root in Africa. All these stimuli from abroad, however, reached the interior of the continent in thin streams and with many interruptions, so that in the interim sufficient time was left for the Natives to assimilate what they had received as far as was congenial to them, and to reject the rest or merely let it die out. Thus the New, at any rate in the centres of its diffusion, meant an enriching and fresh stimulation of organic growth but no break with the Old, and even where this did locally occur it had time to close up. African cultures have always manifested an extraordinary stability and power of assimilation. Neither the migrations of the Hamites and the political upheavals caused by them; nor the settlements of the Arabs and their devastating slave-raids: neither the Indian and Persian immigrants on the east coast; nor even the slave and alcohol trade of Europe have been able fundamentally to change the face of Africa. The Negro has remained and his civilizations have remained; the foreign elements which they adopted have been so completely absorbed and adapted that to-day they appear indigenous.

Indeed, the foreign immigrants adapted themselves in their mode of life and even in their appearance to the indigenous population to such an extent that they themselves became Africans. Certain Arab tribes living in the Eastern Sudan, as well as those round Lake Chad, are through continued intermarriage to-day black in colour, and sometimes it is hardly more than language, religion, and some cultural features that distinguish them from the people around them. Many Hamites are almost as dark-skinned as Negroes, and a number among them such as the Hima have adopted Negro languages. The authenticity of many Fulani, judging by their appearance, is difficult to credit. It is true that Hamites can usually be recognized by their sharper features and often by more slender bodies, but climate, interbreeding, and mode of life have produced so many transitional stages that in many parts of Africa the boundaries of the two races are no longer fixed. The approximation was made easier by the fact that the cultural contrast between the new-comers and the indigenous population was not too great; also the climatic differences, and, in consequence, differences in habits were less marked than those between the Negro and the modern European. The strangers came in small groups and at great intervals, and they left broken bridges behind them. In most cases intercourse with their home countries and the possibility of returning there were excluded; they sought and found a new home in Africa. As the new-comers consisted chiefly or entirely of men, they were obliged to marry indigenous women, which made assimilation easier. As a result they, and more so their children, ceased to be strangers; they became Africans, or rather formed an aristocratic class of African society, which the masses were ambitious to resemble.

Portuguese settlements, which early arose on both the east and west coast, show a transition from older to modern times. These Portuguese colonists have assimilated much of the indigenous mode of life and reveal a remarkable capacity for adapting themselves to African conditions. In some coastal centres their descendants live as half-castes and belong to the better-class Natives. The assertion that those born of unions between black and white are sterile, or that they unite in themselves the less valuable qualities of both races, is not true. If bad elements have been produced by them, it is because they have an ill-

defined position socially, and their education has been
neglected. In cases where mother and father are of
sound body and mind, the children of parents of
different races have, in the opinion of all serious
observers, shown no signs of inferiority.

2

Among the pre-European foreign invasions of
Africa that of Islam is the one which in recent times
has brought about the most visible changes in the
social and political as well as in the religious life of a
large part of the continent. After North Africa had
been conquered by the Arabs in the seventh century,
Mohammedan influence soon began to be felt in the
countries farther south. It may be assumed that from
the tenth or eleventh centuries onwards Mohammedan groups or single traders penetrated into the Sudan
by the trade routes from the Mediterranean. As early
as the eleventh century a Mohammedan dynasty ruled
in Kanem. In the fourteenth century, following the
fall of the Christian Nubian kingdom, Kordofan,
Darfur, Wadai, and Bornu were invaded by mixed
Arab tribes who came from Upper Egypt, and many
of whom gained ruling positions in the new lands.
Even earlier, between the eighth and eleventh centuries, Arab merchants from Morocco and Algiers
had reached the Western Sudan, which had for a long
time previously been in commercial relation with
North Africa. Finally, in the eleventh century, tribes
of nomad Arabs left Egypt and wandered westwards

along North Africa, part of them reaching the Sudan
and forcing the already Islamized Berbers farther
south. Owing to these movements the groups of
people known to-day as Hausa were probably forced
into their present area. At that time they were still
pagan, but from the second half of the fourteenth
century they adopted Islam. By about 1400 the new
religion had spread so far that the countries east of
Lake Chad, and to some extent those west of it, were
covered by a thin but influential layer of Mohammedan culture. These conditions remained almost
stationary, until in the beginning of the nineteenth
century religious propaganda, influenced by political
ambition, was started by the Fulani in northern Nigeria
and the neighbouring lands, and Hausa, Kanuri, and
Mandingo, thanks to the opening up of Africa by the
Europeans were able to carry Islam into unknown
regions. This resulted in the rise of an important
Islamic diaspora in most of the larger places of West
and Central Africa as far as the southern Cameroons.

To East Africa Islam came partly through trading
intercourse over the Red Sea, and through the contact
of South Arabia, India, and Persia with the East
African coast. From the ninth century onwards the
Shirazi civilization, mixed with Mohammedan influences, reached East Africa from the Persian Gulf.
The so-called Shihiri Arabs over a long period migrated into East Africa and settled there as small
traders and artisans. Stronger political forces came
from Hadramaut. At the end of the seventeenth

century a new element came in when the Sultans of Muscat extended their rule over Zanzibar and the continental coast. By their continuous slave raids in the interior they devastated the country, but at the same time spread Islam by trade routes and settlements. As in West Africa, their religious propaganda received a new impetus through European colonization. The present situation is that the whole eastern Horn, except Christian Abyssinia, and a small strip of the coast as far as Mozambique, is Mohammedan, and Islamic communities are also found in many of the important places in the interior.

As has been mentioned, Islam owes its progress in modern times mainly to European colonization. The Mohammedans, as traders and craftsmen, as members of a higher and more civilized race, reaped the first benefit of the *pax Europaea* and the economic progress following in its train. In consequence they came into the foreground, so much so that in colonial and missionary circles a 'Moslem peril' was apprehended.

The bearers of Islam were mostly either political conquerors or merchants. It was to the advantage of the new religion that its first contacts were with Hamitic peoples. Most of the Hamites—Berber, Moor, and Tuareg, Fulani, Hausa, and Somali—are to-day Islamized, and it may well have been that this definitely masculine religion, which moreover had originated in a nomadic people, had a special attraction for them. Islam was bound to impress the Negroes also. It came to them as the religion and civilization of aristocratic peoples who as political masters or as travelled, wealthy merchants and scholars, richly dressed, and with the claim of owning the one true religion, must have appeared superior to the Negroes in many ways. At the same time they were sufficiently akin to them in their habits to live a common social life with them and to become connected with them by blood. The representatives of Islam were people of a higher standard of life, but this was not so different from that of the Negroes as to prevent a new unit arising out of a combination of the two. The new religion and its civilization were assimilated and became African. The process was facilitated by the fact that Islam recognized no race discrimination. The converted Negro was willingly admitted into Islamic society, and to him the Moslem was a brother not only in name but throughout the sphere of social life. It soon became the ambition of the Negroes, primarily of the chiefs and the higher classes, to attain the socially higher status of the Moslem. This meant the adoption of the new religion and this was made easier by the fact that Islam adapted itself in large measure to indigenous customs and views, and that its moral demands were not exacting. This rising into the higher social class has been an essential factor in the advance of Islam. There was also in some cases a desire to escape in this way the oppression and slave raids of Mohammedan rulers, to which they were exposed as long as they remained Unbelievers.

In comparison with these social factors the religious

motives of the conversion to Islam recede into the background. They are not absent, however, and they are in evidence especially where Islam has for a long time prevailed. Faith in the one Allah, who leads no shadowy existence but really rules the world of the individual and leads his faithful into Paradise, and the consciousness of belonging to a world-religion, enhance the feeling of personality. The belief in many gods, demons, and other spirits perhaps does not entirely die out but becomes a superstition and thus sinks to a lower sphere. The numberless charms are replaced by amulets which are an emanation of the infinite power of Allah. The outlook on life becomes freer and broader. The Moslem feels himself to be the possessor of a valuable religious treasure, and it is well known how difficult it is to shake his convictions. His attitude to Christianity is quite different from that of the pagan.

The spread of Islam took place not through what we call 'Missions'. It took the form of a gradual, almost imperceptible transference of culture which included religion. It was distributed in the same way as Christianity in its early beginnings, in a way which may be regarded as the ideal one. Its adherents who travelled to foreign lands were by word and deed confessors of their religion and so won for it new followers. This natural way of spreading was possible for Mohammedanism, because practically all its followers acknowledged their faith daily in their prayers and in other religious observances, and these could not fail to make a deep impression on the African. Missionary activity on a larger scale was never practised; when missionaries were sent from Egypt or other centres, they devoted themselves to lax Mohammedans, not to pagans. The conversion of Africa to Islam thus took place without the employment of a costly apparatus. It was an internal affair of Africa alone, not a proselytizing enterprise of strangers. After the new religion had once taken hold of Africa, its propagators were people who lived in Africa and were or had become Africans. Wherever a congregation, however small, was founded, a Mosque was built and a school which had its teacher. No one ever thought that the money for the erection or the maintenance of such buildings or the payment of the teacher should come from a central institution for the propagation of the Faith. It was from the first moment an understood thing for each congregation that this was its own affair. Islam forged the closest links between itself and the African people. It became a part of this people, and for that reason took such a firm hold that many African tribes can be counted among its most faithful adherents.

Recently the Ahmadia movement has made efforts to gain a footing in Africa. Its representatives, obviously in conscious imitation of Christian mission activity, turn their attention also to pagans.

Islam has had a far-reaching civilizing influence in Africa. It has given the African a greater self-possession and sense of security in his outlook. The membership of a world-wide religious community, the connexion with North Africa, Egypt, and Arabia, the participation in the Moslem brotherhoods, widened the horizon, created new trade connexions, and enriched the indigenous culture in many ways. Trade and industry were not unknown in the Sudan before the arrival of Islam, but under the bond of animistic beliefs and the narrowness of clan life they would have needed, without the many stimuli caused by Mohammedan life, much longer time to attain the high status which distinguish these countries to-day.

The Mohammedan does not fall into such slavish imitation of the white man, as the Negro often does. While many a Negro is proud if he can wrap himself in any old rag thrown away by the European and sometimes makes himself into a ludicrous caricature by so doing, the Mohammedan would not dream of exchanging his flowing *tobe* and his straw hat or cap for articles of European clothing.

Where the influence of Islam is profound, it has done away with many horrors such as human sacrifice, persecution of witches, and cruel ordeals. The misuse of alcohol has at least diminished, and in some areas it has disappeared. In the larger towns of the Sudan Islam has created important centres of Mohammedan learning. The schools of Timbuctoo, Segu, Massina, Kano, Katsena were famous throughout the Mohammedan world. Teachers travelled from town to town and everywhere gathered around them flocks of pupils or opened disputations on learned questions at the courts. It was the pride of rulers like Osman dan Fodio and his son Bello to shine as poets and writers and to draw famous students to their court, so that the whole life of such a centre acquired an intellectual atmosphere quite unthinkable in pagan surroundings. The fact that Islam is a religion of the book makes itself felt in the remotest village with Mohammedan inhabitants. A school is established in which reading and writing are taught, or at least chapters of the Koran are learned by heart under the pretence of being read. However mechanical most of this kind of instruction is, it shows that a certain amount of scholastic education and a respect for learning goes hand in hand with the distribution of Islam. The conservative and even rigid character of Mohammedan education has, however, not adapted these schools to modern demands and made them an instrument of real education. They have remained exclusively religious, and one might say exclusively mechanical, so that their educational value is almost nil. Where a change has come about it is by the efforts of European Governments, who, while retaining for Islam its place in education, have managed to modernize such schools and thus breathe new life into them.

It was to the advantage of Islam that, apart from Arabic, three of the main African languages, Swahili, Hausa, and Mandingo, became vehicles of its ideas. Islamic traders speaking one of these languages spread the language, Islamic civilization, and Islam itself at the same time as their goods. This led to a certain levelling, the elimination of tribal differences, and in not a few cases to the disappearance of tribal units. A number of groups who speak Hausa to-day and have adopted the Hausa ways of life were formerly independent tribes with their own languages. The same process has been going on in the countries of the Mandingo- and the Swahili-speaking peoples. Though this means a loss in tribal individuality, yet on the whole it is a gain; it enabled the Negro to experience for the first time a feeling of solidarity beyond the clan or tribe.

The fact that Islam represents in Africa a higher type of civilization makes it easy to understand why it enjoys the consideration and sympathy of many Europeans and is sometimes recommended as the religion most suitable to the African. Those who take this view should, however, not overlook the fact that Islam fails on certain counts. It may be doubted whether with its higher civilization it has also introduced a higher morality. In the public life of Moslem countries the moral integrity of the rulers and their officials, and the guarantees for well-ordered administration and justice, were scarcely greater than among pagans. Slavery and the slave-trade were recognized institutions. Most wars were undertaken with the express object of capturing slaves and frequently led to great cruelties. The abolition of these abuses was not the result of a reform on the part of Islam but of the intervention of European Governments. The position of women is in no way better in Islam than with the pagans. If among the Tuareg and Fulani, the Hausa and Mandingo, the woman is looked upon as the equal of the man, this is not the merit of Islam. It would be more accurate to say that in contrast to the usages of Islam their ancient customs and views have survived among these peoples. For the advancement of moral and physical cleanliness, hygiene, and the combating of disease Islam has done nothing. More serious than these shortcomings, however, is the fact that Islam does not as a whole seem to be able to lead its adherents beyond a certain stage of culture. To-day in Africa it is sterile. No fresh impulses radiate from it, no powers which foster life and make it a dynamic force in progress. Its atmosphere is rather that of stagnation. There is therefore a danger that the spread of Islam in Africa will lead the development of the Africans into a blind alley. It cannot give to the African the same new power as Christianity, because its own roots are not deep enough in truth, and it does not possess the same capacity for growth.

3

It is difficult to compare the changes brought about by the present European penetration with any earlier ones, so different are they in degree and intensity. Formerly foreign influences came slowly; they either affected only small parts of the continent, or it took them hundreds of years before they spread over a larger district. To-day not a single village remains

untouched and the process of transformation is going
on not only with unheard-of rapidity, but at the same
time with a thoroughness which may be called revolutionary. Primitive cultures are by nature unfitted
to cope with such attacks and must succumb to them.
One day the Negro is a primitive farmer, the next a
proletarian in a European enterprise. To-day he lives
the communal life of collectivism; after a few years
at school he is expected to conduct cash transactions
in a European business. We in Europe have gone
through these changes, but over a period of centuries.
We grew up with the changing conditions and have
struggled with them. They arose from the growth of
our own culture and thus became a natural necessity
for us. For the African they are something strange
that has come to him from without, and therefore can
be looked on only as a disturbing element. European
civilization with its technical triumphs is much too
complicated and presupposes too much knowledge
and ability to be assimilated by the African, i.e. to
become one with his earlier culture. When, as here,
two different worlds clash, the weaker must go to the
wall. European civilization not only claims the right
to preserve intact its own integrity in Africa, but also
it desires to assimilate the African to itself and has
already done so to some extent. According to the
intentions of its masters Africa should become a
province of Europe. Individual parts of Africa should
become affiliated as closely as possible to certain
European powers, and this object is rapidly being

attained. For the African this means that he must abandon his own culture and be satisfied for an indefinite time with the position of pupil and subordinate. He does not mould his own fate or handle his own problems as we in Europe did and do, but strangers mould and handle them for him, according to their plans, not his own. The approximation of the black to the white, aimed at by the latter, is meant only to extend to technical and intellectual matters and does not entail political and social equality. Although opinions may differ on this point, and some colonial powers have more liberal views than others, equality in social and political life, except a few single cases, is hardly anywhere considered. The fact remains that the African is a subject race, and we should be quite clear as to what that means for a race that is struggling to rise and become conscious of itself. With however much goodwill and tact relations are conducted, there will always be the possibility of conflict.

Relations are made easier by the fact that the Negro sees in the white man his ideal. He may heartily disagree with much of what the European does and plans, yet to-day the great majority of the leading Natives in Africa have no greater ambition than to resemble the white man as far as possible. This idea is bound to be decisive in his future development. Even those Negroes who, as educated men and conscious representatives of their race, regard European domination critically or with hostility, claim for themselves the right to possess fully the white man's culture, for they are convinced that they are able to compete with him and hold their own only when they possess his weapons. African leaders disapprove strongly of any attempt to give the Natives an education other than that given to the whites in the country. All proposals to adapt the curriculum of Native schools to their own culture and individuality are treated as attempts to enslave the Natives spiritually and to keep them artificially at a low level.

This attitude must be understood from the particular conditions prevailing in parts of Africa. For the whole of Africa, however, a better policy is expressed in the following remarks by Dr. Willoughby.[1]

'The truth is that nothing is easier than to anglicise the Bantu as far as externalities are concerned, and nothing more impossible than to make them English. If these people can purge their own life of its stains and make it the best that it is capable of becoming, they will not then be British, but they will command the respect of all thoughtful people, and the best service that we can render them individually is to help them to find their better selves and realise the possibilities of their own nature.'

The craving of the African for European education and for the acquisition of European achievements is fully justified and must be encouraged and welcomed without any reserve whatever. With all that the African should realize that his task is greater than that of becoming a second edition of an already existing

[1] *Race Problems in the New Africa*, p. 172.

type. Not imitation but perfection of his own nature
leads to the goal: and the goal for him must be for
his own race, not to be identical, but to be of equal
value with, the white race.

4

Governments, missions, and economic activity are
the three powers which more than others are responsible for the disintegration of Africa. Of these, economic activity is the most conspicuous and perhaps the
most far-reaching. It has brought to the Negro
modern exchange by means of money. This one fact,
by offering him the possibility of earning money and
with it buying European commodities, has through its
powerful attraction shaken the very foundation of the
whole social system. It has awakened desires and at
the same time opened the way for satisfying them.
Formerly the economic life of the individual was
enclosed in the framework of the group, it de-
pended on the assent and co-operation of the chief
and of the community. Now it has broken its bonds
and can function without their help. Formerly a
person was born into a status and had to remain in it.
To-day he can escape from it at will and by his own
efforts, and he can exist outside the group, independent of it. This involves a principle which shakes the
old order at its very roots, for the old order knew no
rise in rank. Status in the group was determined not
by achievement but by descent and the position one
was born into, and he was a bold man who separated

himself from his group. This is no longer so. For many of the younger generation the centre of gravity of their life lies outside the community, and a person of the lowest rank may by skill and perseverance attain a rank superior to that of his chief. Boys when still at school already plan to build up their own life away from the Native village, preferably in a large town, where the pulse of life beats faster and they are not bound by burdensome conventions.

In the old days distinctions between rich and poor hardly existed, and even if chiefs and other important men possessed more than others, they could not do much with their wealth. Nowadays pleasures and social distinctions may be bought with money, and difference in wealth is of greater social meaning than it used to be, not on the positive side alone but also on the negative. If in earlier times there were no rich, there were also no poor, whereas to-day an individual separated from his group can easily become a victim to destitution, especially in the towns.

When a young man wanted to marry, his father or family provided the bride-money for him, and this was divided among the bride's family, so that the marriage was a contract between the two groups. To-day he may obtain a bride with his own money and so become independent of father and family. He can in consequence make his own choice and is not tied to marry the girl whom his relations had decided for him years ago. He may even give the bride-money to the girl herself, so that it is a question of an agreement between two persons instead of two social groups, and hence can be dissolved by either without the interference of other people. Temporary marriages thus develop, the man becoming tired of his wife or the woman running away in order to marry another man and so get another bride-gift.

The centres of diffusion of these powerful changes are towns and industrial areas, and most of all the South African mining districts. The Witwatersrand mine has employed in recent years an average of 200,000 Native labourers. As the people work only for a definite period and then return home, this means that there is a constant coming and going between these centres and the home villages. The labourers are mostly young men who are soon to marry or have recently married; in the latter case they leave their wives behind and these have to fend for themselves. As many of the men on their return go back to the mine again soon, the wife may be alone for ten years or more, except for intervals, and this at the time when a man and woman are at their prime. Cases are not infrequent in which a man leaves a woman in the lurch, and troubles himself about her again only when, after waiting a long time, she has entered a new relationship and he hopes to force compensation for his injured rights from her new husband. The deserted wife bears the burden of her household alone. Although the African woman is used to strenuous work and is accustomed to act independently in all matters of economic life, and although she may up to a certain point count on the help of her family, yet she is in many ways dependent on her husband's co-operation. The fields are no longer properly cultivated, the cattle are uncared for, the huts fall to ruin, and the children are left to their own devices. There are also cases in which the woman, when she has perhaps for years kept house independently, will not again submit to the authority of a husband. The number of children born out of wedlock is increasing, and their fathers are frequently young men who have returned from the labour centres and are used to freedom. If an attempt is made to make them responsible for the consequences of their actions, they can easily escape by accepting a new contract. In the industrial centres and the regions which are subject to their influence, there is universally an obvious tendency to greater sexual freedom. Whereas formerly it was the greatest shame for a girl to have a child before marriage, such events are to-day tolerated with equanimity. The old family laws and bonds are being loosened and often give place to very lax ideas.[1]

In some of the South African Reserves and Locations up to 50 per cent. of the men are continually absent. In Basutoland in the last thirty years 60 per cent. of the able-bodied men have annually worked on the mines. It is obvious that such extreme conditions must affect unfavourably the social and particularly

[1] Cf. J. Schapera, 'Premarital Pregnancy and Native Opinion', *Africa*, vi, pp. 59 ff.

the family life, and are bound to lead to a decrease in the birth-rate.

These dangers have long been recognized by Governments and industrialists, and attempts are being made to avoid them by regulations and inspections of the methods of recruiting labour, by care for the hygienic and social welfare of the workers in the work places, and also by striving to retain unimpaired the connexion of the workers with their families at home. Opportunities of writing letters or having letters written are given to them, and they are helped to send money to their relations through reliable channels. There are also many men who finally settle down again in their own home, willingly submit to the old order and cast off like an old garment the habits learned in mines and on plantations. They may even prove a valuable element in their community with their widened outlook and acquired abilities.

In places, however, where migratory labour has become a fixed habit and affects the majority of the male population, dangerous results are inevitable. In the labour centres the men have learnt an individual freedom of movement which is impossible in traditional village life and threatens to burst the bonds of communal unity. They have grown accustomed to pleasures which can be had only in exchange for cash, and these there are no opportunities of acquiring in the village. Hard work was necessary under the European, but in the leisure hours one was one's own master and pleasant society and distractions were never lacking. These men also find it unreasonable to have to bow to the orders of a chief who has far less experience of the world and of life than they themselves possess, and who is far from always being a benevolent and unselfish patriarch. They have learnt to like individual property and have been obliged to work hard for its acquisition. They are little inclined to share it in the old way with fellow tribesmen and to feel themselves economically one with them. Every one wants to live for himself and arrange his life according to his choice. Their religious faith has been shaken, and it is only with a bad grace that they take part in ceremonies which have become practically meaningless for them. The common life in the old style has lost much of its charm. It appears narrow and antiquated, and it is little wonder that the energetic and enterprising young men, when they have once tasted a freer existence in the outer world, long to return to it. This is in most cases necessary, if only because the money which is brought back is soon exhausted. It is mostly invested in goods, of which a part must be given to relations, so that there is not much left for the man himself. The previous method of investing capital in wives and cattle bore interest through offspring and the work of the women. The sum invested in goods to-day is consumed in a few weeks or months, so that it is not rare for a workman on the day of his return to take an advance from the labour agent on his future new contract.

One great danger of migratory labour lies in the

fact that the man may bring back infectious diseases from the labour centres and spread them in the home village. This not only impairs the health of the people, but is a most serious menace to the reproductive power of the race.

5

The changes in the social structure, which we have described, strike us at first glance as decay. They signify at the same time, however, a transition to new forms, for man as a social being cannot live in isolation and must build for himself forms of social organization. What these new forms will be, we cannot yet see. We are still in the midst of the transition phase and can observe only the first beginnings of the new order. In the old communities the dominant principle was that of the protection and security of the individual. The group took from the individual the largest part of his responsibility, but he knew that he was always in case of emergency covered by the elders of the group. In the new order of things a higher personal responsibility of the individual will be required.

The outstanding phenomenon in social development to-day is the emergence of the individual from the group. As we have seen, the characteristic feature of earlier African society was the predominance of the group, which left only a restricted sphere for the development of personality. It is different to-day, and from this point of view the present processes appear to be rather a step forward as they educate the individual to personal responsibility and break the unrestricted power of the group. True as this is, one would not do justice to the character of group life by saying that it robbed individual life of all significance. The group is never a mere agglomeration of individuals but a well-ordered and articulated whole, in which every individual has a special place and special duties.[1] These may have a social rather than a personal foundation, yet every member of the group knows that the prosperity of the group is dependent on what he does or leaves undone. The responsibility of a mother for her children, of a father for his family, of elder brothers for younger brothers, of the young man to his age-grade companions, and of the old men to the community, has never been strange to the Africans. In many respects the responsibility towards persons in one's own circle was greater in the old order than it is to-day. The cultivation of modern individualism often enough has led to the individual feeling himself responsible for himself alone and not taking even this responsibility too seriously.

It is certainly to be welcomed that to-day more scope is given to personality, for in the history of mankind it has always been the vehicle of spiritual progress. Personality is, however, not created in empty space, but only by intercourse with others. It is not only need and custom which drive man into

[1] Cf. B. Gutmann, 'Aufgaben der Gemeinschaftsbildung in Afrika', *Africa*, i, pp. 429 ff.

the company of his fellows, but the longing for communion born of his innermost nature. He always feels himself to be a member of a human group, and only as such, as a brother among brothers, can he develop his ethical personality and do his life work. For this reason the preservation or new setting up of social groupings is as important for the future of African life as that of individual responsibility: the one is indissolubly connected with the other.

All form is subject to change, and many social institutions in Africa have to-day outlived their purpose. It is only necessary to point out the secret societies and similar associations; there are others of such doubtful value that they could vanish without any serious loss. It is not a question of indiscriminate conservation. We have to discover which of the present forms of life have any vitality in the conditions of to-day; which of them are capable of transformation; and how they can be so shaped as to give the African a home fit to live in. We do not presume to answer these questions, but only pose them for discussion, directing attention to certain points. Two of the most important factors of reintegration, namely administration and missions, are treated in special chapters.

Every man is born into a social organization, into a family, tribe, people, and state. He will always have relations, neighbours, and fellow workers.[1] The

---

[1] Cf. S. Knak, *Zwischen Nil und Tafelbai*, Berlin, pp. 154 ff., *et passim.*

feeling of solidarity with the village and the clan, with men of the same age-grade and with friends in the same association, will remain alive in the future in large parts of Africa. Efforts are being made to-day in European countries to revive associations which had fallen into decay, because the values inherent in them have been recognized. In recognizing these values there is a conviction that in contrast to an atomizing individualism, nothing is more likely to let altruistic feelings gather new strength than the cultivation of such natural bonds. Such institutions are still alive in Africa, and it would be short-sighted to let them die of neglect. Here is a task offering great scope both to the school and to education as a whole. Older pupils and also adults will treat such questions with the liveliest interest and the keenest understanding, for they are concerned with the essence of their own life. Such training in civics should, especially in the higher stages, consist not only of teaching but of actual practice. Unions of pupils can be formed on the model of the age-grades, and thus the natural gradation and leadership, which have from time immemorial been familiar to the Native, can be made efficacious. If a school reckons among its pupils children from various tribes, they will learn to feel themselves to be one with strangers as members of one community. Just as the leading elders of the community play their part in the education of the initiation groups, so the school should become an organic part of the village or tribal community, and

the latter must have the same part in it and feel itself
no less responsible than the missionary or the European educational official. In this case the school can
help to familiarize the younger men with the social
structure of the people, show them its value, and teach
them to regard it with respect.

6

The primitive state, in which one or more clans
lived in a village isolated from the outside world has
vanished to-day. The African has developed a desire
to travel. Profession or inclination takes many people
away from their homes, and there is hardly a large
town which has not its strangers' quarter. Wherever
possible the stranger will settle among the people of
his tribe, who speak his language, because it will be
easier for him to adapt himself thus to new conditions.
At the same time the group is by these additions
enlarged not only in numbers but also in outlook.
People speaking the same language become conscious that they belong together; it will not be
long before, by intermarriage and other associations,
they actually become a new community which has
shed many of its past prejudices. A similar development will take place in large towns where many speaking different languages and belonging to different
peoples are gathered together. At first people speaking the same tongue will live in a separate quarter,
but they inevitably enter into communication with
the rest, and thus become better known to each other.

Naturally in these cases the problem is much more difficult, and it may be a long time before a feeling of solidarity is created among the inhabitants of such cosmopolitan places. There will at first be several communities, each of which exists for itself and gives support to its members. In these cases where it is a question of creating a really new structure, the first stimulus will come from the European rather than from the Native side. Church and school and the associations which radiate from them will become centres of new grouping. Perhaps of even greater importance is the setting up of self-government which will give definite tasks to the separate groups, and at the same time aim at uniting the whole population of the town into a conscious whole.

Different again, but not less difficult, are the conditions in the mines. It remains to be seen whether the knowledge and the responsibility of the white man will enable him to become master of the situation which has arisen here through his action. It also remains to be seen whether he will succeed in creating for the African an existence fit for human beings, and in showing him new possibilities of community life, where now he is threatened with a homeless existence.

The greater mobility of the population at the present time also leads to the inhabitants of a whole colony acquiring a better knowledge of each other. They are subject to the same administration; they have a common school system; common interests arise; Native administration and Native councils include groups which formerly hardly knew each other, but now learn to work for the good of a larger whole. They feel themselves responsible not only for the members of their own group but for a wider unit, which includes groups to which formerly they were indifferent or even hostile. Among the educated classes a lingua franca arises, either the vernacular or European. All this results in tribal differences being felt as less important than formerly and to the whole population learning to look upon themselves as a unity. In other words, something like a national feeling is born.

7

Where members of the white race have settled permanently in Africa questions arise as to the way in which the two races are to live together. Attempts have been made to bring about a geographical separation where the Natives have been assigned areas to live in, as in South Africa, the Transkei, Basutoland, and the Bechuanaland Protectorate, and, in East Africa, in parts of Kenya Colony. If the Reserves are sufficiently large and fertile, it will be difficult to raise objections to such a separation, but the plan, often ventilated, of carrying out segregation in the whole of South Africa would encounter so many obstacles that it seems all but impossible. The Negro has become such an indispensable factor in all the relations of economic life that we can hardly imagine how life would go on smoothly without his co-operation.

The Natives would certainly not move without compulsion from their dwelling places, their pursuits, and their land, and would actively oppose the new plan. They point out that in all previous divisions they have always been the losing party, and they fear that it would hardly be otherwise this time, especially as there must be grave doubts whether there is sufficient land available for the settlement of a large population. Moreover they see in the policy of segregation an attempt of the whites to force the blacks away from European civilization and so to cut them off from the possibility of improvement. Their mistrust is not unjustified. Nobody will maintain that the South African Natives have been treated liberally in the distribution of land, in payment for work done, and in being given opportunities for advancement. They and their leaders have, however, not been discouraged, but have fought bravely for their modest place in the sun. The sole means by which they can conduct this struggle is through education. If this is taken away, they are deprived of hope. They would have schools in the Reserves, but these would offer an education other than that which they desire. There they would also have to go without the stimulus which is to be found in the close association with white men and the necessity of competing with them.

Though a radical separation is impracticable, both races will agree that social intercourse between the two will probably not be the rule, and that consequently they must aim at living peacefully side by side. This necessity is actually expressed in the fact that in almost all places inhabited by members of both races, they choose separate sites for their dwelling places. In Tropical Africa this is to be recommended for hygienic reasons, but it is desirable on other grounds. 'The medicine for quarrelling is separation,' says a Hausa proverb. Each of the two races, the black as well as the white, is sufficiently self-conscious to wish to maintain and develop its own racial quality. By living apart many possibilities of friction and conflict are diminished, and each community can develop its own institutions undisturbed and live its own life. The same conditions have been evolved in North America after long experience and are regarded there as the most satisfactory arrangement by both races.

Of course this living side by side in one place cannot be such that the one section ignores the other. Numerous contacts are bound to exist, through the black men working in the town quarter of the white and with white workmen; by their buying in the shops of the white men and using their means of transport. In certain ways people living in the same place must form a unit, and both sections will realize this. The argument cannot be ignored that if the black men contribute to the maintenance of the community, they have the right to share in its administration and to enjoy through their contribution to taxes the full advantages and services which Western civilization brings to Africa.

It is to be welcomed that among South African

whites the conviction is gaining ground that in spite of social separation the two races must get together and learn to understand each other. These endeavours find their most significant expression in the Joint Councils of Europeans and Natives, which are trying by discussions and consultations to alleviate the racial antagonism and to induce co-operation where possible. In addition to the meetings of the councils and the measures resulting from them, the movement has had a remarkable success in repeatedly initiating European-Bantu conferences. Whatever the immediate consequences of these efforts may be, they prove the possibility of that which was formerly held by most South Africans to be impossible, namely, that members of the two races, with approximately the same level of education and with serious goodwill, can discuss together on an equal footing their common weal and so open the way to co-operation.

8

In districts under strong European influence groupings have arisen which closely follow modern European models and are mostly in opposition to the political and economic domination of the Europeans. The leaders of these movements are intellectuals. Their adherents spring principally from groups of workers. Their weakness is that their leaders often lack the necessary qualities of leadership, and their appeal is mostly to the detribalized. Hence they

hardly find a footing among the real indigenous population. The number of members is subject to strong
fluctuations, as the majority are soon disillusioned
and leave the association as soon as they see that the
hopes held out have not materialized. Neither the
African National Congress nor the Industrial and
Commercial Workers' Union of Africa has hitherto
been able to effect any substantial improvement in the
condition of the Natives. The same is true of the
Congress of British West Africa, which is a union of
the educated classes and at its meetings discusses the
problems of English West African policy. There is
no doubt, however, that all these movements contribute to creating a feeling of solidarity among the
Natives, and it is regrettable if its driving power is
opposition to the white man.

Latterly communism too has been striving to find
adherents in Africa. Its successes up to now have been
but small, but it is not impossible that sooner or later
the doctrines it preaches will find attentive hearers; it
has *one* strong side which must not be ignored. Communism preaches seriously the brotherhood of all
men. It promises the Negro complete social and
political equality. Here are the men who look upon
the black man as really an equal and make no evil
distinctions as do all the rest, not excepting the
Christians. It would be strange if this gospel did not
make the Negro listen.

The problems connected with the present disintegration and reconstruction of African society are as manifold as the African population itself, and any attempt at pronouncing general recommendations for its solution would be futile. What is necessary is a considerable number of detailed studies carried on among groups living under various conditions,[1] such as (*a*) tribal areas where there are no European settlers and planters and the new influences come mainly from the administration, missions, and commerce; (*b*) tribal areas from which there is an extensive emigration of males to industrial centres or plantations for work; (*c*) tribal areas in which there is an intensive economic development in Native-grown products; (*d*) areas with European settlers; (*e*) Natives in urban areas; (*f*) Natives living on plantations; (*g*) Natives in mining areas; (*h*) the detribalized African; (*i*) Natives living under direct and under indirect rule; (*j*) a study of new social groupings forming under the impact of European penetration.

[1] Cf. *Five Year Plan of Research*, p. ii.

XIII

THE CLASH OF RACES

I

WHEN primitive peoples have come into close contact with Western civilization, the consequence for them has frequently been either retrogression or destruction. Examples of this can be seen in North America, Australia, many Pacific Islands, and parts of South Africa. Analogous conditions have resulted in earlier times from the clash of stronger with weaker peoples. In Africa men apparently of Negro race appear to have advanced in prehistoric times northwards into what is at present the Sahara, until they were forced back by light-coloured people.[1] The question whether similar effects will take place as a

---

[1] P. Laforgue, 'Le Préhistoire de l'Ouest-Africain', *Africa*, iv, pp. 456–65.

result of the modern European penetration of Africa cannot yet be answered. The general view is that the vitality of the Negro and his adaptability to new conditions of life are too great for him to be in danger of racial extinction.

Close contact between two races at different stages of civilization gives rise to a series of social problems which have not been adequately studied. Up to the present, investigators have been content with examining the effect of this living together on the lower race, in this case the African. Equally important are the changes taking place among the whites, when they live as a dominant caste among the Negroes. Their views on the dignity of labour and on social behaviour to inferiors may be deeply influenced. A sense of superiority and a feeling of caste may arise among them. Dependence on the manual labour of the other race in combination with an unfavourable climate can lead to deterioration in efficiency and moral standards. It is difficult even for highly placed Europeans who live in constant contact with a race having a lower standard of living to maintain their own higher level. In South Africa the poor whites, who are in danger of sinking to the level of the Natives, present a practically insoluble problem.

The present population of Africa[1] according to recent census figures is about 130 millions, possibly less, making a density of four persons per square

[1] R. Uhden, *Die wirtschaftlichen und bevölkerungspolitischen Möglichkeiten Afrikas*, Koloniale Rundschau, 1931.

kilometre. In the steppe lands, most of which do not allow of agriculture but are fit only for cattle nomads, as, for example, in the region south of the Sahara, there is scarcely one person (in French Equatorial Africa 1·5) per square kilometre. Even in the forest district of the Congo where there is an abundant supply of rain the population reaches only 1–1·5 per square kilometre. The savannah lands show a relatively dense population. In northern Nigeria the density rises to almost 46. The greatest congestion is found in the oases of the Sahara and in a few favoured places, as on the southern slopes of Kilimanjaro, where 125 persons live on one square kilometre. Kavirondo is also a densely populated country. The greatest density is reached in Egypt. The valley of the Nile has 400 persons per square kilometre, and the purely agricultural Egyptian province Menufie 684.

Even when desert lands are not considered, the population of Africa compared with other parts of the globe with an equally good climate is extraordinarily sparse. The actual space available for habitation is not occupied as it might be. Let us take as an example the region of the savannah north and south of the primeval forests, that is, from the source of the Niger to the Nile-Congo water-divide and down as far as the Zambesi. This area embraces 5·6 million square kilometres. If one assumes, in analogy with the savannah districts of India, the possible population density to be 90, these areas might support 504 million people, that is more than the present population of Europe. The tropical rain forest and the areas of the warm-moderate climate of Abyssinia, Angola, and South Tanganyika can naturally support a higher rate of population. The estimates of the possible total population of Africa fluctuate between 1,000 and 2,000 millions. The lowest estimate is that by Shantz and Marbut who, basing it on an investigation of the soil, give 1,085 millions. If we accept this figure as approximately correct, it means that eight times as many people could live in Africa as there are actually to-day, assuming that orderly conditions prevail, and that the land is being cultivated intensively with all the aids of technical and artificial fertilization.

As there are other parts of the earth which are over-populated, and as the population of the earth is continually increasing, the time is within sight when the land to be disposed of in Africa will be occupied, and the question then arises who will be the occupants.

South Africa is to-day, not numerically but culturally, predominantly a white man's country. The black man has had to retreat before him in all spheres of life, in the same way as one or two centuries ago the Hottentot and Bushman had to give way to the black new-comer. In other parts of the continent in which it is or seems to be possible for the white man to reside permanently and establish his family, settlements of whites have been formed. Although the question whether a settled white population in the African highlands can find all the conditions of life fulfilled has not yet been fully investigated, it is likely

that these white settlements will increase, in population as well as in area. The highlands in Kenya, Tanganyika, and Angola which are considered as suitable
for European colonization embrace a round million
square kilometres, to which are to be added approximately 1·20 million square kilometres in South Africa.
About 2·20 million square kilometres, therefore, or
three-tenths of the whole continent can be considered
as possible for white settlement. General Smuts has
put forward the idea of 'a strong forward movement
in the policy of settling the high lands of Eastern
Africa which stretch in an unbroken belt, hundreds
of miles broad, from Kenya to South Africa', aiming
in this way 'to establish in the heart of the African
continent and as a bulwark of its future civilization
another white dominion'. It will hardly be possible
to execute this ambitious plan, for the broad, unin-
terrupted girdle of highlands does not exist, and there
are Native inhabitants in a considerable part of the
land. Nevertheless such an appeal will not fail to
fascinate people, and the fact remains that in the last
few years the white population of East Africa has
shown a steady tendency to increase, a tendency which
is certain to go on. Whilst fully recognizing the fact
that the black man will profit from the presence
of the white, nevertheless every penetration of the
white man simultaneously means a forcing of the
Negro into the background.

Three million whites are to-day living in Africa.
Among these the Greeks, who came through Egypt

and are penetrating farther and farther into Africa, represent a special feature. In Egypt they are numerically the strongest white colony, but they have spread also in the Eastern Sudan, in Uganda, Kenya, and Tanganyika. In almost all coastal regions and also farther inland Syrian traders have settled. Both they and the Greeks have an advantage over northern Europeans in that they are accustomed to a warmer climate and can live permanently in countries where it may be impossible for northern Europeans. The same is true of the Portuguese and in North Africa of the large groups of French and Italian settlers, who find here a climate perfectly congenial to them.

Another remarkable fact is the immigration of Indians to East Africa. Since the War their number has been doubled and to-day amounts to 100,000. Like the Greeks they are chiefly traders, craftsmen, technicians, and employees of European firms. They are generally thrifty, lead a good family life, and have many children. East Africa is thus in an increasing degree becoming a natural outlet for the surplus population of India. The Indians seldom mix with Natives and they retain an active connexion with their homeland, whereas the Arabs have always shown a tendency to merge into the Africans and thus lose their significance as an independent racial element.

All the immigrants, Asiatics as well as Europeans, are in certain respects superior to the Natives. They can become the Africans' teachers and thus be a factor in raising the cultural level. At the same time they will inevitably limit the space available for the African. Although strangers, most of them enjoy greater political rights than the Natives. They are also stronger economically. The Native is always with them the employee, never the employer. In the regions where the stranger settles permanently he acquires a portion of the land, and generally of the best land. The Native must withdraw and be satisfied with land which is less suited to the foreign settler. In other vocations too the Native is at a disadvantage. The stranger will soon learn how to reserve the best-paid positions for himself. In East Africa the Indians hold positions for which the Africans could equally well be used. This situation is, however, changing. The education of the Native is making such progress that he will soon be able to fill in increasing degree posts which used to be held by Indians, though as a trader the African may for a long time to come not be able to compete successfully with the Indian.

We have in North America a stock example of how the population movement of the Negroes formed itself in a white man's country under the intensive influence of European civilization. The comparison between Africa and America is not permissible without qualification, yet it may be instructive for our problem. In parts of South Africa conditions exist to-day which are not unlike those in North America, although it must be borne in mind that in South Africa the Negroes are in a majority and at least part of them still live within their old tribal bonds. The

American Negroes after their liberation had lost all
social ties and lived under wretched conditions. A
rise into higher social classes was made extremely
difficult for them, and this is still partly so to-day. On
the other hand, life in a country with an advanced
civilization offered them strong stimuli, and, in an
increasing degree, possibilities of attaining better
standards of life. Those who attempted to climb up
the ladder had to fight hard. While some succeeded,
many remained behind in the competition or did not
even try. The great majority has not risen beyond the
scale of an unskilled labourer. In spite of all disabilities, however, they have succeeded in evolving new
forms of life for themselves and have become at home
in America. They are not welded into a social unit
with the white Americans, but they have built up
a Negro society of their own, which in every place
where they are numerous forms separate social, religious, and to some extent also economic units. It
is wrong to think of the North American Negroes as
scattered fragments. They form communities which
are adequate for them, and in which in spite of all
difficulties they know how to assert themselves and
develop their own racial character. Although the
American Negroes desire in the first instance to be
American, their consciousness of race and their pride
of race are, at least in the higher classes, on the
increase. Nothing has contributed to produce this
attitude more than the opposition on the part of the
whites against which they had constantly to fight.

'White Americans are welding Negroes, first, into a Race despite their mixed blood; and secondly, into a fighting economic unit. It is impossible to starve twelve million people in a world of plenty unless they are incurably stupid.'[1]

The North American Negro population rose between 1830 and 1930 from 2,382,000 to 11,891,000. This fivefold increase was a unique example of how a relatively primitive race of men in a completely strange environment and under entirely changed conditions of life not only maintained itself but grew in an amazing measure, while the American Indians within the same period sank into insignificance.

In spite of their marked increase, however, the proportion of Negroes in the total population is diminishing. In 1830 it was 18 per cent., in 1930 only 9·7 per cent., and in the same time the proportion of the whites rose from 81·9 per cent. to 88·7 per cent. On the other hand, the contribution of both races to the increase in population has remained fairly equal, among the whites in 1830: 33·9 per cent., and in 1930: 14·8 per cent.; among the Negroes in 1830: 31·4 per cent., and in 1930: 14·8 per cent. The increase of Negroes in urban areas between 1890 and 1900 was 35·4 per cent.; between 1910 and 1920: 32·2 per cent.; in rural districts from 1890 to 1900: 13·6 per cent.; from 1910 to 1920:−3·3 per cent., that is to say, a decrease of 3·3 per cent. in the rural population.

The mortality among Negroes is throughout higher,

[1] Dubois in *The Crisis*, 1932.

and the birth-rate lower than among the white population. The death-rate per 1,000 for Negroes is about what it was for whites thirty years ago. The rate for whites in 1900 was 17·1 per cent., that for Negroes in 1926 17·3 per cent.[1] From statistics covering most states it is seen that the birth-rate for the white population exceeded by 9·4 and that for Negroes 7·5 the death-rate. Circumstances are least favourable in urban districts; whereas in the country districts there was a surplus of 10 for both races, in towns it is for the whites 8·8 and for the Negroes 3·3. Generally speaking, in North America between 1910 and 1927 the death-rate among whites decreased by about 23·9 and among Negroes by 15·8.

In view of the unfavourable conditions in the towns it is of particular significance that the Negroes, who used to live predominantly on the land, are thronging into the towns. The latest census reports that in 1930 43 per cent. of the Negroes lived in cities, compared with 34 per cent. ten years ago. New York has a Negro population of 327,000, Chicago 233,000, and Philadelphia 190,000. Between 1920 and 1930 37,590 Negro farmers lost their farms. Land operated by white farmers increased 34 million acres and that operated by Negro farmers decreased 3,835,000 acres.[2] The influx to the towns is welcomed by many Negro leaders, for, as they say, quite different possibilities of rising are offered there than on the land, where the

[1] M. Work, *The Negro Yearbook*, 1932.
[2] *The Crisis*, Dec. 1932, p. 380.

Negro is too often a victim of exploitation. This may
be correct or not, but it is certain that with the increase
in the urban Negro population the proportion of the
blacks in the total population of the country is continually decreasing.

In South America circumstances are different, in
that the climatic conditions are more favourable for
the Negro race, and one can hardly speak of a social
discrimination between black and white. South
America is inhabited by 64 millions, of whom only
30 millions are pure breeds, the rest being mixed.
Here again Negroes are falling behind in the increase
of the population. In 1819 the proportion of whites
was estimated at 24 per cent., that of the Negroes at
52 per cent., and of all mixed breeds at 17 per cent.;
in 1912 the corresponding figures were for the whites
36 per cent., for Negroes 19 per cent., and for mixed
breeds 36 per cent. The natural increase of the whites
is given as 1·2 per cent., that of mulattoes as 0·93 per
cent., and of the Negroes as 0·62 per cent.

2

The population problem in Africa is most acute in
the south, because the white race has made its home
there beside the Natives. In recent years statements
have repeatedly been issued which give, and are
meant to give, the impression that the Natives are
rapidly increasing and are becoming a danger to the
whites. These statements are partly misleading. In
the census of 1921, to 1,000 whites there were 27

children under one year of age, to 1,000 Asiatics
and cross-breeds 30, to 1,000 Negroes 50 children.
But this does not take into account that among the
Negroes the infant mortality is extraordinarily high,
reaching very often 50 per cent. and more of the
children born, and if children of ten years old were
counted, the proportion of the races would be quite
different. From the census of 1921 the Census Direc-
tor, Mr. Cousins, draws the conclusion that in fifty
years South Africa will have a white population of
6·5 million against a black population of 16·5 million.
This assertion has been justly questioned, and Mr.
Roberts[1] is probably nearer the truth when he assumes
that the Native population of the Union of 1947 onwards will remain stationary with about 6·3 millions.

The total non-European population of the Union
increased between 1911 and 1921 by 15 per cent.; the
European in the same period by 19 per cent. From
1891 to 1911 the increase of Natives is said to have
amounted to 69 per cent.; if this is correct, the following decade saw considerably less increase. In reality
the apparently immense growth of the earlier census
periods is explained by the fact that the figures are
partly rough estimates. Doubtless those of the last
census are more reliable, and from them it may be
concluded that the Native population is growing
more slowly than the white, so that here conditions

[1] 'A Statistical Inquiry into the Population Problem of
South Africa', *Transactions of the Royal Society of South Africa*,
vol. xiii, Pt. iii, pp. 201–44.

are developing analogous to those in North America. The coloured people in South Africa increased between 1911 and 1921 by 3·23 per cent. only.

In Basutoland, according to the official census reports, the Native population had grown between 1904 and 1911 by 15·55 per cent.; and between 1911 and 1921 by 23·43 per cent., that is, by 8 per cent. more than in the Union. The increase is very unevenly distributed over the districts, whereas in one district it ran to 85 per cent., in another it amounted hardly to 5 per cent. This shows that it is not exclusively an increase by birth but is to be accounted for rather by immigration. According to Buell[1] it is the opinion of Government physicians that the birth-rate of Basutoland is now declining.

From other parts of Africa only isolated reliable figures are available. In Uganda in spite of favourable economic and social conditions the population has for years remained stationary and only recently shows a slight tendency to increase.

In the colony of Sierra Leone the total African population has grown from 1881 to 1921 from 60,000 to 84,000, that of the Creoles (descendants of repatriated slaves) has, on the other hand, declined from 35,000 to 28,000. The increase in the African population amounting to 40 per cent. in 40 years includes a considerable immigration from the Protectorate and from other parts of West Africa. The town of Bathurst had, according to the last census, in a population

[1] *The Native Problem in Africa*, i, p. 170.

of 10,859, 350 births (32 per 1,000) and 383 deaths (35 per 1,000). On the other hand, favourable conditions obtain in the Municipal Area of Lagos. According to the latest census the birth-rate has increased from 3·002 in 1921 to 3·494 in 1930, while the death-rate during the same period declined from 2·472 to 2·016. The decrease in infant mortality has also been satisfactory, the figures being 284·8 for 1921 and 129·1 for 1930. This remarkable result is no doubt due to untiring activity in the sphere of hygiene.

In Nairobi and Mombasa in 1931 the death-rates were for Europeans 4·78 and 5·03 respectively, and for Africans 15·23 and 16·17 respectively.

Careful investigations have been carried out by Dr. O. Fischer in the village of Ipole in Unyamwezi.[1] This village had 234 inhabitants. Of the 158 adults 120 were Christians and 38 pagans, 66 men and 92 women. Of 91 women 269 children were born, 137 boys and 132 girls. Of these 142 died, which gives a mortality of 52 per cent., among boys of 58 per cent. and among girls of 48 per cent., so that the preponderance of males at birth was not only levelled but reversed. On an average there are 2·9 births to a woman, of these 1·5 die as infants and 1·4 survive. According to Dr. Fischer the proportion in other parts of Tanganyika is better, the average birth-rate being 4, of which 2·3 children survive.

In his monograph on the Lobi[2] H. Labouret re-

[1] Published in *Die evangelischen Missionen*, 22, i, pp. 3 ff.
[2] *Les Tribus du Rameau Lobi*, Paris, 1931, p. 52.

cords the results of his observations, which he made as to the descendants of 25 women at the age of 45 from 4 different villages. The 100 women had given birth to 370 living children, of whom 318 reached the age of puberty.

M. P. Ryckmans has made minute investigations on the movements of the population in the Belgian Congo. As far as we know, they are by far the best work that has been done in this sphere in Africa, because they go into the problems of method with the scientific thoroughness which alone can lead to reliable results. In his study[1] he gives some typical examples of his previous investigations. According to these, conditions vary considerably in various parts of the Congo. In the Territory of Katakokombe on the Sankuru, the number of those counted amounted in 1925 to 52,987, of whom 15,879 were children. In the year 1930 the whole population, both counted and estimated, had decreased to 50,114, of whom 13,116 were children. Thus there had doubtless been a decrease of population here. In striking contrast were the conditions in the territory of Madimbe, in which the population was 95 per cent. Christian, and where all the births and deaths were registered. Here the excess of births over deaths was in 1929 33·8 per cent., and in the year 1930 41·3 per cent. Of the total male population 17·5 per cent. were the fathers of four or more children, and every 100 women had 245

[1] *Notes sur la Démographie Congolaise*, Brussels, 1931 (Institut Colonial Royal Belge.)

children ; in the Chefferie Kekemba there were 380
children to every 100 women. The sexes were of equal
number within a few dozen. Sankuru seemed to be the
only district in which the population was decreasing,
and this was the more remarkable as the recruiting of
labour had for a long time been on a smaller scale than
elsewhere. M. Ryckmans' opinion is that the chief
reason for this too low birth-rate is the relaxation of
morality, and that the recruiting acts only indirectly,
because it entails a loss of morality.

It may be hoped that similarly exact observations
from other parts of Africa will soon be available, and
we shall then be able to gain a clearer idea of the
movements of the population and the reasons which
govern them. It may, however, be asserted that while
the population is decreasing in parts of Africa, it is
growing slowly in others, but there is nowhere any
sign of a rapid increase. Among the factors which
have an unfavourable effect on the growth of population are the following :

(a) Life in towns. Housing conditions in many
African towns are miserable for the poorer population
and in the highest degree prejudicial to health. Life
in the towns offers temptations which loosen the
bonds of family life and lead to the decay of morals.
People easily accustom themselves to irregular work
and thus to insufficient nourishment. The younger
people are apt to spend a disproportionately large
part of their money on pleasures, and many contract
contagious diseases.

(*b*) Detribalization. It has on occasions been asserted that the detribalized Natives have shown an insufficient increase or none at all. The latter statement is probably an exaggeration. On the other hand, the constant decrease of Creoles in Sierra Leone is disquieting and similar conditions prevail in Liberia. It is assumed that since the foundation of the Republic 25,000 Negroes have come from America and that the number of 'Americo-Liberians' to-day stands at 12,000–15,000. By detribalization in the wider sense we must understand every loosening of the social bonds going on to-day in many parts of Africa, which almost always leads to decay of morality and therefore to a decrease in the birth of healthy children.

(*c*) Migratory labour. Its effects are particularly dangerous where the men have accustomed themselves to live for the greater part of their time in the work centres, and can pay only short visits to their homes in between contracts. Many of them are demoralized in the work-places or carry contagious diseases to the rural districts.

(*d*) A danger to the normal increase also exists where the Natives, whether in towns or in the country, for example, as squatters, live in poor and depressed circumstances and have no possibility of rising.

(*e*) Infant mortality. Epidemics. Insufficient nourishment. It is possible to combat the last three, and the fight against them should be carried on with greater energy than hitherto. It ought to be possible to reduce infant mortality, which is now very high almost everywhere. Medical measures taken by the Government and by missions should be intensified in order to save the African children for their mothers. The woman educator will find ample scope for her activity among the Native women and girls. Appreciation must be awakened of cleanliness, of proper feeding and the rational care of children, and, above all, of healthy family life. Native nurses, midwives, medical helpers, and doctors should be trained and set to work. Here the Native administration can find ample occupation. A fine example of this is given by Nigeria, where in 1932 134 dispensaries, financed by the Native administration, were established. They are staffed by attendants who have had their training in Government Medical Stations. It is planned to expand these centres of health propaganda and education into rural health centres when the medical assistants now under training are available for service. In raising the standard of life and educating the people to a cleanly life, in the suppressing of many prejudices, superstitions, and beliefs in magic, the school too can render yeoman service.

The increase of population was certainly small before the arrival of the European. The inability to combat disease, high infant mortality, wrong and partly inadequate feeding, internal wars, and the slave-trade were all obstacles to a healthy growth of population. A new menace to the vitality of the race to-day lies in the European penetration. Many diseases were first introduced by the Europeans; others developed and became more widely spread than before along the trade-routes which the European has created.

On the other hand, the interference of the white man has had favourable results. The example quoted by Ryckmans, according to whom the best conditions as to population are found in a district almost Christianized, is probably no accidental coincidence, for similar reports are available from other parts of Africa, though not yet in sufficient quantities to enable us to make conclusive comparisons.

It must be admitted that the African, who is directly or indirectly affected by European influence, lives in certain respects under better conditions than his predecessors. The worker in the mines is more amply fed than many a peasant was in the old days. His needs have grown, but so too have the means for satisfying them. In many regions prosperity and therefore the whole standard of life have risen. Every one has the certainty that he will enjoy in peace what he has acquired. In illness he can have assistance for himself and his family. The whole outlook on life has become freer and wider. There are many who to-day are in possession of richer values of life than previously. Where before there was stagnation, to-day there is movement. The African no longer leads a secluded existence, but shares in the life of humanity, and has to win his place in competition with other races. If the presence of the European brings danger to him and to his race, at the same time it offers him undreamed-of possibilities.

It is sometimes maintained that the African derives the greatest benefit from the European in places where the white man has settled permanently, and where the Native enjoys as a labourer an intensive training for work. It is true that in this way the Native will improve his knowledge and methods of work and receive many new impulses, but the assertion that such conditions are the best guarantee for his progress appears to be exaggerated. It is hardly right to say that in South Africa the situation of the Negro is more satisfactory, his possibilities of life greater, and his general progress in economic and social conditions more conspicuous, than in other parts of the continent. More than 80 per cent. of the Native population there is illiterate, and only 25 per cent. of the children of school age actually attend school. It should be admitted that recently improvements and progress have been made, and that in many quarters there is a growing feeling of responsibility for the welfare of the Natives. Conditions, however, are far from being more satisfactory than in many parts of West and East Africa where the European population is less dense.

Of the more than 1,600,000 Natives who live as squatters, tenants, and servants on European farms, that is, in the most immediate proximity for training for work under the white man's guidance, a South African says:[1] 'The native squatter is the most backward of all his kind, divorced from his tribal life, untouched by civilizing influences.' Professor Mac-

---

[1] S. G. Millin, *The South Africans*, p. 260.

Millan[1] is of opinion that 'the Natives of the Union, as a whole, are a community dragging along at the very lowest level of bare existence'. Experts seem to agree that the situation of the Native population in the Union has permanently deteriorated in the last few years. These facts must be carefully considered in trying to find out how far the Negro will be able to hold his own when he lives among a higher race. We should always try to understand his position in the whole setting of life and should not be misled by improvements in certain spheres. Thus the Negroes of North America have in many respects made educational progress, nevertheless 'the proportion of school attendance has increased but slightly during the last ten years and has hardly kept up with the increase of the population'.[2] The same state of things is reported from Cape Colony: 'the enrolment has not even kept pace with the normal increase of population, and the percentage of the number of Native children of school-going age in the Province actually attending Government-aided schools has definitely fallen.'[3]

3

The European's position as a dominant power in Africa has been made easy by the fact that he was since his first arrival an object of admiration to the

[1] *The Cape Times,* 20 April 1926.
[2] *Twenty Year Report of the Phelps Stokes Fund,* p. 34.
[3] *The South African Outlook,* 1 August 1932, p. 142.

African. He was looked upon as a superior being, possessing every desirable object and being capable of doing almost anything, a man by nature a ruler to whom one willingly submitted. The African has indeed had some bitter experiences of this same European. In the whole of the eighteenth and the first half of the nineteenth centuries the slave-trade flourished. It would be unjust to lay the blame for this shame of humanity entirely on the white man. Africans owned and traded slaves long before European vessels came to their shores, and Africa had been a slave-exporting country probably for thousands of years. The European traders would never have been able to purchase so many slaves if the Africans themselves had not offered them for sale, and if the European conscience had not brought the slave-trade to an end, it would still exist in many parts of Africa. With all this the guilt of the European in this trade still remains great enough, and it is not the only thing he has on his conscience in Africa.

In the early days of European penetration the white people who went to Africa were not all of the finest type. Traders and adventurers were sometimes unscrupulous in their dealings with Africans. Administrators made mistakes from inexperience. Native institutions were disregarded, political independence was taken away from them, their chiefs were deposed for reasons which the Natives could not understand. Most of this belongs to the past, but what remains is still enough to be a source of bitterness:

the annexation of land; unfair taxation; disabilities in education and in finding a place in life; exclusion from higher occupations; and a social discrimination which is carried out in part of the continent with unnecessary severity.

The African forgets quickly. The present generation would know hardly anything of the slave-trade to America if their European teachers had not told them of it. Bad treatment and exploitation by the whites did not appear to them so execrable as we judge them to-day. The white man was the great and sometimes hard chief; did they not have to submit to similar treatment from their own rulers, and should not he who has the power also use it?

The two races have gradually learnt to understand each other better. The African of to-day knows that the presence of the white man has become useful, even indispensable to him. He is conscious that the larger part of what he has gained under the guidance of the white man would be lost again if the white man were to leave Africa. Similarly, the attitude of the white man to the black has become more reasonable. The European trader who seeks a market for his goods in Africa has the greatest interest in allowing the Natives to achieve a competence which will enable them to become his customers. The Government is working in the same direction. It must be to its interest that there should be a just compromise between groups and races, and that they should work side by side in harmony. Naturally enough; the attitude of the European employer, who has to rely on the African labourer and often has reason for dissatisfaction with him, is different. His argument runs as follows: 'If the Native owns enough land to be able to live on it comfortably, he will not come to the European as a worker, or at most only for short periods. It is therefore better to limit his conditions of life, or to tax him so highly that he has to seek a part of his subsistence elsewhere than in his own concerns. School education should not be over-stressed, for the educated Native will have little inclination to hire himself out as a worker and will try to find other occupations, in which he will perhaps compete with the white man. It is the Government's duty to see that the European employers have sufficient work-men, and its Native policy must be arranged accord-ingly. It must also leave the employer sufficient liberty to train his workers as he thinks necessary.'

It doubtless demands patience from the European employer to turn the Native into a useful worker. To many Natives the journey to the mines or the plantation is nothing but an interesting adventure. They think less of the work they will be doing than of the new experiences they hope to enjoy. They are unaccustomed to the work, and, as soon as the charm of novelty has worn off, it becomes weari-some. If they can kill time in any other way, in idle-ness or gossip, they see no harm in it.[1] The worker's

[1] Cf. W. C. Willoughby, *Race Problems in the New Africa*, Oxford, 1932, pp. 188 ff.

thoughts are much more in his home, where his people lead a pleasant life, than in his work. He perhaps does not realize that he has entered on a fixed contract for a certain time. When he sees that his employer insists on the observation of the contract, and all possibilities of escape are closed to him, he may bow to his fate but will do his work grudgingly and carelessly. On receipt of bad news from home, he feels it to be a bitter wrong if he is not allowed to travel back to his people. He will probably forfeit his contract and his wages rather than neglect a duty to his people or disobey a call from the leader of his clan. He left his home only with the chief's consent, and when the latter calls him back, it is natural for him to follow the call. It will only in rare cases be possible for him to take his wife with him to his place of work because accommodation is lacking. Moreover, the wife herself will be disinclined to go with her husband. In her home she is under the protection of her clan, and loyalty to it is much too strong to allow her to go among strangers with a light heart, and to entrust her destiny to her husband alone.

Employee and employer do not understand each other, not only because they speak different languages, but because they live in different worlds. The relation of employer and employee is something strange to the Native. When he worked at home, perhaps under the guidance of an elder, he was allowed a free hand to do his work when and how he liked. With the European he is obliged to work exactly on instructions and without interruption. If his work does not please the foreman, the latter will talk to him in no gentle terms and threaten to deduct something from his wages. The Native looks on this as nothing but malice, and takes refuge in obstinacy. If the employer is not able to put himself into the position of the worker, his patience is soon exhausted, the relations between him and his employees become strained, and discontent and insubordination result. From this purely negative attitude there may arise, where large numbers of Natives are concerned, and where they live long enough in the same place, an entirely new feeling of solidarity, which is based on opposition to the white man and his power over the black. The Natives came to the work-place as members of quite different tribes, differing in speech and manners, often prejudiced against each other and full of dislike. But even in a crowd so casually gathered together a certain feeling of unity cannot fail to arise. Groups enter into relations with each other because they are all fellows in the same misfortune. It is here that the naïve, innocent, and loyal attitude of the African to the European is lost. The worker will always find a ground for complaint, justified or not, against his employer. If any one appears who can express these complaints intelligibly and in violent terms, the opposition to the white oppressor soon makes itself heard. Political leaders and agitators play a sinister part in South Africa. Doubtless some among them have deserved well of their people. They have strengthened the consciousness of race and shown the Natives that, in spite of their subjection, they still are a power and able to fight with success for their aims, if only they unite. Some of them are, however, betrayed into such exaggerated language, their demands are so limitless, and they ignore actual facts so completely, that they run the risk of doing more harm than good to their compatriots. It is made easier for them to influence their hearers because they speak to people who are separated from their homes and perhaps suffering from home-sickness, or to such as have severed their connexion with tribal life but are not yet separated from it widely enough to have lost the living memory of it in their hearts. In both cases they are people who look upon the old tribal life in a golden light as compared with the miserable present, and the agitators are very clever at exploiting this mood. One agitator says in his address: 'Brothers, let me remind you of what you all know. Before the white man came to Africa, the whole of this great and beautiful country belonged to the Blacks. We were what the white man calls "barbarous". But we had a social system which worked well. In our tribal order material possessions were owned communally. Man, woman, and child shared alike in the good things of life. If I had a bag of maize and my neighbour had none, it was a matter of course that I should share with him. When the missionary came to us he said: that is right; if you help one another, God in heaven will rejoice. But when we came to the great

towns, we saw that it is the way of the white man to
grab as much as he can. The most esteemed thing
among them is he who has grabbed most, stamped on
his rivals and himself come to the top. Either the
missionary did not know all these things or else he
betrayed us. So it comes that we have no success in
business. If you wish to climb high, you must give
up such unpractical Christianity. The white people
who live here in splendid houses and have many
motors do not go to church, they have no time for
the God of the Christians, they scorn him. . . . Christianity is the religion of the white man. They say the
devil is black. If we blacks take a god, then we will
have him a black god; and when we want to paint
the devil, we will paint him white, for the white people
are devils.'

A great deal must be deducted from such perora-
tions as rhetorical exaggeration, but the impression
still remains that this is the voice of the disinherited,
who expresses his disillusionment with the white man
— a mood, though not in any way general, to be met
with in certain Native circles in South Africa. It is
sharpened by the feeling that it is a difference of race
on which the discrimination depends. The Negro
may have the same qualification as his white fellow-
worker, but he must not aim at attaining the same
position. The white workers in South Africa refuse
to admit the blacks into their organizations. The
Industrial Conciliation Act of the Union of South
Africa denied to all Natives, subject to the Passport

Laws, the right of forming labour combinations, which means that the Natives of South Africa have only in Cape Colony, where there are no Passport Laws, the possibility of organizing themselves for the protection of their interests.

It is almost inevitable that difficulties in the relations of the two races in a country like South Africa should exist. White South Africans rightly point out that it is their duty to preserve Western civilization unimpaired in their country and to maintain a standard of life corresponding to this claim. However justified this attitude is, every white South African will admit that it includes the responsibility for the lower race. The Natives are entrusted to them, and the administration of this trusteeship will always be an unfailing criterion for true human culture. Maintaining cultural superiority cannot mean suppressing the justified aspirations of those who are willing and capable of contributing their share in the development of the common homeland.

A seeming contradiction in the attitude of some South African Natives consists in the fact that they feel the European to be their adversary, while they look on European civilization as something desirable. This paradox is, however, easy to understand. The Negro's civilization is shattered. Return to it is impossible, and even where it remains comparatively intact, it is not in a position to hold its own against that of Europe. If, therefore, the Native desires to venture on the struggle of existence against the European, he must meet him with his own weapons. To do so, he requires European knowledge and skill, which have given the white man his superiority. He does not want to assimilate them in the measure and in the same manner which the European will allow him, but in unrestrained liberty. It can be understood therefore that men like Mr. D. Jabavu reject the catch-word of a development of the Native 'along his own lines' and see in it a means of keeping the African in his place. Where detribalization has so far progressed that social cohesion among Natives has practically disappeared, and they have become individuals in the same sense as Europeans are individuals, it is natural for Africans to aim at an education equal to that pro-vided for the white race, and it is noteworthy that in America a similar tendency is developing. 'The general movement of Negro education (in the United States) as regards standards, methods, and objectives is now decidedly in the direction of that prevailing in white education. This is necessary and inevitable.'[1]

No wonder if in this unequal struggle the Negro is apt to lose his balance, at least as far as the leading classes are concerned. He has assimilated European culture in the school, perhaps even in his parents' home. He nourishes his intelligence from the books and newspapers read by the white man. Intellectually he may feel himself the white man's equal, sharing the same ideas and values. Socially and politically the

[1] *Twenty Year Report of the Phelps Stokes Fund*, 1911–31, New York, 1932, p. 33.

gulf between the two races remains. It is bridged in many individual cases by personal tact and kindness, by acts of social welfare, by friendly relations between masters and servants which are by no means rare. Yet with all this it is clearly brought home to the consciousness of the educated man that he is a member of an inferior race.

Cases in which the black man is the white man's equal in achievement are, however, exceptions. The white man possesses qualities and powers which are, as a rule, not, or not yet, found in the black man, and which therefore mark out the former as called upon to lead and rule. This develops a feeling of inferiority in the black man from which the educated classes in particular suffer, and which they try to counteract. The way of doing this is often naïve. The wearing of European clothes, whether rags or the most up-to-date style; using European furniture and European forms of social intercourse; adorning the Native language with European expressions; using bombastic phrases in speaking or writing a European language: all these contribute to a feeling of equality with the European and his achievements, since in the old primitive view external similarity implies internal equality. The criticism of European Governments and of Europeans in the Press and at public meetings, and the making of impossible claims, are intended to prove that the Africans are in no way inferior, and will not submit to any slights.

The same desire to vindicate the African against

the European is shown in a more sympathetic way in the attention which is being devoted to ancient African culture. It has latterly become the fashion among educated Africans, in America as well as in Africa, to speak of Africa as the cradle of civilization, so that one might be led to believe the great-grandfathers of the present Negroes built the Pyramids, the Tombs of the Kings, and the Sphinx. Much trouble is being devoted to discovering close connexions between the religions, the political institutions, and even the languages of the Negroes and those of the ancient civilized races of Asia and Europe. All such efforts are fruitless, for they have nothing in common with scientific research and therefore lead nowhere. They are welcome, however, as showing that educated Negroes are beginning to think of their past and their own culture. There is nothing in their past or in their culture of which they need be ashamed, for all mankind has passed through certain phases of development, some faster, and others, less favoured by fortune, more slowly. Honour is due to those people who respect their past and study their own civilization in order to understand it and learn from it. Up to the present the study of African cultures has been principally carried on by the European, but we do not doubt that the Africans will more and more take their place beside him. There is already a series of works by African authors which show that they are capable of so doing. When they have learnt more thoroughly than at present how to approach their task with the same careful preparation and scientific methods as are thought necessary for such studies in the rest of the world, every one will welcome their co-operation.

If pride of race is such a mighty weapon in the hands of the white man, why should it not be the same for the Negro? Should it not be quite as possible for him, as for the other peoples and races of the earth, fully to develop his own racial type with the resources which modern civilization offers to us all? With the powers and gifts which come to him from his own past, can he not contribute to mankind through art and science, and through forms of political and social life, something which no one but he himself can give?

If that is to happen the European will have to give the African a fair chance. In most parts of Africa that can be done without any difficulty, and it is in fact taking place. It is less easy where, as in South Africa, the European has made his home. Here a wise policy will not shut its eyes to the necessity of seeking for a solution which will give equal justice to both sides. No one can ignore the fact that, as in the whole of Africa so also in the south, the Natives are on the path of progress. It would be unreasonable to deflect them from this path or to forbid them to go beyond a certain limit of culture. Prosperity and progress can only hold sway permanently where all sections of the population see an open road before them, but not if one section of the population finds itself enclosed within artificial barriers. Real prosperity is that in which the whole population shares according to the measure of its economic capacity. The more the Natives cease to be poor and are able to acquire wealth, the more will the economic life of the country flourish, and the more will the white population profit by it. A poor and dejected population is always a burden and a danger for the country.

The white man in Africa claims to lead his own life, and he should therefore be courageous enough to give the black man at his side the opportunity of doing likewise. In his communal life, in which he will live segregated from the white man, he should, within the legal ordinances which are valid for all, be free to carry on his activities unhindered, and to create his own forms of life. There will be opportunities enough for him to be active in his own community among men of his own race, as an official, policeman, craftsman, storekeeper, engineer, house-builder, journalist, doctor, teacher, and preacher. What seems more natural than to give the inhabitants of Native townships a local self-administration, and in this way educate them for responsible activities? As matters stand at present, the Native doctor will hardly ever have occasion to deal with white patients. What should prevent him, though, from putting his knowledge and skill at the service of his countrymen? Why should a Native doctor or house-builder be more undesirable than a Native journalist or political agitator? Should it not be possible to look at these problems in the same generous way as is expressed in a statement of the South African *Medical Journal*, when it speaks of 'the vital necessity of not separating, in deference to local prejudices or political considerations, the health interests of the Native from those of the European'? The same article goes on to say:

'We need not go into social and economic distinctions nor need we discuss whether or not adequate and reasonable provision can be made to prevent the mixing socially of nurses or students where such mixing is regarded as an offence or a misfortune. But we see no necessity whatever for putting ill health and the training of Native nurses in a separate water-tight compartment, and it is our sincere conviction that the attempt to do so simply creates an unhealthy atmosphere of suspicion that in the long run will do an infinity of harm.'

Ultimately, however, the future of the Negro throughout the whole of Africa lies with the Negro himself. No education, however wise, no provision, however benevolent, can lead a race to full manhood. The race itself must blaze the trail and must decide to follow it. For the African the present hour is an hour of decision, and he should be ready to meet it with all his senses awake. European and other races will gain a further footing in Africa and extend their influence, and the problem for the African Native is to find out how far he will be able to maintain himself side by side with the foreigner and compete with him successfully. The African must realize that through all the present changes and those yet to come his future is at stake. *Tua res agitur*: 'you are being weighed in the balance.' 'However much the European may do for you, the decisive thing is what you do for yourself, and still more what you yourself are.' In the last resort the fate of the African depends not on the will of the white man but upon what the African himself makes of himself. Should leaders arise who are conscious of their responsibility, who can succeed in making this responsibility a vital force in those who follow their leadership, then the African will emerge from the upheavals of to-day as a new human being, and the co-operation of the white and the black will be a blessing to both.

EPILOGUE

THE survey in the preceding chapters has thrown into relief some aspects of the present situation in Africa. It shows the urgency and complexity of the problems and their importance to humanity. To solve these problems a knowledge and an insight are called for which can be acquired only by patient observation and study, and often by re-thinking ideas which may seem familiar to people with African experience. Disinterested investigation which seeks nothing but the truth is what is needed. Scientific methods are considered indispensable to-day in studying any problem of human life, and this is true for Africa in the complicated situation which the intervention of the European has created there. The task of scientific investigation is so great, and from the nature of the present situation so urgent, that it can be successfully undertaken only by international co-operation and the co-ordination of all sincere efforts to reach a deeper understanding.

The International Institute of African Languages and Cultures was brought into existence to encourage such international co-operation. Its aims differ from those of existing institutions of anthropological and linguistic research in that it attempts to study not merely the facts of African life and society, but the process by which these are being transformed through the introduction of European civilization. It desires to arrive at an understanding of the socio-

z

logical situation as a living whole, to study the forces which are changing African society, and the ways in which they are doing this. A scientific training in modern methods of anthropological, sociological, and psychological research is an indispensable preparation for those who would undertake such inquiries.

The study of cultural change embraces questions which are not ordinarily regarded as belonging to anthropology, such as the effect of economic development, the position of natives in industry, the African as an independent producer, the many problems involved in the education of less developed peoples, questions of nutrition, and population movements. But though such questions are sociological rather than anthropological, a thorough knowledge of anthropology is necessary for understanding them.

It is obvious that all such research must be based on a knowledge of the native language. The languages of Africa are also important as the instruments of education and the vehicle of literature. Orthography, the production of a vernacular literature, the utilization of language for educational purposes, as a social bond, and as the means of cultural expression, are some of the problems which demand careful study.

The study of African institutions requires the cooperation of Africans, and from the beginning the Institute has endeavoured to obtain their collaboration. Africans have contributed to the Journal of the Institute, they have advised on questions of orthography, and there is reason to hope that before long they will be taking an effective share in research. The most fruitful work will result from a collaboration between European and African.

The Institute rests on the conviction that research, while remaining strictly scientific in its outlook and methods, should be related in the most intimate way to the living forces in African life. The aim of this book has been to make clear the connexion between research and the practical interests of those who are taking an active part in the rapid transformation of the African continent.

SOME RECENT BOOKS IN ENGLISH DEALING WITH AFRICAN PROBLEMS

GENERAL

Bovill, E. W., *Caravans of the Old Sahara*. Oxford University Press for International Institute of African Languages and Cultures. 1933. See Chap. XII, Disintegration and Reintegration.

Buell, R. L., *The Native Problem in Africa*, 2 vols. New York: The Macmillan Company. 1928.

Driberg, J. H., *At Home with the Savage*. London: George Routledge & Sons, Ltd. 1932.

Huxley, Julian, *Africa View*. London: Chatto & Windus. 1931.

Jones, T. Jesse, *Education in Africa, being the Report of the Phelps Stokes Education Commission in South Africa*. New York: Phelps Stokes Fund. 1922.

——, *Education in East Africa, a Study of East, Central and South Africa by the second African Education Commission under the auspices of the Phelps Stokes Fund in co-operation with the International Education Board*. London: Edinburgh House Press. 1925.

Lugard, Lord, *The Dual Mandate in British Tropical Africa*. Edinburgh and London: W. Blackwood & Sons. 4th edition. 1929.

Murray, A. Victor, *The School in the Bush*. London: Longmans, Green & Co., Ltd. 1929.

Oldham, J. H., *White and Black in Africa*. A critical examination of the Rhodes Lectures of General Smuts, London: Longmans, Green & Co., Ltd. 1930.

Oldham, J. H. and Gibson, B. D., *The Remaking of Man in Africa*. Oxford University Press. 1931.

Orde Browne, G. St. J., *The African Labourer*. Oxford University Press for International Institute of African Languages and Cultures. 1933.

Richards, A. I., *Hunger and Work in a Savage Tribe*. London: George Routledge & Sons, Ltd. 1932.

Seligman, C. G., *The Races of Africa*. London: Thornton Butterworth, Ltd. 1930.

Smith, E. W., *The Golden Stool, some Aspects of the Conflict of Cultures in Modern Africa*. London: Holborn Publishing House. 1926.

Smuts, J. C., *Africa and some World Problems, including the Rhodes Lectures delivered in Michaelmas Term*, 1929. Oxford University Press. 1930.

Thurnwald, R., *Economics in Primitive Communities*. Oxford University Press for International Institute of African Languages and Cultures. 1932.

Willoughby, W. C., *Race Problems in the New Africa*. Oxford University Press. 1923.

Africa, The Journal of the International Institute of African Languages and Cultures. Oxford University Press. Vols. I–VI (Proceeding). Contains articles on all the most important problems affecting the African native.

LANGUAGE

Meinhof, C. and van Warmelo, N. J., *Introduction to the Phonology of the Bantu Languages*. Berlin: Dietrich Reimer. 1932.

Werner, A., *The Language Families of Africa*. London: Kegan Paul, Trench, Trubner & Co. 2nd edition. 1925.

Werner, A., *Structure and Relationship of African Languages*. London: Longmans, Green & Co., Ltd. 1930.

Westermann, D., and Ward, Ida C., *Practical Phonetics for Students of African Languages*. Oxford University Press for International Institute of African Languages and Cultures. 1933.

MONOGRAPHS ON SPECIAL PEOPLES

Driberg, J. H., *The Lango*. London: T. Fisher Unwin. 1923.

Earthy, E. D., *Valenge Women*. Oxford University Press for International Institute of African Languages and Cultures. 1933.

Junod, H., *The Life of a South African Tribe*. Neuchâtel: Imprimerie Attinger Frères. London: Nutt & Co. 2nd edition rev. and enl. 1927.

Mair, L., *An African People in the Twentieth Century*. London: George Routledge & Sons, Ltd. 1934.

Meek, C. K., *A Sudanese Kingdom*. London: Kegan Paul, Trench, Trubner & Co. 1931.

Rattray, R. S., *Ashanti*. Oxford University Press. 1923.

——, *Religion and Art in Ashanti*. Oxford University Press. 1927.

——, *Ashanti Law and Constitution*. Oxford University Press. 1929.

Schapera, I., *The Khoisan Peoples of South Africa*. London: George Routledge & Sons, Ltd. 1930.

Seligman, C. G., and B. Z., *Pagan Tribes of the Nilotic Sudan*. London: George Routledge & Sons, Ltd. 1933.

Smith, E. W., and Dale, A. M., *The Ila-Speaking Peoples of Northern Rhodesia*. London: Macmillan & Co. 2 vols. 1920.

Stayt, H. A., *The BaVenda*. Oxford University Press for International Institute of African Languages and Cultures. 1931.

Westermann, D., *The Shilluk People*. Philadelphia: Board of Foreign Missions of the United Presbyterian Church of North America. 1912.

PRINTED IN
GREAT BRITAIN
AT THE
UNIVERSITY PRESS
OXFORD
BY
JOHN JOHNSON
PRINTER
TO THE
UNIVERSITY

For Product Safety Concerns and Information please contact our EU
representative GPSR@taylorandfrancis.com
Taylor & Francis Verlag GmbH, Kaufingerstraße 24, 80331 München, Germany

www.ingramcontent.com/pod-product-compliance
Lightning Source LLC
Chambersburg PA
CBHW070547270326
41926CB00013B/2230